THE BURDEN OF REFUGE

The Burden of Refuge

THE SINDHI HINDUS OF GUJARAT

Rita Kothari

Orient Longman

ORIENT LONGMAN PRIVATE LIMITED

Registered Office
3-6-752, Himayatnagar, Hyderabad 500 029 (A.P.), India
E-mail: cogeneral@orientlongman.com

Other Offices
Bangalore, Bhopal, Bhubaneshwar, Chennai, Ernakulam,
Guwahati, Hyderabad, Jaipur, Kolkata, Lucknow,
Mumbai, New Delhi, Patna, Pune

ISBN 13: 978-81-250-3157-4
ISBN 10: 81-250-3157-X

Typeset by
Trinity Designers & Typesetters
Chennai 600 041

Printed by
S S Colour Impression Pvt Ltd.
Chennai 600 106

Published by
Orient Longman Private Limited
160 Anna Salai
Chennai 600 002
E-mail: chegeneral@orientlongman.com

The maps in this book are not to scale. The external boundaries and coastline of
India as depicted on pages 178 and 179 are neither authentic nor correct.

For
my father
Laxmandas Makhija
and
my daughter
Shamini Kothari

Contents

Acknowledgements

The origins of this book lie in personal experience. Abhijit Kothari made me see the academic validity of this personal experience. I am most grateful to him.

Many friends and colleagues have contributed to this book: Sarvar Sherry Chand for her intellectual and emotional support, Achyut Yagnik for taking me to the first conference where the Sindhi experience of Partition was being discussed and his subsequent inputs, Nandita Bhavnani for her generous sharing of knowledge and material on Sindh, Mimi Chowdhury for being the first person from the publishing world to acknowledge the validity of this project, Prof. Jan Bremen and Prof. Ghanshyam Shah for their deeply moving interest in the project, Prof. Vai Ramanathan for sending me books and dissertations from the U.S., Lata Parwani for sharing her unpublished work and Paul D' Souza S.J. for patiently waiting for me at airports and outside visa offices in Delhi, Susan George for editorial expertise and more. I am grateful to all of them.

Several institutions and people associated with them lent their valuable support: the Institute of Sindhology, Adipur, Kutch (Sahib Bijani and Lakshmi Khilani), Gujarat State Archives (Dinesh Bhatt), Fr. Cedric Prakash at PRASHANT, Ahmedabad, Karamat Ali and B.M. Kutty at PILER, Karachi, Social Science Regional Council (SSRC) and the University Grants Commission. I thank all of them.

My Karachi friends – Saghir Shaikh, Salam Dharejo, Brij Jesrani, Khalique Jonejo, Yousif Hyder Shaikh and Shoukat Hossain Shoro – opened up homes for me and extended to me warmth only Sindh can offer.

I took generous help from several people without whom my fieldwork would not have been possible—Dr. Girish Kazi and Thakur Motwani (Surat), Jeetu Ramnani (Kalol), Prem Goplani (Bhavnagar), Rajendra Makhijani (Godhra), Dr. Jetho Lalwani, Umesh and Vinod Makhija (Ahmedabad), Murli (Vadodara), Jayant Relwani (Rajkot). Vidya Tewani helped me with library and human resources. Thanks, Vidya.

I thank Prof. Radha Kumar for her critical evaluation of this book and the management at St. Xavier's College, Ahmedabad for their support.

I have enjoyed working with Orient Longman and especially wish to thank the editors Hemlata Shankar and R. Sivapriya.

My gratitude to my families – Makhijas and Kotharis – is difficult to articulate. Should I just say, thank you?

Finally, thanks to all the proud and dignified Partition survivors from Sindh to whom this book owes its existence.

Rita Kothari
August 2006
Ahmedabad

Preface

At the turn of the previous century, my grandfather who lived in Shikarpur, Sindh, moved like a temporary migrant from Sindh to Bukhara and back. Shikarpur was the heart of commercial activity in Sindh, and his foray into Central Asia was part of a financial network which developed in the second half of the eighteenth century. This surge of Indo–Central Asian trade lasted until the time of the Russian Revolution. In 1947, my father moved from Sindh to India and his movement was part of a historical exodus of Partition migrants from Sindh. In the 1960s, my cousin moved from Bombay to Hong Kong and like many other Sindhis, made a niche for himself in the electronics market until Hong Kong ceased to be a British possession and joined China. All three men represent different diasporic moments and also voluntary and some not-so-voluntary contexts of crossing borders and the consequent separation from "a real and/or imaginary homeland" (Braziel and Mannur 2003, 1). The three moments also reflect the frequent subjection of the Sindhi community to larger historic forces. For the purposes of this book, my concern lies in the movement my father and one million odd Hindus of Sindh made—the contexts that made them feel that they must leave their land, and the consequences this has had on them and the two successive generations that grew up in a divided India.

In the academic and literary discourse on Partition, it is a fact little documented and discussed that like the Punjabis and Bengalis, the

Indian Sindhis also had a homeland in what is now Pakistan, and that there was a mass exodus of over 700,000 Sindhi Hindus from the province of Sindh during 1947.[1] The Sindhis drew little attention from the state and subsequently, from Partition Studies, because they had arrived 'safely'. The Sindhi story of Partition does not live up to the archetypal images of blood and gore. There were few instances of violence in Sindh, and many cases of loot and hooliganism, but these occurred some months after Partition. They are considered, by both the Hindus and the Muslims of Sindh, as results of the influx of Indian refugees into Sindh, and not as reflections of communal tensions within the province. This changes the contours of the Sindhi experience of Partition, which was perhaps more traumatic in its moment of resettlement in India, than in the departure from Sindh.

It is an equally unacknowledged fact that there was no 'Indian' part of Sindh that the Sindhis were coming to. Sindh, in its entirety, went to Pakistan, and a majority of the Hindus who constituted its religious minority, fled from the province. Thus one of the richest, globally diasporic communities arrived in India as stateless and penniless immigrants and restarted life amidst the resentment and reluctance extended by host communities. The religious minority of Sindh was now the linguistic minority of India, accompanied by a considerable diminution in their social standing. In fact, their Hinduness, the chief reason for their migration, was also put to question in states like Gujarat and Rajasthan, and in parts of Uttar Pradesh. As a community that ate meat, eschewed traditional Hindu practices such as untouchability, and hailed from 'Pakistan', the Sindhis were considered 'Muslim-like' and 'untouchable' in staunch vegetarian states such as Gujarat and Rajasthan.[2]

The over-pragmatic Sindhi did not 'indulge' in nostalgia for the

1. This figure is based on a comparison between the censuses of 1941 and 1951 which shows a reduction of the Hindu population from 857,716 to 133, 572. Another study (Thakur 1959/1997, 30) mentions that 1.25 million refugees from Sindh came into India.

2. The synonymy between Sindh and Pakistan, and by corollary 'Muslim', has persisted to such a degree that in the year 2005, there was a petition filed in the Supreme Court to remove the word 'Sindh' from India's national anthem. See "Delete 'Sindh' from National Anthem", 3 January 2005, *Indian Express*.

homeland for he became the petty and pushy trader who undercut profit and thus re-established himself once again as one of the most successful businessmen. The community's collective forgetting enabled individuals to become model migrants who got on with life and were soon established and affluent, almost as if Partition had never happened. Save a handful of Sindhi writers (who speak largely to their own tribe because nobody else reads them) and the surviving members of the migrant generation, a large majority of the Sindhis in India hardly ever think of themselves as a post-Partition community. The migrant generations seldom told stories about their past to the younger generations, or perhaps, the latter had no desire to hear them. The shared codes of language, legends and community networks also became difficult to sustain because the Sindhis have been dispersed across many states in India. Their inability to 're-create' a Sindhi history and culture in a divided India contrasts with their phenomenal economic success, making them textbook examples of migrant adjustment.

There is little incentive to speak in Sindhi because it is not a language that the Sindhi needs for educational or business opportunities. Moreover, the Sindhis of India are surrounded by negative stereotypes which also make the post-Partition generations avoid speaking the language to an extent that makes Khushwant Singh remark that the Sindhis will soon become, "a relic of the past" (10 July 2004, *Tribune*). Besides the loss of language, the Sindhi story of 'success' after Partition also fails to register the loss of unique socio-religious traditions that beautifully amalgamated elements from Sikhism, Hinduism and Sufi Islam. The desire to be like everybody else has made the Sindhis iron out the distinct features that were a result of their long-standing proximity to Islam and Sikhism. The losses incurred by the Sindhis remained unacknowledged by both non-Sindhis and the Sindhis themselves, and yet, they are manifest in the fragmented and ruptured history of the community. As a member of this community, I too was busy shedding the elements that identified me as a Sindhi. Given below is an account of my personal journey towards this book.

PERSONAL CONTEXT

It is difficult to go back in time and locate the precise moment when my discomfort as a Sindhi in Gujarat led me to a larger historical pursuit. Did it happen when I found that discomfort mirrored in many other Sindhis—anxious to discard the language, or to hide it behind the mask of Hindi, to claim 'difference' from a 'typical Sindhi', to maintain silence about family and home, to follow the practices of their Hindu Gujarati neighbours? I suspected that there was a sense of 'shame' in being a Sindhi and recognised its contours. For instance, at least five Sindhi female students in my college had put down Hindi as their mother tongue in their admission forms, although they spoke only Sindhi at home; the posters of a cultural organisation in Vadodara that carry the caption "Speak Sindhi, feel no shame"—all these indicated poignantly how Sindhiness was an undesirable identity, at least in the state of Gujarat. I was also intrigued by the fact that I never had a simple, straightforward answer when people asked me, "Why do you go to temples as well as gurudwaras?" "Why do you worship both Krishna and Shiva?" After marrying into a genteel, upper caste Gujarati family of Ahmedabad, I also noticed how people who have had an unbroken past and unbroken traditions, legacies and heirlooms, enjoy a far more coherent sense of identity than the one I experienced. This sense of fragmentation was much stronger in me than in my sisters, who have married into Sindhi families and hence, have little else to compare themselves with. At the same time, they have also expressed from time to time their dislike of being Sindhis. I remember when I decided to learn to read and write the Perso-Arabic script of the Sindhi language, my sister Mala remarked, "Are you mad? What have we achieved by learning Sindhi? You were lucky to go to an English medium school, why bother with this now?"

Whether the disavowal of Sindhiness I had observed in myself and others was a Partition phenomenon common to all Sindhi generations, or unique only to the Sindhis of Gujarat was something I could not judge then. It is true that in Gujarat, as elsewhere in India, the Sindhis live amidst many negative stereotypes about appearance (they are always fat), hygiene (they are dirty), and a general lack of education and sophistication. More importantly, the 'success' of a community that progressed from rags to riches evokes suspicion about its business ethics. Like the Jewish moneylender, the Sindhi businessman is a disliked figure, and very often, the laughing stock in Hindi cinema, who simply keeps saying, "*Vadi saiin*". However, there is a different sharpness and contempt in the perception of the Sindhi in Gujarat. There are two contexts to this dislike: firstly, the Sindhis came to the mercantile state of Gujarat as competitive traders, who very often threatened local business; secondly, the Sindhis were a meat-eating community hailing from an Islamic province, arriving at a staunch vegetarian state. All of this has made the Sindhi identity in Gujarat a negative one, a fact that has been internalised by young Sindhis who are anxious to erase and/or modify this identity.

I began my study by conducting preliminary interviews of Sindhis in the state of Gujarat. The first interview was with my father, Laxmandas Makhija, who told me, "I have not met a single Sindhi who has lost a loved one during Partition. The Sindhi Muslims were very good to us." Fed on Bhisham Sahni's novel *Tamas* (2001) and on the blood-curdling account in Khushwant Singh's *Train to Pakistan* (1988), I almost felt let down. And yet, this was an intriguing discovery. Why was this fact not recorded in all the studies of Partition I had read so far? There must have been something unique about the Sindhi identity that allowed Sindhi Hindus to leave Sindh physically unscathed. Perhaps it was necessary to start from this point – the Sindhi identity in pre-Partition Sindh – and trace its history through the trauma of Partition, the migration and the resettlement process, to understand the shaping and re-shaping that it underwent. Perhaps the manifestations of the present have their roots in the past. I therefore defined my central question as: How has Partition affected the Sindhis in small and big ways, and was a sense of shame one of its consequences? Although the hypothesis inherent in this question was yet to be tested, and the parameters of my study to be defined, it seemed to me then that further investigation rested on meeting with Sindhis of different generations in Gujarat and recording detailed oral narratives. I tried to acquire knowledge of historical Sindh through published literature and through interviews with the first-generation migrant Sindhis.

Confirmation of disavowal of Sindhiness seemed to come largely from the second and third generations. In the labyrinth of voices and words that surrounded me, I tried to locate the precise point of rupture.

While this process was going on, Gujarat experienced one of its most shameful and violent traumas in 2002. On the 27th of February 2002, over fifty-eight passengers travelling in the Sabarmati Express from Ayodhya to Ahmedabad were killed in a fire set by an angry mob at Godhra. The fire was set to one of the train's coaches as it passed through Godhra. The passengers in the torched coach were karsevaks—volunteers and supporters of the Vishwa Hindu Parishad (VHP, a Hindu fundamentalist outfit) involved in the reconstruction of the disputed temple in Ayodhya. The Godhra violence, perpetrated allegedly by the Muslims of Godhra (known as the Ghanchi Muslims), is still under investigation. The aftermath of the incident at Godhra, now known as the 'Gujarat carnage' – supposedly Hindu reprisal for the Muslim violence – took the form of an ethnic cleansing, in which, amidst what seemed like a failure of the state's law and order machinery, about two thousand Muslims across the state were killed and many thousands more displaced. This breakdown of democracy has by now received much attention from scholars of different persuasions (Agnivesh and Thampu 2002; Engineer 2003; Varadarajan 2002). The unexpected and disturbing participation of Dalit and tribal groups (hitherto unconcerned with Hindu religious fundamentalism) in the violence has also been taken into account (Sethi 2002). However, the Sindhi involvement in these riots has evoked no special comment, although the worst massacre of Muslims took place in Naroda Patiya, Ahmedabad, a constituency dominated by Sindhis. Maya Kodnani – member of the state legislative assembly (MLA), Bharatiya Janata Party (BJP), Naroda constituency – expressed no public apology for what happened in her constituency. On 24 March, a chain of shops owned by Sindhis in Revdi Bazaar in Ahmedabad was torched. While talking to my cousins Umesh and Harish Makhija, who also conduct business in Revdi Bazaar, I heard them say that this was the usual "Sindhi–Muslim tit for tat".[3] I was given to understand that the Muslims and

---

3. See "Retaliatory attacks on Hindus", 24 March 2002, *Times of India*.

the Sindhis have always been at each others' throats. Gradually, I found out that violence between Sindhis and Muslims was not new in Gujarat. It had precedents in the city of Ahmedabad during the riots of 1969. The P. Jaganmohan Reddy Report on the 1969 riots lists Sardarnagar as one of the affected areas. The account below testifies to the Sindhi participation in the riots of 1969. The geographical distribution also throws light on the possible advantage of sheer weight of numbers that the Hindus (in this case, Sindhis) have over the Muslims in the area.

Sardarnagar Police Station has an area of 38 square kilometres; Sardarnagar has a population of 100,000 approximately, of which 98,000 are Hindus and 2,000 Muslims.
Muslims pockets in predominantly Hindu localities:
        Muslim Mohalla in Naroda village.
Hindu pockets in predominantly Muslim localities:
        Nil.
Mixed localities:
        Nil.

Practically the whole area is Hindu dominated but in several places like Saijpur Bogha (Jikar Hasam Chali, Pathan chawl, etc), Kavdajini Chali, Mahavirnagar, village Hansol, Kubernagar, Sardarnagar and in the industrial area which has recently developed, there are scattered houses of Muslims.

Shri S. J. Mehta (G.W.21) who is the Police Inspector says that the limits of his Police Station adjoin Sherkota, Gomtipur and Madhupura Police Stations of Ahmedabad city. It also adjoins Kujad and Dabhoda Police Stations of Ahmedabad District. The 'Sindhis' are in majority and most of them are residing in Kubernagar and Sardarnagar areas. (Reddy 1971, 28)

Moreover, the presence of the Sindhi element in the 1969 riots is confirmed by some peoples' memories.[4]

4. My colleagues Sarvar Sherry Chand and Fr. S. Rappai, S.J., remember that the Sindhis were involved in the 1969 riots as both perpetrators and victims. A respondent named Ashok Lilani, who now lives in Kalol, told me that he had to move from Ahmedabad because his shop had been burnt down by the Muslims during the riots of 1969 (personal interview). On recalling the incident he said, "Even now when I think of those days, a shudder runs through my body." His mother Radha Lilani used the same words when describing her Partition experiences of 1947.

The strain in Sindhi–Muslim relations goes back to the 1950s, when the Sindhis settled in Godhra, and has continued sporadically through the 1980s (see the discussion in chapter 5). This seemed to contradict the Sindhi experience of Partition. It was also surprising that the Sindhis of India who had lived in close proximity with the Muslims in Sindh and had been deeply influenced by them in terms of language, food, clothes and script, should have developed such hatred for them. While the Sindhis of Gujarat show no desire to accept the Muslims, they in turn remain rejected and marginalised by the mainstream Hindu Gujaratis who think of the Sindhis as 'dirty', 'shrewd' and 'Muslim-like' people. Was the Sindhi hatred for the Muslims a result of this marginalisation? Or did its context also lie in pre-Partition history? My inquiry could no longer be limited to examining only the Sindhis' sense of shame. A series of other questions would also have to be answered after the 'Gujarat carnage': Were the Sindhis of Gujarat retaliating for their sufferings during Partition and settling old scores, so to speak? Or had living in Gujarat created communal tendencies in them that had hitherto not existed? Was their newly acquired Hindu identity a result of their efforts to shed their sense of stigma? The aggressive collaboration of the Sindhis with Hindutva in Gujarat drew my attention to a new set of questions. Although some of these questions may also be relevant for Sindhis living in other states, my gaze rested on Gujarat—a state that had shown blatant discrimination against religions different from Hinduism and Jainism. My research, which lay fallow during this stressful period in Gujarat, re-emerged with a different emphasis. It was clear to me that Gujarat would be the arena of investigation not least because it includes one-third of the Sindhi-speaking population of India. It is here that the Sindhis seem to have paid heavy prices for assimilation. They have not only cast off their language, modified their clothes and food habits, but have also lost a very integral feature of their history—their syncretism. In my interview with her, Maya Kodnani mentions how because of Muslims, the Sindhi Hindus suffered on two counts. First, they got driven out of their homeland, and second, they faced rejection in Gujarat because they hailed from what is now Pakistan. As a result, they have not been integrated into the mainstream and in order to do so, says Kodnani, they must go back to being 'proper' Hindus—eat vegetarian food, observe Hindu rituals and stay away from Muslims. Has her own life been a step in that direction?

If it seems from the above that the scars of Partition persist at all moments, I have also witnessed moments when the 'fact' of Partition is made irrelevant and ridiculous. Perhaps that is where our lessons lie. For instance, on my way to Karachi from Mumbai I met a young man named Khubchand who was returning from his fifteenth visit to India. He is a Sindhi Hindu from Pakistan whose parents stayed back during Partition. His father is a landowner in Mirpurkhas and at the time of Partition, he did not find it easy to sell land and convert his estate into cash. It seemed pointless to him to go as a poor man to India; instead, he preferred to stay a rich man in Pakistan. Khubchand is twenty-one years old. He has extended the family business to Karachi. His father looks after the lands, and in addition Khubchand is a trader of rice in Karachi. He is happy living in Karachi, a city which according to him is far more 'modern' than Bombay. Through his contacts in the embassy, he manages to acquire a visa whenever he wishes to visit India, and as he puts it, enjoy "the best of both worlds".

The so-called bitterness of Partition turned into casual moments of laughter when, after a nice meal and conversation with three Sindhi Muslims, I was told by one of them in Sindhi, "It's such a shame you had to go through so much to visit Sindh. These borders and rules simply don't make sense." Sagely and sincerely, I nodded in agreement, only to throw my head back with laughter when at the very next moment he said, "But yaar, you must return our Kashmir to us." On another occasion, I was with a group constituting of both Hindu and Muslim Sindhis in Karachi. In the course of our conversation about my research, Omar Memon told me, "I hope you will mention in your book that Hindus used to exploit the Muslims, they would charge usurious rates of interests and usurp Muslim homes and jewellery." Before I could answer, someone jested, "You know, Omar is reminding himself of that, Rita. His grandfather managed to get a large Hindu property when his next door neighbour left, and this is Omar's justification for that guilt! He is wondering if Hindus like you will take that property back!"

The physical and psychological borders drawn during Partition also disappear when Sindhis of both religions meet at literary conferences organised by world Sindhi associations, or when delegations from India visit the dargahs of Shah Latif and Sachal Sarmast in Pakistan. Such moments are not rare among the Sindhis and they define the historical character of a Sindhi. The disappearance of such historical 'Sindhiness' from the lives of the Sindhis of Gujarat, who seem to have disposed of a religio-cultural pluralism and their mother tongue in order to erase their Sindhiness, is a matter of sad concern. Equally sad is the fact that the Sindhis in India – known only for shrewdness in business – were in Sindh, its cultural elite; their philanthropic contribution is evident even today in the libraries and hospitals they had established, and in the schools and colleges they had managed. The relics of the Sindhi Hindu's past in Karachi and Shikarpur speak of a very different Sindhi than the one stereotyped in India. This book tells the story of this rupture over three generations. It takes the reader from the present Gujarat of this preface to the pre-Partition past of the Sindhis and back to Gujarat, where we find the Sindhis rejecting their Sindhiness and anxious to embrace more mainstream identities.

1 Introduction: Sindh and its People (1843–1947)

In Sindh, they [Hindus] eat meat, are addicted to spirituous drinks. They do not object to fish and onions, and drink water from inferior and superior castes.

—*Gazetteer of the Bombay Presidency,* 1880

Hinduism and the culture of Sanskrit literature has been so completely swept away from Sindh's borders that it is now a country without caste or Brahmans.

—Ernest Trumpp

From incomprehension and ignorance to dislike, there have been many ways of imagining what Richard Burton calls "an unhappy valley" (Burton 1851/1998). Our inquiry into the present of the Indian Sindhis must begin with their past when they lived as a Hindu minority in Sindh. The post-Partition tribe of Sindhi writers in India tends to build a history of Sindh by showing how it was the 'cradle' of the

Indus Valley Civilisation with Mohenjodaro in Larkano, Sindh, as concrete testimony of its claim. While this view enables a minority community like the Sindhis to invest a sense of gravity in its smudged and inaccessible past, it is not my concern here. This book deals with the present of the Sindhis and their contextualisation in the nineteenth and twentieth centuries.

The Hindus of Sindh, who form the chief focus of this study, bewilder anyone with a well-defined notion of Sanskritic Hinduism. With a blithe disregard for differences between castes, or between Saivism and Vaishnavism on the one hand, and with their simultaneous visits to tikaanas (Sindhi temples), gurudwaras, and Sufi dargahs on the other, the Hindus of Sindh practised a form of Hinduism that was influenced substantially by Sikhism and Sufism.[1] They shared the context of Sufism with the Muslims of Sindh, who formed its chief majority, and both communities had a long-standing tradition of worshipping Sufi pirs.[2] This overlapping context between the Hindus and the Muslims of Sindh was made possible by centuries of proximity going back to the first Arab invasion of Sindh by Muhammad bin Qasim in A.D. 711. Sindh was under Muslim rule for eleven centuries, a period long enough to ensure that the Hindus were, either through migration and/or conversion, reduced to being a religious minority.

---

1. The Sindhi practice of Sikhism is very intriguing indeed, making Raymond Williams remark that the Sindhis are "on the boundary between Sikhs and Hindus" (in Ramsey 2004, 61). Even today, post-Partition Sindhis do visit traditional gurudwaras and occasionally hold weddings there. They also have their own gurudwaras which have not only the holy text of the Sikhs, the Guru Granth Sahib, but also, sometimes, pictures of Hindu deities. This coexistence of Hindu gods and the Guru Granth Sahib is unacceptable to the post-1980s practice and understanding of Sikhism, and that censure has made Sindhis reduce their overt affiliation with Sikhism. Harjot Oberoi's work on Sikh identity (1994/1997) argues that prior to the nineteenth century, Sikhism did incorporate Hindu elements but gradually lost its heterodox elements.

2. In his study on the Sindhis of Lucknow, Steven Ramsey (2004) shows how the Sindhis defy religious borders due to their being intersected by three different traditions—Hinduism, Sikhism and Sufi Islam, and also how they find it increasingly difficult to fit into the mainstream notions of religion in India. In a telling way, his dissertation begins by recounting Dr. Rochal Das's (a Hindu Sufi who lived in Pakistan and was the disciple of a Muslim pir) visit to Lucknow to bless a Sindhi gurudwara.

Despite this, the Hindus were Sindh's most wealthy class; they almost entirely dominated the trade and bureaucracy. When a majority of them left Sindh during the Partition they left behind them a huge vacuum in the economy and, significantly, also in the educational and philanthropic institutions that even today speak of their once strong presence in the life of the province. This part of the book is about pre-colonial life in Sindh; it provides in broad terms an introduction to the province and its people.

Since Muhammad bin Qasim's invasion in A.D. 711, Sindh was ruled by a series of monarchs from the Arab empire, the Ghaznavids, the Sumras, the Sammas and the Mughals. Further evidence of this province's extreme remoteness may be garnered from the fact that with the exception of Sumra and Samma rule, the centres of administration were almost always outside Sindh. Until the late ninth century, Sindh was a part of the Arabian Caliphate. The caliphs ruled from various centres of the Arab world, appointing governors in Sindh. Under Sultan Muhammad of Ghazni (988–1030) Sindh was once again governed by a series of governors whose administrative headquarters lay outside Sindh. Under the Delhi Sultanate and the Mughals, the centre was obviously Delhi.

Arab dominion of the area was overthrown by the Sumra dynasty (1058–1249) who were indigenous Sindhi Muslims. In the fourteenth century, the Sumras were replaced by the Samma rulers in Lower Sindh (1351–1517). The Sammas were fiercely independent and rebelled against the Delhi Sultanate. The capital of these early dynasties was the city of Thatta.

During this period, Persian replaced Arabic as the official language, Sufi mysticism evolved, and poetry of a very high order was produced. It was during the Samma rule that Humayun came to Sindh. The Sammas were replaced by the Arghuns (1519–54) and the Turkhans (1554–1625), both dynasties from the north. In 1592, the Turkhans were defeated and Sindh was annexed by Emperor Akbar. Sindh remained under Mughal rule until the invasion of Nadir Shah the Persian in 1739, when, after a gap of 1500 years during which the region had been ruled by a number of local rulers from the subcontinent, Sindh once again returned to the Iranian empire. From 1739 to 1783, Sindh was ruled by the Kalhoras. Iran's dominion of Sindh however, did not last very long; the Talpur Mirs took over the reins in 1783. It was from the Talpur Mirs that the British annexed Sindh in 1843.

Sindh had always been isolated from the main centres of power in India. Although it shared its eastern borders with Rajasthan, its southern boundaries with Gujarat and its northern tip extended as far as Punjab's southern most limits, it remained cut off from the rest of British India by the Arabian Sea as well as the desert of Kutch. However, it was more than just relative geographic distance that cut Sindh off; it seemed to be beyond the sphere of central administration in both pre-colonial and colonial India. It was geographically and culturally close to the southern and eastern parts of Baluchistan. As a frontier province, it evoked little interest, as it did not seem to belong properly to either India or Central Asia (Markovits 2000, 216). Until the British merged Sindh with the Bombay Presidency in 1847, it remained remote and peripheral from the main centres of India. This part geographical, but largely cultural distance also played a sizable role in the evolution of Sindh's distinct religio-cultural identity.

Furthermore, vast stretches of uninhabited land dependent on the mercies of the river Indus and a people who seemed uncivilised and backward made it at an altogether unattractive and out of the way region. Apart from the awkwardness of physical location, Sindh was "like the rest of India at the time of the [British] conquest, a peasant society ruled by despots of either the imperial or local variety. It was like India, essentially a 'medieval' society with no inkling of democratic practice. There was however a very significant difference between Sindh and the rest of India. Sindh was the only province of the subcontinent which was overwhelmingly Muslim in population. In Sindh 75% of the population was Muslim, whereas in the Punjab and Bengal, their majority provinces, little over 50% were Muslim" (Khuhro 1981, 170). It must be kept in mind that Sindh had been a part of the Muslim world from the time of Muhammad bin Qasim's conquest in A.D. 711, to its annexation by the British from the Talpur Mirs in 1842.

The province of Sindh witnessed the longest period of proximity between Hindus and Muslims, and although the relationship was neither equal (the former were a religious minority) nor harmonious, it was the most intimate on the subcontinent.

At this juncture, it is crucial to qualify that the opposition of 'Hindu' and 'Muslim' in this narrative is somewhat artificial, for not *all* Sindhis in all cases saw themselves in terms of their religious identity. The territorial identity of living in Sindh and the linguistic identity conferred by the Sindhi language were very strong in Sindh, evident even today in the Sindhi Hindu and Sindhi Muslim interaction across borders.[3] This book uses these terms to build an atmosphere of colonial India when indistinct identities were moving towards hard-lined ones, culminating in a parting of ways during Partition.

IMAGINING SINDHI HINDUS

Since Sindh had traditionally been a country of immigrants, its population was very mixed (Cheesman 1997, 34). The inhabitants of Sindh included, among others, the Hindu Rajputs who had been residents of the region at the time of Muslim conquest (tribes such as Sammos, Sumros, Unars, Jats, Mohanos and others). A large number of Lohanas who had emigrated from Punjab in the distant past, and the Lohanas from Kathiawar who had escaped from religious tyranny in medieval Gujarat, were also part of the varied population. According to Berumal Advani, the origins of most Sindhi Hindus can be traced to Kutch (from where they escaped during earthquakes), Kathiawar (due to fears of religious conversion), Rajasthan (due to political instability) and Punjab (due to the conflicts between the Sikhs and Aurangzeb) (1946/2001, 7). The Muslim population fell into three broad categories—Sindhis, Sayyids and Baluchis; also present were the smaller communities of the Memons, Khojahs and Pathans (Cheesman 1997, 35).

3. This explains to an extent the phenomenon of cyber-relations between Sindhis in India and those from Pakistan. It is one of the many manifestations of a strong linguistic identity that overcomes religious barriers.

A majority of the Sindhi Hindus belong to the trader caste called the Lohanas found in the western region of India, but they classified themselves on the basis of occupation, as the amils and the bhaibands. The use of this form of classification rather than caste hierarchy has operated as a marker of identity among Sindhis. Historically speaking, the Hindus who served in the courts of the Kalhoras were called the amils, meaning literally, people who implement orders (*hukm ka amal karna*). Gradually the word also came to refer to educated people (people with learning or ilm). The amils were the literate Hindus who worked as administrators from the seventeenth century onwards and usually lived in bigger cities like Hyderabad and Karachi. Operating as revenue collectors and consultants, the amils of Sindh were an important class. The non-amil or the bhaiband section of the Hindus was engaged in trade. From running small shops and lending money, to managing international business operations, they did it all. A non-amil Hindu in Sindh was referred to by the ubiquitous term of 'vaaniyo', i.e. bania or trader. If the amils took financial decisions in court, the Hindu banias controlled the economy outside the court; the Sindhi Hindus formed Sindh's administrative backbone from the eighteenth century onwards.

A narrative of persecution?

The Sindhi Hindus were a religious minority in a province that had had four centuries of unbroken Muslim rule. Naturally, the Hindus were subject to the political will of the Muslims, making some post-Partition Sindhi Hindus look back upon their past as a narrative of persecution (See Malkani K.R. 1984; Thakur 1959/1997). In the assessment of the history of Sindh, a pro-Hindu scholar is likely to assume that the Hindus necessarily experienced not only political, but also religious domination. The heavy Islamic influences upon the Sindhi Hindus are unmistakable, manifest in external matters such as food, clothes, language and even a socio-religious world view that departs significantly from Hinduism. Moreover, conversions from Hinduism into Islam had been to a greater or lesser extent an ongoing phenomenon. All these factors lend themselves to a view that the Hindus were not able to practise their religion freely and that they lived at the mercy of their Muslim masters. This view would be fallacious if it did not take into account the peculiar dynamics of Sindh where its religious minority was also the most prosperous section of its society. Undoubtedly, political power was with the Muslim majority, but neither Muslim political rule nor Hindu subjugation to Islam was absolute. In his *History of the Hindu Sindhis*, Berumal Advani describes how Muslim rulers from Muhammad bin Qasim to the Talpur Mirs (who were defeated by the British) had different religious ideologies and different dominions in Sindh (1946/2001). For instance, Muhammed bin Qasim's control in Sindh lay largely in and around Shahdadpur while the native Rajputs of Sindh continued to rule other parts. Similarly, the Abbasid caliphs of Baghdad who ruled Sindh in the eleventh century levied religious tax on the Hindus but let them exercise linguistic and political freedom. While the Kalhoras and the Talpur Mirs enjoyed considerable political domination over the Hindus, they also employed the Sindhi Hindus in key positions at court. Although the history of Sindh is peppered with accounts of conversion, both forced and voluntary, it would be a falsification of the complex political economy of Sindh to assume that any one community was constantly victimised.

A well-known Gujarati writer and nationalist Kakasaheb Kalelkar, on visiting Sindh, gathered that "the Muslims of this region recognised the skills of Amils and handed over administrative power to them. The Muslims themselves were peasants, cowherds and craftsmen. Time and again, they needed money, so they would go to the Hindu Bhaibandh [trader]. If the Bhaibandh found anything objectionable in government, they would go straight to the Mirs and threaten to leave. The Mirs would assure them of religious protection. After hearing this from the Hindus of Sindh, I never believed that religious conversion in a Muslim province was always by force" (1984, 305). The debate about the issue of conversion is thus indeterminate. However, what can be established with certainty about Sindh, and especially with reference to the Sindhi Hindus, is that centuries of proximity with Islam and cultural distance from India modified its religious practices to a significant extent.

Socio-religious outlook: Absence of caste

Colonial historiographers were struck (and even disappointed) by the loose and somewhat blithe interpretation of Hinduism in Sindh. It is difficult to provide a comprehensive account of the Sindhi Hindus' socio-religious life, which departed substantially from the textualised version of Hinduism and also incorporated elements from Sufism and Sikhism. However, some broad features – such as the caste system and its consequent ideology of pollution – provide an insight into the unusual version of Hinduism in Sindh. The Hindus belonged mostly to the three upper varnas—the Brahmins, the Kshatriyas and the Vaishyas. It would appear that the members of the fourth varna, the Shudras, had been converted to Islam during the successive Muslim regimes (Kripalani 2004, 4). The Brahmins, Vaishyas and Kshatriyas interdined and intermarried. Significantly, the Brahmins in Sindh were not its most privileged social set. They constituted a small and negligible group in a mercantile community that performed certain rituals during festivals, but did not represent any sacerdotal powers. In the process of contextualising the emergence of the nineteenth-century reformer Sadhu Hiranand, Gobind Malhi notes, "Sindhi Hindus were very much unlike Hindus of the rest of India in religious beliefs and social customs. Where Sindhi Hindus believed in the oneness of God under the dual influence of Islam and Sikhism, Hindus in the rest of India had multiple gods and goddesses. Idolatory and all its attendant rituals were conspicuous by their absence while the Sindhi Hindus were in Sindh. The caste system as generally understood was non-existent in Sindh. Brahmins, poor and ignorant, formed a negligible minority" (1988, 3; also see Gidumal, 1882). Partly as a product of the Sindhi Hindus' mercantile ethos that privileged the rich bania in its social hierarchy and partly as the result of Sindh's cultural isolation from the rest of India, the province evolved its own distinctive socio-religious outlook. For instance, the Brahmin of Sindh had a laidback approach to his own learning and practices. He did not follow the norms of purity and ate meat, drank liquor, and mixed with other castes, evoking Richard Burton's severe remark, "The Brahmin of Sindh can put any Brahmin of India to shame" (1851/1993, 273). While the position of the Brahmins in Sindhi Hindu society is fairly clear, there is some ambiguity about its untouchables.[4]

Socio-religious outlook: Syncretism

Sindh's unorthodox version of Hinduism must be seen as a historical outcome of several contexts and it would be a fallacious and unqualified conclusion to think that 'pure' Hinduism was not allowed to exist in Sindh.[5] The Sindhi Hindus' non-textualised version of Hinduism was an outcome of three predominant influences—Islam, Sikhism and

4. In terms of theory and practice, the Sindhi Hindus did not practise untouchability in Sindh. The only exception to this, notes Kripalani, were the scavengers whom nobody (including Hindus and Muslims) touched because of the work they did and the manner in which it was done (the night-soil was carried in baskets). Nobody felt polluted by touching anyone, and even the scavengers were allowed to draw water from the same well (2004, 7). Having said that, it must also be qualified that the census of Sindh in 1931 records more than fifteen scheduled communities (see Satyani 2005). It is difficult to know how in the absence of untouchability in the social space, untouchability continued to exist in self-perception. It is perhaps safe to conclude that while the Sindhi Hindus did not (and still do not) have a rigid ideology of pollution, they were not without condescension towards certain sections of society. Also, since the artisan class in Sindh was almost entirely Muslim, it points to a context when caste discrimination did exist and led to a massive conversion from the so-called lower castes. It seems more likely that the Sindhi Hindus did have caste practices which, over a period of time, went out of use. Its traces may have remained in forms of social behaviour, but the rigidity about physical touch had disappeared.

5. This view is reinforced by the fact that most of the population in Sindh converted to Islam sometime between the fifteenth and eighteenth centuries (Markovits 2000). However, it is difficult to determine whether these were always involuntary conversions: the Sindhi Hindus also converted to Islam as an extension of identification with the rulers. In a study on the Arya Samaj (1983, 36), Gobind Chellani remarks that the educated classes among the Sindhi Hindus liked to dress and talk like the Muslims, and sometimes showed an alarming inclination towards conversion. The truth about conversion probably lay between the two extremes of voluntary and forced.

Sufism. In fact, even Islam in Sindh was not its textualised Koranic version, but one influenced by Persian Sufism. It created in Sindh a scope for eclectic practices. The ideology of Sufism rests upon a spiritual path to devotion without any intermediation by mullahs and ulemas. Although some of its forms were fairly orthodox, Sufism in Sindh derived sustenance from the secular forms of poetry and music. Even today, Sufism considers poetry and music closer to divinity than texts. The most inspired mystics such as Shahbaz Qalandar and Shah Abdul Latif evoked far more devotion than abstract concepts of God. This philosophy left neither Hindus nor Muslims untouched, so that Shah Abdul Latif provides definition to Sindhis of both religions. The greatest saints in Sindh were enshrined as pirs and their mazhars (burial places) were places of pilgrimage for both communities, as is the case with Shahbaz Qalandar of Sehwan. The importance of this tradition in Sindh cannot be overstated. As far as the Hindus were concerned, it created for them an ethos in which they did not grow up thinking of Islam as inimical. Not only that, shared geography, history and socio-religious practices made identities spill over into each other. In their practice in Sindh, and to a certain extent even now, Sindhi Hindus have a strong legacy of Sufi thought. In Sindh, a Hindu world did not occlude visits to the dargahs, or fasting for a pir or syed. This non-Sanskritic Hinduism made rigid visitors squirm, but it also served as a context for creating a more pluralistic way of life in matters of religion. It was of little significance then that Sufi thinkers like Shah Abdul Latif, Sachal Sarmast and Sami were of Muslim origin. They served as immortal icons held far more dear than the figures of Rama and Krishna. In his book *Sindh and its Sufis*, Jethmal Parsram describes the religious tradition of the Sindhis as one of negation. He remarks, "Sindh originally Hindu, has been more or less in close contact with the Greek, the Scythian, the Arabian, the Persian and the various sub-nations of Islam; as a result it has been flattened into a state of negation. It is a province which, in the matter of race, is neither Ancient Indo-Aryan nor Arabian Semitic, but it is a conglomeration of many elements" (1924/2000, 49).

It can be concluded from the above discussion that the Hindus and Muslims of Sindh did not enact their traditional roles and were bound by the humanism of Sufi philosophy. As Ramwani notes, "The Hindu of Sindh ceased to be a Hindu, and the Muslim ceased to be a Muslim. Islam came to Sindh in the form of Sufism, Guru Nanak's Sikhism came without its Khalsa element, all forms of religious thought changed their nature in Sindh" (1987, 136). As far as social interactions were concerned, the Hindus and the Muslims participated in each other's religious practices and the boundaries dividing their worlds were quite porous. At the same time, my conversations with the migrant generation also testify to the exclusivist practices of the Hindus against the Muslims. Hindus, by and large, did not accept cooked food from Muslims, and in public places there were separate water arrangements for Hindus and Muslims. It is difficult to judge the measure of this phenomenon, but it seems that at railway stations and restaurants, there would be separate water for Muslims and Hindus (referred to euphemistically, as *rangeen paani* and *safed paani*, respectively). Hindus would attend religious and social functions at a Muslim house, but take their share of uncooked food. It is possible that such practices came into existence or increased in colonial Sindh when the Hindus felt fearless enough to show such discrimination. We shall return to this gradual metamorphosis of social relations later. For now, it is important to keep in mind that the Hindus and Muslims of Sindh shared an intimacy of relations, though this was not necessarily harmonious. It is best described as one in which "hostility mingled easily with amity" (Markovits 2000, 50).

A background of some common practices was also overlaid by an agrarian economy, both of which increased mutual inter-community dependence. According to Gita Viswanath, the Hindu–Muslim configuration contributed a workable harmony rather than an "inherently benevolent human nature" (1999, 135). Be that as it may, the identities of Hindus and Muslims in pre-colonial Sindh were relatively porous. In the shared folklore and music of Sindh, elements of Vedantism merge with Sufism and it is difficult to know where one begins and the other ends. In his autobiography, Kripalani mentions how his brother "left the Hindu fold, with his wife and daughter, and became a Muslim. This was out of conviction. He had studied Arabic and Persian. In the new faith he was immediately accepted as a great and learned Maulana. He was tall and handsome, endowed with an attractive personality, and converted several young men of the community to Islam" (2004, 11). Kripalani also states that he continued to be dear to the family and was also a bit of a Hindu and a bit of a Muslim. Such voluntary conversions, not just from stigmatised communities, but also from socially privileged groups were common in Sindh. Thus the socio-religious interaction in Sindh evolved out of a unique local history and must be viewed in its own context.

Centres of power

The paradox of the Sindhi Hindus who (especially now) see themselves as direct descendants of a pure Aryan civilisation, but who practise a Sufi-indoctrinated version of Hinduism, is one among the many in Sindh. Equally intriguing is the fact that a religious minority with little political power controlled the economy of Sindh. Trade and finance were in the hands of the Hindus, while political power was the preserve of the Muslims. No matter how rich a Hindu bania was, he still owed allegiance to the natural leaders of Sindh—the Mir, the pir and the wadero. These three centres of power characterised the political sphere in Sindh. The Mirs were clearly the royalty, the ruling dynasty who lost Sindh to the British in 1843. The pirs were the various spiritual heads of Sindhi society. They claimed holy lineage and provided spiritual support, advice and direction largely to the Sindhi Muslims, and also to some Hindus. The political control of the pirs would come into play when Sindh faced issues of local governance (Ansari 1992). The wadero, literally meaning the elder (of the community) complemented the pirs by providing secular support. The wadero was most often an established landowner and the village chief. His authority was drawn from his social and economic superiority, handed down to him over generations. Even after the fall of the Talpur Mirs, "the pir and the wadero shared the leadership of Sindhi society" (Cheesman 1997, 38). If the Mir, the pir and the wadero represented power at one end of the spectrum, the haaris or the cultivators of Sindh represented the other. The haaris – the landless labourers of Sindh – were (and still are) its most disempowered section. They were mostly Muslim and had neither economic nor political power. Somewhere in the middle of the spectrum were groups like the Baluchis, who constituted one-fifth of Sindh's Muslim population. According to Cheesman, the Kalhoras of the eighteenth century brought the Baluchis with them as part of their army. Their military history and fierce code of honour made them a potential threat to the British in the nineteenth century. Thus, political power, although a preserve of the Muslims, was far from uniform.

At the same time, "Commerce in Sindh owed its existence to the Hindus, who used to finance the state, and exercised a great influence over their Mohammedan masters in spite of those masters often oppressing and always affecting to despise them," remarks the controversial Seth Naoomal in his much discussed memoirs (1915, 9).[6] It may be worth asking, as Markovits does, how did a religious minority in a Muslim-dominated province where most of the population had converted between the fifteenth and eighteenth centuries, control trade and finance? One answer to this question lies in the population and demographic distribution of Sindh. Although Muslims did form the numerical majority of Sindh, they lived in villages as landowners, feudal lords or labourers. In the words of the famous traveller Richard Burton, "throughout Sindh, the Hindu element preponderates in the cities and towns, the Moslem in the

6. Seth Naoomal Hotchand was one of Sindh's richest and most influential figures in the nineteenth century. Ill-treated by the Talpur Mirs, he played a significant role in facilitating the British annexation of Sindh. In the rewriting of Hindu history as one of subjugation under Muslim rule, Seth Naoomal has acquired considerable significance for having brought an end to Muslim rule. According to the writer J.M. Girglani, "There are different ways of looking at history. The earlier criticism of Seth Naoomal was written during an era when the freedom struggle and Gandhian philosophy provided the paradigm of Indian intellectualism. But today when secularism has got perverted into a prop to minority communalism and majority denigration resulting in the partition of the country and communal bloodshed, the conduct and actions of Seth Naoomal would appear to be quite justified and laudable. Let us admit that the advent of British rule in Sindh saved the Sindhi Hindus from the possibility of total serfdom or total conversion" (2003, 3).

country: the former everywhere represents capital, the latter labour" (1851/1993, 298). The levels of literacy among Muslims were very poor and landless labourers formed the bulk of Sindh's Muslim population. Another factor that may account for the somewhat unusual prosperity enjoyed by them is that the Hindus of Sindh were free of some of the religious injunctions borne not only by the Muslims of Sindh but also certain Hindu communities of India. For instance, the Muslims could not engage in money-lending because of an Islamic injunction against riba (charging interest). The Hindus of Shikarpur (like the Jews in Europe) emerged in the eigthteenth and nineteenth centuries as a powerful class of moneylenders. The Sindhi Hindus did not bother with inhibitive rules regarding pollution. Unlike the upper castes of India, they could travel by sea and mix for commercial reasons with other races without the fear of pollution. Even at the risk of generalisation it must be said that the Sindhi Hindus were an enterprising and shrewd community, who managed to turn a disadvantageous situation into one of advantage. By the time the British conquered Sindh, this community had had over two centuries of experience in finance. The Hindu amils operated unobtrusively as diwans and munshis in the courts of the Kalhoras and Mirs. If they saw profit in mastering Persian and adopting Muslim ways, they took a pragmatic stand and did what they had to. Their affluence was one of the most unusual aspects of this back of the beyond province. For instance, Seth Naoomal had a firm based in Karachi with agents in Bombay, Kutch and Calcutta. In 1832, the manager of Naoomal's Calcutta branch bought a European ship and put it under an English master on a salary of Rs. 400 per month (Cheesman 1997, 49). Markovits' study (2000) on the Shikarpuri merchants provides a mind-boggling picture of the vast operations of Sindhi Hindus in the remote places of the world. It also helps put in perspective the much-resented affluence of the Hindu banias, accrued not entirely from the exploitation of poor Muslims but also from enterprise.

The foregoing discussion provides in broad strokes the socio-religious world view of the Sindhi Hindus, and also the political economy of Sindh. We observe asymmetries in the distribution of economic and political power. At the same time, the political economy of Sindh had internal checks and balances so that the bania could not abuse his economic power and the Muslim ruler could not abuse his political power. This interdependence contained conflicts and created an ethos of intimacy. Concurrently, Sindh's geographical and cultural isolation made for a distinct and local evolution of a socio-religious world view that allowed neither the Hindu nor the Muslim to be rigid and orthodox. It made for identities that were porous and fluid. The arrival of the British, which forms the focus of the next chapter, was to cause alterations in the socio-economic life, which also influenced the fluidity of identities. The following discussion is based on the colonial experience of Sindh.

2 Colonial Sindh (1843–1936)

We have no right to seize Sind, yet we shall do so and a very advantageous, humane and useful piece of rascality it will be.

—Charles Napier

Sindh is very differently situated from any of our old possessions and even from most of our recent possessions...

—Sir Bartle Frere

The British annexation of Sindh in 1843 created a heated debate. Charles Napier's smug and famous message 'Peccavi' (a pun on sin and Sindh) to the governor general in Bombay has masked in popular memory his own admission of the grey nature of the victory. Napier's dubious feat of conquering Sindh happened at a time when liberal English opinion was weighted against conquering new territories. Multiple interpretations prevail on why the British needed a backward province like Sindh that had until the nineteenth century never drawn colonial attention. According to Markovits, the opium trade from Malwa to China through Sindh was one of the reasons why the British wanted Sindh. Despite several efforts to monitor this lucrative business, the British had not succeeded in keeping a check on it (2000, 42). Access to Sindh would give them access to the opium route and their own share in the business. Apart from this economic aspect, the British also needed Sindh for military reasons. Sindh was strategically located—it was the gate to Khorassan. In the mid-nineteenth century, the British feared invasion from Russia, and Sindh offered the possibility of fortifying the British-ruled part of the subcontinent. Thus the "British joined the invaders and conquerors who had gone before—the Mughals, the Persians, the Afghans and most recently, the Baluchis in seeking to wrest from Sindh and its river, strategic, military and economic advantages to strengthen and consolidate their imperial rule in India" (Jones 2002, 1). Moreover, after the defeat of Napoleon in 1815 in the Peninsular War, the British administrator Charles Napier or rather the "crude soldier" needed to get something right (Choksey and Shastry 1983, 14). Sindh represented new booty to a frustrated English officer. Sir Charles Napier was appointed the commander of the British troops in Sindh in 1842, when Lord Ellenborough was the Governor General of India. Once Sindh was annexed, Napier had complete control over a province that was far from the affairs of the Bombay Presidency. It gave Napier enough opportunity for high-handedness, leading to his humiliating departure from the province in 1847.[1]

The Napier period of administration lasted only for four years and did not witness any significant administrative reform. It was left to his successor, Sir Bartle Frere, to initiate the process of a serious engagement with Sindh. Frere merged Sindh with the Bombay Presidency and made it a part of the same administrative unit. Although this move would not improve the economic life of Sindh, it brought a sleepy and isolated province in contact with events in mainstream India. Frere found Sindh abysmally lacking in modern facilities

---

1. It inspired his brother William Napier to 'set the record straight' and attempt to vindicate him in a book, *The History of General Napier's Conquest of Scinde* (1857/2001).

and systems. Upon his arrival in Sindh in 1848 he noticed that there
was "not a mile of bridged or of metalled road, not a masonry bridge
of any kind—in fact not five miles of any cleared road—only a set of
barracks of higher class than 'temporary', not a single dawk bungalow,
serai, or dharmashala…" (in Choksey and Shastry 1983, 35). Frere's
own efforts at devising a canal system and irrigation policies were
often frustrated because the infrastructure was extremely poor, the
officers in Sindh not motivated and the language (Sindhi) unknown
to British administrators. The harsh climate of Sindh, its rocky terrain,
the feudal nature of its society (with its large illiterate population),
repressive pirs and waderos made the province "one of the least lovely
in India" (in Cheesman 1997, 14). A posting in Sindh was almost a
punishment. Given such indifference from all quarters, the effect of
direct policies in Sindh was slow, and signs of colonial modernity,
few. Scholars who have written extensively on Sindh (Choksey and
Shastry 1983; Cheesman 1997; Khuhro 1999) demonstrate two chief
areas of concern – education and land reforms – both of which had
far-reaching effects. This chapter discusses British education and land
reforms to show how they, perhaps willy-nilly, benefited the Hindus
and caused a serious imbalance in the socio-economic relations between
the Hindus and the Muslims. While the differences in class increased,
they also happened to correspond with an increasing awareness of
religious differences, so that the rich-Hindu–poor-Muslim discourse
was grafted onto the social consciousness of Sindh. With new prospects
of economic power in colonial Sindh, the old and symbiotic
relationship between the wadero, the amil and the bania which had
tended to cut across the Hindu/Muslim and urban/rural divides
weakened (Ansari 2005, 23). This tipping of the socio-economic
balance in colonial Sindh led to the increasing political mobilisation
of the Muslims who began to see themselves as an exploited, under-
represented and backward group. This consciousness had its own role
to play in certain kinds of pre-Partition politics. This chapter provides
a hundred-year trajectory of Sindh, from the point of its annexation
and immediate inclusion in the Bombay Presidency to its separation
from the same in 1936.

LANGUAGE AND EDUCATION

One of the first systems the British needed to put in place was the language of communication and administration. In pre-British Sindh, Persian was used as a language of administration in the courts of the Kalhoras and the Talpur Mirs. Some sections of the Muslim religious elite and teachers such as the Syeds, and the Hindu amils who had worked as revenue officers and ministers in the courts of the Talpur Mirs were well-versed in Persian. However, a large majority of the province spoke only Sindhi and did not know Persian, Sanskrit or Hindustani, any of the languages the British officers would have been conversant with. Sindhi was a new language for the British despite its roots in Sanskrit, because the mountain languages of Central Asia had influenced it considerably. At the same time, it was imperative to retain Sindhi as the official language of the province because it was the only common, spoken language in the province. The difficulty now lay with the script. Sindhi did not have a uniform script because different people wrote it in different scripts. The Nanakpanthi section of the Hindus (the followers of Guru Nanak) used the Gurmukhi script, while the Hindu banias and small shopkeepers maintained their accounts in Khudawadi or Hatkai (a script devoid of vowels). The literate sections among the Muslims who had attended indigenous schools run by the Syed community and the Hindu amils who had studied in such schools wrote in the Perso-Arabic script. Considerable deliberation was necessary before the British could arrive at a consensus about the script (Khuhro 1999, 230–40). When the decision was finally made in favour of the Perso-Arabic script, it was done because, as Barrow Ellis, the deputy commissioner mentioned, "...while the great majority of the population of Sindh consists of Mahomedans, it is imperative on us that we should not deter them from entering the public service and debar them from means of instruction in their own language, by the universal adoption of a Hindu-Sindhi character, which the Mussalmans would never adopt" (in Khuhro 1999, 239). Ironically, it was the Hindus who mastered Sindhi in the Perso-Arabic script much more easily than the Muslims and cornered most of the official

jobs. This was largely because the Hindus made themselves the chief
beneficiaries of the new education.

Once the steps towards determining an official language had been
taken, deciding the educational policy was not difficult. The British
administrators in Sindh hailed from the Bombay Presidency and were
thus steeped in the education system of Bombay. As a consequence, it
was decided that the language of primary education (i.e. up to the
seventh standard) would be Sindhi, while that for higher studies would
be English. With this in mind, the British government approved schools
that followed the state policies of instruction and supported them as
'grant-in-aid' schools. Once the British machinery was well-entrenched
in Sindh, a host of schools run by Christian missionaries, Parsis,
Gujaratis and Hindus cropped up. Since Karachi became the British
capital of Sindh, most of the modern schools were established there; a
number of schools were also set up in the bigger towns of Sukkur,
Shikarpur and Hyderabad. In this new scheme of things, education in
Sindhi became almost an entirely urban phenomenon. The
responsibility of providing education to rural children fell upon local
and municipal boards which were supported by the government only
partially. Simultaneously, indigenous schools run in pre-colonial Sindh
through the patronage of the courts or rich zamindars stopped receiving
financial help from the government.

While these developments may appear neutral and were similar to
the educational systems and reforms elsewhere in the Bombay
Presidency, the consequences for Sindh were fairly drastic. Jones'
research on the social demography of Sindh shows how Sindh had a
sharp urban–rural divide corresponding with the Hindu and Muslim
populations respectively. The data below from Jones (2002, 2–3) serve
to highlight this severe demarcation.

The urban–rural divide

In 1931, the Hindus numbered 1,015,225 or 28% of the total
population while the Muslims, by far the largest community, totalled

2,830,800 or 70% of the population. The rural–urban settlement patterns in Sindh tended to follow along communal lines.

Table 1: Sindh's population by religion and district

District	Hindus	Muslims
Karachi	162,111	465,785
Hyderabad	198,684	460,920
Nawabshah	115,899	377,746
Larkana	113,040	577,899
Sukkur	177,467	440,148
Thar Parker	218,850	245,964

Source: Data from Jones (2002).

Thus the Hindu populace, particularly the upper castes, was concentrated in the cities, towns and larger villages of Sindh, while the vast majority of the Sindhi Muslims lived in small villages in the rural areas. On an average, the Hindus in the towns outnumbered the Muslims by 29%. In sharp contrast to this, in the rural areas there were three times as many Muslims as there were Hindus.

Table 2: Hindus per 100 Muslims in urban and rural areas by district

District	Urban	Rural
Sindh (overall)	129	25
Karachi	96	9
Hyderabad	180	28
Nawabshah	235	26
Larkana	105	15
Sukkur	155	22
Thar Parker	272	86

Source: Data from Jones (2002).

Since a large section of the Muslim population lived in villages as a cultivating or landowning class and the newly established schools were very much an urban phenomenon, access to education was both difficult and expensive for them. As people living in rural areas, they had to make do, if at all, with schools run by local boards (with inadequate funds from the government) or the fast-declining indigenous schools such as the madrasas.

The *Gazetteer of the Province of Sindh* (1927) shows the following enrolment figures for Hindus and Muslims in the urban cities of Karachi and Hyderabad in 1916:

> The total enrolment of a government school—the Narayan Jaganatha High School—in 1916 was 477 students, which also included Jains, Parsis and Jews. The number of Hindu students was 350, while that of Muslims was 12.
>
> The enrolment of students in a private mission school, the Church Mission High School, in the same year was 417, out of which 256 were Hindus and 35 Muslims.
>
> D.J. Sind College in Karachi, Sindh's most prestigious college, showed an enrolment of 268 students in 1915–1916, which included 181 Hindus and 39 Muslims.

Since the majority of Hindus lived in the cities and the majority of the Muslim population was distributed in the villages, the Hindus became the chief beneficiaries of the new education system. As functionaries of the old regime where they were used to working as clerks, ministers and revenue operators, the Sindhi Hindus equipped themselves for jobs in the British system. Adeel Khan, as he traces the process of pre-Partition politics in Sindh, on examining the stark contrast between the literacy levels of the two communities, remarks, "The immense poverty of the Muslims, the stranglehold of the oppressive feudal system, the lack of education facilities, and the high cost of whatever educational institutions were available—all worked against the 'luxury' of education. By the end of the nineteenth century only 1.4% of the Muslims (who accounted for 78% of Sindh's population) were literate" (2005, 130).

As the new education appeared unsuitable and inaccessible to Muslims and their indigenous education through the madrasas suffered due to lack of government funds, the Muslims of Sindh were caught in a vicious cycle where the lack of education made the processes of empowerment unavailable and their disempowerment led to a lack of education and service opportunities. The impact of this phenomenon upon the sociology of Sindh manifest itself in serious class and communal cleavages. By the beginning of the twentieth century, there was a considerable discrepancy between the two communities: literate Hindus formed 9.3% of Sindh's population, while literate Muslims formed 0.74%. For a community that formed the majority of Sindh's population, the Muslims appeared to be the least represented in government and administrative structures. With the exception of its landowning class (the waderos) and the religious elite (the pirs), most Muslims had access to neither capital nor civil services. In its self-perception, the Muslim community saw itself as severely under-represented and found the Hindu share in government services disproportionately high. This feeling was not without justification. For instance, in 1895 the Hindu share in the judiciary alone was 80% and there was not a single Muslim magistrate (Khan 2005, 131). Hence the Muslim resentment of the 'over-representation' of the Hindus in government jobs was understandable.

Simultaneously, the Muslim community also incurred a drastic loss through the colonial policies on land. The following discussion shows how land reforms in British Sindh led to the indebtedness of the Muslim landowner and the rise of the Hindu moneylender.

The Hindu moneylender: From peti to kheti

The land reforms initiated by the British had far-reaching effects on the predominantly agricultural economy of Sindh. Agricultural stakes in Sindh were higher than those of other provinces because climatic conditions were harsh. Save parts of central and northern Sindh (which benefited most from the river Indus), a large portion of land was desert-like. What the British needed was an effective land policy that would increase their own revenue without upsetting the traditional agrarian arrangement. Choksey and Shastry's study on land and irrigation policies in Sindh demonstrates the long delays and ineffectual modes of policy implementation (1983). The tale of establishing an effective irrigation system in Sindh, note Choksey and Shastry, began in the 1850s and almost ended with the opening of the great Sukkur Barrage in 1935. In order to understand the changes effected by the British in the agricultural economy of Sindh, it is important to have a look at the system they were encountering.

The traditional agrarian arrangement mainly involved the waderos and the haaris, both Muslims. The waderos were the landed gentry of Sindh who possessed tremendous social and political prestige in the villages. The haaris or the landless cultivators of Sindh were its poorest section and formed a majority of the Muslim community. The haaris were far too poor to own any capital, equipment, or even seeds and manure, to till the land. They would borrow money from the Hindu banias in exchange for their agricultural produce. The wadero would not lend money to the haari because his religion prevented him from charging interest. Every village in Sindh had Hindu shopkeepers who could spare cash and did not mind an occasional foray into money-lending. The political regime of the Mirs had put enough fear in the Hindu bania not to charge very high rates of interest. The Hindu bania was also not allowed to own land; hence, the incentive for his involvement in land was not very high in pre-colonial Sindh. The responsibility of looking after the land and its cultivation did not interest him, especially at a time when agriculture in Sindh did not yield good produce. For instance, when the British wished to confer an uncultivable land as jagir (endowment) upon Seth Naoomal, the rich Hindu merchant well-known for helping the British conquer Sindh, his reaction was, "I wished to secure a *peti* [a cash box] whereas he [the collector] proposed to force upon me *kheti* [farming] which would necessitate my supervision and attendance all the year around..." (1915, 180).

However, there is a change in this scenario due to the land reforms introduced by the British. The British imposed a mandatory tax on all cultivable as well as non-cultivable land, which increased the burden of payment on the waderos. Owning land brought them prestige and some agricultural produce which they shared with the haari. As long as this situation prevailed, they stood to gain some but lose nothing. The policy of imposing a mandatory tax on land in colonial Sindh, known as the Diffused Resettlement Act, drew the waderos into a quagmire of debt. The wadero's reluctance to sell ancestral property and his inability to understand financial matters, made him mortgage his property. The most likely candidate for this kind of transaction was the bania who did not mind charging usurious rates of interest in the new dispensation. In the process, the Hindu bania/shopkeeper who occasionally lent money now became a regular moneylender with whom the haaris as well as the waderos mortgaged their possessions. Even today, in post-Partition Sindh, Muslim Sindhis share jokes about the shrewd bania who used to mislead the rural and uneducated Muslim with his 'complex' arithmetic:

> *Panj baaro assi…*
> *Daha siraikki chhad,*
> *Navve te sahi kar!*

> Five times twelve is eighty…
> Never mind ten,
> Sign for ninety!
> (Khalique Jonejo, personal interview)

As things stood in 1896, the Hindu bania turned moneylender possessed 42% of the arable land in Sindh, a result of the land transfer from the waderos to the Hindus. The indebted wadero had been signing his land off to the Hindu moneylender—a phenomenon peculiar to the economy of Sindh in the nineteenth century.[2] The haaris of Sindh continued to be poor, and since they lived in a dispensation where the British were not bothered about them, the Hindus charged them usurious rates of interest while the waderos gave them no land rights for tilling. The haari was thus caught between two exploitative agencies—both sanctioned, at least initially, by the British government. According to Richard Burton, "there are few

---

2. David Cheesman's study (1997) on money-lending in rural Sindh discusses the contexts that led to the ruination of the peasantry and the transfer of land from the wadero to the bania.

districts in this part of Asia where the cultivators are not bankrupt, only prevented from failing as it were, by its being the interest of the creditor not to ruin his debtor beyond a certain point" (1851/1993, 299). He describes the way by which this comes to pass in Sindh:

> The peasant paid one-third of the produce of his fields to the ruler, Amir, governor, or collector: we will suppose that he paid it in kind, to make the hard condition as favourable as possible to him. Upon the next moiety, or two-thirds, he and his family had not only to subsist till the next harvest, but also out of it he was required to economise so as to have the resources to sow his fields when the season came round. Here lay the difficulty. The peasant could not save; and if he could, he would not save, so when seed was required, he went to the Hindu, the usurer and attorney of the little parish; and, after immense trouble, he borrowed, at the rate of about cent per cent, mortgaging at the same time the coming harvest, the smallest quantity of grain deemed necessary. He was then a ruined man. (299)

The implications of these imbalances were not only feudal but also communal since the creditors were always Hindu and the debtors, Muslim. In the discourse on exploitation of the peasantry in Sindh, especially the one encouraged by the Muslim League in the twentieth century, the wadero was absolved. The villain was the 'omnipresent bania', an eyesore to rural Muslims because his success was suddenly visible.

The British were disconcerted by the debts of the waderos, since the waderos occupied a very crucial position in society; they were the "governors who governed Sindh" (Cheesman 1997, 219). Dislodging the waderos from their traditional seats of authority did not bode well for the British who had not intended to upset the traditional balances in Sindh; the dissatisfaction of the Muslims in Sindh could very well take the colonial regime with it. In Cheesman's words, "Within a couple of decades of the British conquest, a number of officers serving in Sind began to suspect that the Waderos were getting the worst of the competition. They were floundering in a mesh of debt and usurious interest payments. Their estates were breaking up and passing on to their Hindu creditors" (52). The British instituted immediate corrective measures at the end of the century by introducing the Sindh

Encumbered Estates Act in 1876, in accordance with which, they took charge of mortgaged land and paid off the waderos' debts to the bania by overseeing cultivation. According to Markovits (2000), this may have caused a reversal in land transfer in the twentieth century. Nonetheless, to the rural Muslims, the Hindu rack-renter – the moneylender – was living off the wadero and the haari and was solely responsible for the increasing poverty of the Muslim community. When the political mobilisation of Muslims took on particularly communal hues in the twentieth century, the Hindu moneylender was to become the chief villain of the script about the Muslim community's poverty.

It can be concluded from the discussion above that as in education so in agriculture, the Muslims were losing their influence and hold (Khuhro 1999, 293). The British concentration on urban education and the withdrawal of support from traditional Muslim education caused a very sharp contrast to emerge in class, in status and in the general processes of empowerment and modernity. Simultaneously, rural Sindh also witnessed the rise of the Hindu moneylender who owed at least some portion of his prosperity to the indebtedness of the Sindhi Muslim. From a shopkeeper or trader, the Hindu had risen to be a landowner cum moneylender who in the perception of the Muslim charged usurious rates of interest and showed no concern for his impoverished Muslim brethren.

THE RISE OF KARACHI

The people of Sindh were watching the drastic changes taking place in the sociology of Sindh. As the British government's slow-moving schemes began to materialise, Sindh became far more integrated with the rest of India than before. By the second decade of the twentieth century, Karachi had a premier airport and one of the four busiest ports in the country. The "opening up of Sindh" (Ansari 2005, 23) and the rise of Karachi upped the economic opportunities, creating far more competition in business and bureaucracy than before. One of the most frequently articulated grievances that the Muslims had against the Hindus amils was their over-representation in bureaucracy.

With the rise of Karachi, this grievance against the Hindu amils would collapse with all 'outsiders' who take from Sindh what rightfully belongs to Sindhis. But that is something I would like to deal with later. For now, let us look at Karachi and how it stood out in Sindh as its most important business hub.

The British decision to make Karachi the new commercial capital of Sindh led to a large influx of 'outsiders' – Gujarati and Kutchi traders, Parsi contractors, Jewish merchants, Punjabi businessmen – into Karachi towards the end of the nineteenth century. By the early years of the twentieth century, Karachi had become the most successful trading city of Sindh; it had large harbours and was well linked by rail and even by air. The *Gazetteer of the Province of Sindh* (1927) shows the rise in the rate of migration to Karachi per decade:

1881 – 18%
1891 – 16%
1901 – 23%
1911 – 22%
1921 – 21%

Within forty years of the advent of British rule, the value of trade handled by Karachi had multiplied seven times over—it exceeded six million pounds annually (Ansari 2005, 25). While Karachi brought Sindh into the sphere of hectic commercial activity and network of communications, it also created new and distinct insecurities amongst the Hindus and Muslims. As far as the Hindu traders of Karachi were concerned, the new entrants in business were giving them stiff competition. The Sindhi merchant class organised under the 1860 Karachi Chamber of Commerce was the first body to express resentment at the dominance of the Bombay traders. The Muslims of Sindh began to wonder why despite being a numerical majority they were not represented in Sindh's most important trade centre. In their self-perception this served as one more reason for the belief that the Muslims of Sindh did not enjoy just desserts 'in their own land'. This phenomenon was also consolidated further by a rising political consciousness among the Muslims that they needed to organise and seek greater representation.

Political consciousness among the Sindhi Muslims

New elite spokesmen like Hassan Ali Effendi and Rais Ghulam Bhurgri were the first to articulate the economic unrest among the Muslims of Sindh. Effendi, a leading Muslim educationist, established the Sind Mohammedan Association (SMA) in 1883 which was one of the formative organisations that claimed to represent the Muslims of Sindh and lobbied for a 'fair share' in terms of education, agriculture and political representation. Effendi represents the rise of a small but influential Muslim class that was exposed to western education and felt strongly about the backwardness of the Sindhi Muslims. The purpose of the SMA was to ensure that the Muslim community received the benefits accruing from British rule, specifically in getting fair treatment for Mohammedan representation in municipalities and district local boards, and in the legislative councils (see Khuhro 1999; Jones 2002). This was the first time leading Muslims got together to protect the interests of the community. A corollary organisation, the Sindh Madrasa was set up (again by Effendi) in 1885, swiftly marking the increase in political awareness.

Rais Ghulam Bhurgri had the chance to project Sindh on a wider stage when he was elected to the Bombay Council, where eventually he also became a participant in the newly formed Muslim League, as well as in the Congress. At the turn of the twentieth century, Bhurgri set up the Sindh Zamindar Association (SZA), an organisation that looked into assessment rates and legislation regarding land alienation. Simultaneously in 1865, the Bombay government extended to Sindh its Act of 1863, ordering the establishment of local funds and the creation of committees and municipal bodies. Subsequently, the Morley Minto reforms in 1909 also gave opportunities for fulfilling political aspirations and projecting the issues of Sindh on a wider scale. This new leadership emerged from the landed elite—the Mirs, pirs and waderos. Sindh's religious elite had a particularly significant part to play; Sarah Ansari's study (1992) shows how the pirs used their religious legitimacy for electoral gains. These early organisations played an important role in helping the Muslims shape the campaign strategies, which they would use effectively while seeking the autonomy of Sindh from the Bombay government.

During the early stages of Muslim politicisation, Sindh was not operating along sharply drawn communal lines. For instance, Bhurgri when he was the secretary of the Congress session in 1917 had the support of not only Shaikh Abdul Majid Sindhi and Shaikh Noor Mohammed but also of people like Harchandrai Vishindas—individuals concerned with the poverty of the rural masses in Sindh. In fact, some Hindus like Jairamdas Daulatram and Dr. Choithram Gidwani continued to be part of rural upliftment programmes until Partition. Similarly, before Effendi set up the SMA, he was associated with the Sindh Sabha, a quasi-political association with both Hindu and Muslim membership, concerned with airing the views and grievances of the natives in newspapers and on platforms. When the SMA was formed, Hindus were allowed to become honorary members (Khuhro 1999, 173).

Both the Muslims and the Hindus of Sindh, hitherto cut off from the activities and concerns of mainstream India, increasingly began to engage in greater dialogue with all-India Hindu and Muslim organisations. Among the Muslims this dialogue manifests in greater political awareness. An influential episode in this regard is the Khilafat Movement, a campaign triggered off by British hostility towards Turkey during the First World War. It threatened the religious and political authority of the Caliph of Turkey and as a response of solidarity, branches of the All-India Khilafat Conference were established in various parts of India. In Sindh, they were established by Sheikh Abdul Majid Sindhi, a Hyderabadi journalist, and Abdullah Haroon, a Karachi merchant, both of whom played a prominent role in the province's subsequent political affairs (Jones 2002, 7).

It seems fitting to me that, at this eventful juncture in the socio-political lives of the Sindhi Muslims, we now take our leave of them for a short while, in order to turn our gaze to the changes that were being effected in the social, political and religious lives of the Sindhi Hindus. Due to the increased interaction with mainstream India resulting in attempts to become 'proper' Hindus, we see transformations in the collective consciousness of the Sindhi Hindus gradually leading to a narrowing of self-definition.

SOCIO-POLITICAL CHANGES AMONG THE SINDHI HINDUS

At a time when some of the Muslim zamindars and pirs were involved in the Khilafat, the Hindus of Karachi and Hyderabad had also opened themselves up to a range of anti-imperialist activities, especially from 1900 to the 1930s. When the revolutionary Khudiram Bose from Bengal was hanged in 1908, young Sindhi Hindus in Hyderabad put up his portraits in their houses. When Gangadhar Tilak was sentenced to six years' imprisonment, many young men began to sleep on the floor. Narayandas Malkani mentions in his autobiography how this defined the beginning of a 'nationalist career' for him. Choithram Gidwani remembers collecting funds for Madame Bikhaji Cama, the Indian revolutionary in Paris. In 1910, J.B. Kripalani, Choithram Gidwani and others set up the Brahmacharya Ashram in Hyderabad to create patriotic feelings among young men and also to help revolutionaries in hiding. Secret help was extended to Rashbehaari Bose (the mentor of Subhash Chandra Bose) to aid his escape to Japan, via Afghanistan. Tilak's visit to Sindh in 1920 evoked a very warm response. All these unconnected gestures were consolidated when Gandhi first visited Sindh in 1916. Like the protagonist of Ram Panjwani's novel *Kaidi,* who moved from the violent means of Bengali extremism to Gandhian philosophy, the Hindu nationalists shifted their focus. Gandhi visited Sindh seven times between 1916 and 1934, and found life-long supporters in Acharya Kripalani, Choithram Gidwani, Jairamdas Daulatram and Allah Baksh Soomro (who later became the chief minister of Sindh once it secured its independence from the Bombay Presidency, and was assassinated in 1942). It may be possible to establish a synonymy between Gandhi and the Congress; both evoked fairly positive responses in Sindh from 1910 into the 1930s.

Social reform

The combination of western liberal education and the nascent nationalism of the nineteenth century created a context for reform in India, the nature and thrust of which varied from community to community.[3] Multiple and heterogeneous efforts at redefining 'self' and one's socio-religious life – emerging out of the specific contexts of the nineteenth century – are included in the umbrella term 'reform'. The difficulty in using the term reform is further compounded by other theoretical considerations of whether reform was a temporal or a thematic phenomenon. Sindh in the nineteenth century was not isolated from the kind of self-critique that characterised urban sections of Bengal and Maharashtra.

In the social lives of the Sindhi Hindus, the year 1869 when Navalram Advani from Hyderabad, Sindh, visited Calcutta and was influenced by the Brahmo Samaj, is a landmark. Advani belonged to the educated section of Sindhi Hindu society (the amils) and was a deputy collector. He also established the Sikh Sabha (later renamed the Sukhi Sabha) in Hyderabad. It was an institution devoted to the propagation of Guru Nanak's teachings, in continuity with the Sindhi Hindus' spiritual affiliation with Sikhism, contributing to the community's atypical practice of Hinduism.[4] Therefore, when Advani encountered Keshub Chander Sen (one of the founders of the Brahmo Samaj) and through him the Brahmo Samaj, the institution seemed to him consistent with the forms of theism and caste tolerance as practised by the Sindhi Hindus. The Brahmo Samaj is based upon a monotheistic worship of the Vedic Brahma and eschews ritualistic Hinduism. This found an echo in the educated Sindhi Hindus, especially those from Hyderabad, who were introduced to it by Advani.

3. For instance, the generalisations about reform in Bengal cannot be applied to Gujarat, which responded more in economic terms—such as indigenisation of industry (Kothari 2004).

4. The Sindhis in India continue to visit gurudwaras, and sometimes also built their own gurudwaras with Hindu gods on one side and the Guru Granth Sahib on the other. It is more common to see Sindhis celebrate Guru Nanak Jayanti than Ramnavmi. It must also be added that the Sindhi version of Sikhism precludes the tenets of khalsa or preparation of armed defence.

This phenomenon in the last decades of the nineteenth century marks the beginning of Hindu 'reform' in Sindh (Malhi 1988). What especially attracted Advani to the Brahmo Samaj was not so much its religious reformism, but its thrust towards educating women, the prohibition of sati and the encouragement of widow remarriage. Sindhi Hindu women in the nineteenth century practised purdah and lived a completely closeted life. Advani noticed that even in the most 'liberal' city of Hyderabad which had a large population of educated Hindus, there were no women who did not observe purdah. Levels of illiteracy were high, child marriages pervasive and girls were hardly ever sent to school. Centuries of life in a relatively isolated province, proximity with Islam and the feudal system in Sindh had made Hindu women virtually indistinguishable from their Muslim counterparts.[5] Advani took along with him other amils of Hyderabad, amongst whom was also his brother Hiranand, and upon his return to Sindh, set in motion concrete reforms. The outcome was the well-known Navalram Hiranand Academy, one of the earliest schools offering modern education in Sindh. A contemporary of Advani, Dayaram Gidumal who studied law at Elphinstone College, Bombay, came back to Sindh and established the Sindh Sabha in 1892. The Sindh Sabha had a much broader base than the Sukhi Sabha for it aimed at addressing the social upliftment of Sindh as a province. It paid particular attention

5. In the "socio-religious vulnerability" (Chowdhury 1996, 2308) of the early decades of the twentieth century, the Sindhi Hindu man was concerned with creating a distinct Hindu identity not only for himself but also for the Sindhi Hindu woman. For instance, an organisation called the Om Mandli established by the diamond merchant Lala Lekhraj Kriplani in 1937 in Hyderabad, did not have an overt communal or even revivalist stance, but was somewhat Brahminic about its woman followers who were its chief target. It played an important role in the redefining of Sindhi Hindu women in a new context, where they needed to be distinguished from Muslim women. The Om Mandli was interested in recruiting young women who were made to lead a celibate life and wear saris (as opposed to the salwar kameez the Sindhi Hindu women wore) so that they looked like a cross between a Bengali bhadramahila and a Christian nun. While in Sindh, the Om Mandli came under severe criticism by Hindus who considered it a disruptive force in family life. The British government banned the Om Mandli barely six years after its inception, but it revived with a different form and thrust in post-independence India. The impact of the Om Mandli was nowhere close to that of the Arya Samaj in Sindh, or to its own renewed avatar as the Brahmakumaris (see Chowdhury 1996).

to the development of schools and colleges, and was also supported by other communities such as the Parsis and the Muslims. Apart from Dayaram Gidumal, the leading members of the Sindh Sabha were Daulatram Jethmal (the founder of the D.J. Sind College), Udaram Mulchand and Hussain Ali Vakil. Although there was some resistance from the Muslim community, especially with respect to women's education, the Sindh Sabha was successful in drawing support from broad sections of Sindhi society and its role never became divisive.

Emancipatory and liberal reforms in nineteenth-century Sindh (as elsewhere in India) however, were largely restricted to the educated classes, particularly the amils.[6] The foundations of liberal Sindhi institutions began to shake in the tumultuous decades of the early twentieth century, especially in response to all-India events such as the Hindu–Muslim riots in the Maharashtra of the 1920s, the campaigns against cow slaughter, the establishment of the Hindu Mahasabha and the Rashtriya Swayamsevak Sangh (RSS), and also in response to events within Sindh.

The Brahmo Samaj must be recognised as a non-divisive and cosmopolitan beginning to reform movements in Sindh, and as the years passed, this kind of liberal reform would shrink to the more 'purificatory' practices of the Arya Samaj. In fact, the Brahmo Samaj in the form that Advani established did not survive for very long. From very early on in the twentieth century its foundations weakened in the face of controversies regarding conversion and increasing internal factions in Bengal. Sindh did not have a strong missionary movement and yet the perception of the Brahmo Samaj as an ally of Christianity did not leave Sindh unaffected.

During the divisive years of the Khilafat and Non-cooperation in the 1920s, civil spaces were also divided along communal lines so that Sadhu Hiranand the reformer was shocked to find in his own school, separate water arrangements for Hindus and Muslims. When he attempted to drink 'Muslim' water and break the barrier, students from both communities condemned his act. This, notes Malhi, was

---

6. Out of this trend emerged the well-known figure of T.L. Vaswani, whose Vaswani Mission in Pune is currently the largest Sindhi organisation devoted to self-reliance among women.

"the end of a cosmopolitan reform in Sindh. These were the contentious years" (1988, 43).

The Arya Samaj

A new strand within reformism was about keeping Hindus within the 'fold' and/or bringing them back to it; in Sindh it was expected to prevent conversions from Hinduism into Islam. From within the reformist groups in Hyderabad, there emerged concern over conversions of the amils into Islam. The amil affiliation with Islam (at least in terms of outward appearance—clothes, facial hair and language) was quite strong and identification with the rulers, with whom the amils worked closely, sometimes led to conversion. It is within this context of the peculiar political and ethnic solidarities of the early twentieth century that we must examine the emergence of the Arya Samaj in Sindh.

Although the Arya Samaj originated in the vision of Dayanand Saraswati who was from Gujarat, one of its most fertile spheres of influence was Punjab, and eventually its neighbouring province, Sindh. The Arya Samaj was founded in 1875 with a view to combating conversion and providing Hinduism its due place among competing religions like Islam and Christianity. Revivalist organisations such as the Arya Samaj forged an all-inclusive Hindu identity (as opposed to caste identities of Brahmins, Vaishnavs, etc.) to create notions of collectivity that could withstand threats from Christianity and Islam. It aimed at taking Hindus 'back to the Vedas' and reinstating a 'pure' state preceding the Puranas and other later accretions in Hinduism. This made the Arya Samaj eschew caste distinctions, which it saw as a post-Vedic phenomenon that went against the grain of pure Aryan identity. While this side of the Arya Samaj is concerned with social equality, the institution itself was formed as a response to new threats posed by missionary activity in the nineteenth century. If Punjab showed a tendency towards conversion into Sikhism and Christianity (Sharma 2000, 95), Sindhi Hindus were prone to converting to Islam. In either case, certain tools were handy, shuddhi (a purificatory rite by which the converted were brought back to Hinduism) being one of them. The Arya Samaj's practice of taking Hindus back into a purer, Aryan practice of religion extended to a literal re-conversion in the name of shuddhi. Untouchables in Punjab who had converted to Christianity and Hindus in Sindh who had converted to Islam were thus brought back to the Hindu fold. It brought the Arya Samaj in direct confrontation with other religious groups and led to sporadic religious tensions such as the Larkano riots of 1927.

When the Arya Samaj planted itself in Sindh in the mid 1920s, its combative role as an organisation that brought 'converted' Hindus 'back into the fold' had already been well established in Punjab. According to Gobind Chellani, a rising tide of amil conversion into Islam was the chief context for the arrival of the Arya Samaj in Sindh (1983, 53). It is difficult to determine the precise number of people who were drawn into the revivalist vortex or of those who refused to participate. According to the figures available on the Arya Samaj in Ahmedabad, Gujarat, it currently has 8000 members. There are strong affiliations with the Arya Samaj among some Sindhis in Mumbai and Ulhasnagar, Maharashtra, and in Ajmer and Jaipur, Rajasthan. The respondents from these organisations trace the existence of the organisation in Sindh. Gobind Chellani's book on the Arya Samaj in Sindh provides a list of over ninety well-known Arya Samajis from Sindh. The chairman of the Arya Samaj in Sindh was Shri Khemchand Gurnomal Shuddhimal and he was so committed to the cause, says Chellani, that he was "rightly called the Savarkar of Sindh" (52). Both Chellani and K.R. Malkani recount frequent incidents of conversion among the amils of Hyderabad and the controversial case of Tharumal Makhijiani who had converted to Islam but later wanted to revert to Hinduism. The furore surrounding this incident and the division of opinion in the Hindu panchayat as to whether re-conversion should be allowed, serves as a prelude to the arrival of the Arya Samaj. As far as the case of Tharumal Makhijiani (1878) was concerned, the Hindu panchayat in Hyderabad pronounced judgment against re-conversion. However, this set off intense debates about what seemed like a rise in conversions, because other amils (such as Moorajmal and Deoomal who had converted in 1891) had also converted to Islam, and whether they could be re-converted became a subject of contention. Consequently the issue led to seeking 'outside' help and Diwan Dayaram Gidumal wrote to Swami Shraddhanand of the Arya Samaj in 1893, asking the institution to intervene. As a response to Gidumal's request, Pandit Lekhrajani Arya and Pandit Puran Anand reached Sindh. The first public meeting of the Arya Samaj in Sindh was in 1893. The two pandits worked day and night, and the moment they came to know of someone with the slightest desire to change his religion, they would not leave him alone till he had changed his mind (K.R. Malkani. 1984, 9; Chellani 1983, 57).

During the 1920s, the Arya Samaj became particularly active and contributed directly to Hindu–Muslim confrontation. Interestingly, as the extract given below testifies, the Samaj was less interested in cultivating the spirit of Hinduism than in ensuring that the Hindus remained Hindu:

> The mass conversions of Muslims to Hinduism assumed significant proportions only in the 1920s, in the backdrop of concerted efforts by the Muslim and Hindu elite to inflate their numbers so as to enhance their political bargaining power. The Arya Samaj was particularly successful among Muslim groups which were only partially Islamised and had still retained many of their old Hindu customs and beliefs. Thus, for instance, the Sheikhs of Larkano (Sind), a low half Muslim–half Hindu caste, were converted by the Sukkur unit of the Arya Samaj as early as in 1905. Similar was the case with the Sabrai Labanas of Ludhiana (Punjab) and the Marwaris of Ajmer (Rajputana), who, like the Larkano Sheikhs, followed a curious mixture of Hindu and Islamic practices.
>
> It is interesting to note that these group conversions to Hinduism organised by the Arya Samaj entailed essentially the giving up of certain Islamic customs such as the burial of the dead, '*nikah*', the visiting of *dargahs*, and circumcision, rather than the imparting of Hindu religious knowledge to the new converts. This was possibly because the *shuddhi* movement was motivated far less by the desire to promote spirituality and moral and religious values than by strong anti-Muslim passion. (Sikand and Katju 1994, 2215)

There was also a gradual move to de-Arabise the Sindhi script and use the Nagri, along with a move to teach Hindi and Sanskrit instead of Persian. Choithram Gidwani (who later became a well-known Congress representative) travelled through Sindh advocating the use of the Nagri script. In addition to these 'reforms', the Arya Samaj also organised bahasbaazi (debates between Hinduism and Islam) in Hyderabad and Larkano. Chellani records a 'successful' debate on scripture in 1929 with the Anjuman Naseet Islam and the Arya Samaj representing Islam and Hinduism respectively. The Arya Samaj emerged 'triumphant' by showing that they knew far more about their scriptures than the representatives of Islam. The Arya Samaj contributed directly to the creation of mutually exclusive categories such as Islam and Hinduism. By 1923–24, the Khilafat and Non-cooperation movements were abandoned, creating a sense of vacuum after an intense period of nationalist sentiments. Khuhro offers a useful comment on that period: "In India the ugly head of communalism reared itself...the high passions aroused by mass movements resulted in turning those movements into religious frenzy...communal bitterness and strife spread throughout India in the '20s and its effects were felt in the peaceful, tolerant atmosphere of Sindh as well" (1982, 26). After the late 1930s, the Muslim League was more than happy to take these increasingly solidified communal categories further to the point of Partition.

Of course, not every Hindu was an Arya Samaji nor was every Arya Samaji a Hindu fundamentalist. For instance, notes Lakhmi Khilani, "Our family forbade us from reading Dayanand Saraswati's *Satyaprakash*. I can't remember exactly what reasons they gave, but they must have considered it a disruptive text" (personal interview). Khilani is one of the directors of the Institute of Sindhology in Kutch, Gujarat. The institution is based upon the principles of Sufi syncretism that binds the Sindhis of India and Pakistan. It is possible that there were many other families like Khilani's which may help us to put the success of the Arya Samaj in perspective. But it is also a historical fact that the Arya Samaj paved the way for organisations like the Mahabsabha and the RSS. A strong propagator of the Arya Samaj in

Gujarat, Gangaram Samrat clearly and proudly admits such interconnections, "Arya Samaj has always supported RSS. I did too. I never went to the shakhas, but the RSS had my support. And for that reason, my sons are with the Vishwa Hindu Parishad, the present-day avatar of the RSS" (personal interview). According to Kirat Babani, Gangaram Samrat and his kind represent one of the two strands within the Arya Samaj; people like Tarachand Gajra and Choithram Gidwani who were secular, represented the other (personal interview). Nevertheless, the combative role of the Arya Samaj is captured in the words of one of its admirers who says, "To an extent that tit called for tat, the Arya Samaj played a useful role" (K.R. Malkani 1984, 85).

The move from the Brahmo Samaj to the Arya Samaj marks a narrowing of identities and what follows then is a network of Hindu-centred organisations, which supported each other, if not in methods, at least in ideology. By the 1930s, notes Malkani, Sindh was a fertile land for various reformist activities, a garden with many birds singing in it. All these diverse strains, he claims, merged together with the arrival of the RSS.

THE SEPARATION OF SINDH

We have looked at how while reformist organisations were modifying the socio-religious outlook of the Sindhi Hindus, colonial intervention in land and education policies had widened class cleavages in Sindh and led to the awakening of political consciousness among the Muslims of Sindh, who felt they had been under-represented and exploited in the nineteenth and the twentieth centuries. The discussion that follows shows the Sindhi Muslims' campaign for the separation of the province of Sindh from the Bombay Presidency as a step towards greater autonomy and progress. The move for making Sindh autonomous was not initially speaking a 'Muslim' need. A Hindu named Harchandrai Vishindas first articulated it in a political forum of the annual session of the Congress held in 1913. According to Vishindas,

On the conquest of Sind by the British in 1843 it was administered as a separate Province with Sir Charles Napier as its Governor. After his departure in 1847, it was annexed to the Bombay Presidency and still continues to be so, although in several matters the Commissioner in Sindh, unlike the Commissioners of the other Divisions, of the Presidency, has been invested with the powers of the local Government. Still the province possesses several geographical and ethnological characteristics which give her the hall mark of a self-contained territorial unit. The Punjab has been long casting very covetous eyes upon this Province and urging her claims to an annexation, which became most insistent after the announcement of territorial changes by His Majesty the King Emperor at the last Delhi Durbar. But Sind set her face resolutely against all such blandishments and prefers to continue a part of the Bombay Presidency until such time as destiny permit her, to her own advantage, to attain to Provincial autonomy. (in Khuhro 1982, 1)

Vishindas's argument for the distinctness of Sindh and its religious and cultural disparities with the Bombay Presidency was partly true and partly based on the business-minded community's veiled desire to extricate itself from having to compete with the much more powerful Bombay interests (Ansari 1992, 111; Sathananthan 2000, 228). At the same time, some notice of Sindh's affinity with Punjab rather than the Bombay Presidency had been taken even during the annexation of Sindh in 1847. Hence Sindh's distinctness was not a new issue. When the argument for Sindh's autonomy re-emerged, alongside of Harchandrai Vishindas, Rais Ghulam Mohammed Bhurgri also brought it up in the Bombay Council. This was in the context of 1914 and 1918 when the Montague Chelmsford Report (which for the first time committed India to the evolution of a parliamentary system of government) appeared. Encouraged by the liberalising nature of the report, the Sindhi Hindus and Muslims – represented by Vishindas and Bhurgri – articulated the same demand couched in different words. According to them, the commissioner's rule in Sindh was oppressive and autocratic and the Bombay Presidency did not care about Sindh; therefore, the commissioner's post in Sindh should be abolished and the province left to its own devices. At this stage, the Congress supported the argument through the Sindh Provincial

Conference; however, the response of the Sindh Muslim League and even of the Sindh Mohammaden Association were lukewarm.

The subsequent years passed desultorily, with occasional spurts of interest in pursuing the matter of separation. In fact, the death of Bhurgri in 1924 would have perhaps brought an end to the issue. This however, was prevented by two very significant events that happened during this period. The impetus that fuelled the move towards Sindh's autonomy came from the Khilafat Movement that had created a pan-Muslim leadership in India, and thence, interest in collective action in Sindh. The Khilafat also provided to the issue of separation a new, young and enthusiastic leadership in the form of Abdul Majid Sindhi who whipped up propaganda for separating Sindh and put forth the issue at various venues, such as the annual sessions of the Congress, All-India Khilafat and also the All-India Muslim League. A very significant outcome of the propaganda was also the support from two new leaders, Mohammad Ayub Khuhro and Sayed Ghulam Murtaza Syed—both of whom would play key roles in the Pakistan movement. Both these men were young and members of the Bombay Legislative Council. They belonged to the influential landowning families in rural Sindh and, "represented a new breed of leadership: rural based, progressive-minded, less obsequious to the British and militantly pro-Muslim" (Jones 2002, 19).

It is important to remember that from the inception of the subject of a separate Sindh in 1913 by Harchandrai Vishindas, until almost 1927, the movement for separation had support from both the Hindu and the Muslim communities. In fact, as Lata Parwani (a) mentions, "While the political rhetoric in the public arena was cast in communal terms, there were no clearly defined 'Hindu' or 'Muslim' positions. Real divisiveness arose from an unease regarding the financial viability of the province, and more importantly from a perceived threat to the privileged status of the societal elite, Hindus as well as Muslims". The movement was thus not cast in Hindu or Muslims terms but was based on whether it was profitable for Sindh to continue being a part of a government that wrought damage rather than benefit to the province. Apart from Harchandrai Vishindas, supporters of the issue included Durgadas Advani, Nihalchand Vaswani, R.K. Sidhwa and Naraindas Anandji. The famous Congress representative Jairamdas Daulatram also agreed with the movement in principle, though not always with the arguments (see Khuhro 1982). The first reference to the fact that the separation would benefit the Muslims more than the Hindus is to be found in a speech by R.R. Cadell, Commissioner of Sindh on 31 May 1927.

> I would like to say a word about another development and that is the growth of provincial feeling in Sind, the feeling that it should stand on its own legs and not be attached to a Presidency in many respects alien to it. That feeling has undoubtedly increased of late years. Of course there are many side issues. The Mahommedans may be influenced in favour, because it will add a province in which there is a Mahommedan majority. For the same reason the Hindus of Sind would rather adhere to Bombay with its Hindu majority." (in Khuhro 1982, 23)

Cadell's language exposes the divergent responses towards the issue of separation. Although not all Hindus ceased to support separation, there was a definite shift in their attitude towards the subject after 1927, a response perhaps to the communal tensions in the India of the 1920s, but largely the result of an event in Sindh itself—the Larkano riots of 1928.

In the biography of her father, Mohammad Ayub Khuhro (a Muslim League leader who is remembered very negatively by the migrant Sindhis of India), Hamida Khuhro mentions that when her father was visiting Larkano in March 1928, a sudden riot broke out:

> The riot had been caused by the activities of the Hindu fundamentalists of the shuddhi, Arya Samaj and Hindu Mahasabha movements who were busy scouring the countryside at the time trying to find and "reconvert" or shuddhi (purify) any person they suspected had been converted from Hinduism.

She further says,

> It was clear that the Hindu extremist organisation like the shuddhi and Mahasabha movements were bent upon stirring up communal trouble. In this case they had got hold of a woman who had been

married for more than fourteen years and had several children. She was bribed and threatened into abandoning her home and testifying against her husband which resulted not only in personal tragedy for her household but also started the first communal riot in Sindh. (1998b, 72)

The riots were 'ably handled' by Mohammed Ayub Khuhro who took stern steps against some of the Hindus in Larkano. Chastened by this event, some Hindus such as Virumal Begraj, Professor Chablani and Mukhi Gobindram hotly protested separation. The Sindhi Hindu's perception that a separate Sindh was a conspiracy to keep the Hindus in fear and under economic disadvantages in a Muslim majority province began to gain ground from this period onwards. The Sindhi Muslims' consequent opinion that the Hindus considered only their vested interests and did not wish the welfare of the poor Muslims of Sindh also became a part of the discourse on separation.

The Hindus articulated their opposition on grounds of financial viability, by saying that the province of Sindh was not self-sufficient. However, it betrayed a fear of a *dyatko raaj* (N. Malkani 1973, 112), which, roughly translated means, 'rule by illiterate Muslims'. Hiranand Khemsingh, a prominent Hindu barrister and member of the Bombay Legislative Council publicly asked how the Muslims, only 0.3% of whom were educated in the English language, would manage to run a government (in Jones 2002, 24). To the Muslims, the Hindus were a hindrance in achieving a just Muslim nation, a project that drew the interest of the Muslim League now. The Hindu Mahasabha also jumped into the fray and made up for the dilly-dallying Congress stand on the issue. Thus, an intensification of communal perceptions characterised the debate around the separation of Sindh in the decade of the 1930s and made the whole movement a complex part of Sindh's history.

In 1932, the Muslims under the leadership of Abdul Majid Sindhi formed the Sindh Azad Conference to bring together all Sindhi Muslims – the emergent middle class as well as the landed aristocracy – who supported the cause of an autonomous Sindh. But it was also at this point, says Nuruddin Sarki,

...that Mahasabhaites and Leaguers could not see eye-to-eye in the assembly. I also think that the Sukkur Barrage issue had some role to play in increasing the bitterness. The British had to borrow a huge loan to build the Sukkur Barrage and they wanted to tax the rural Muslim zamindars to recover that cost. The Hindus did not back the Muslims even in this issue which happened around the same time as the separation. (personal interview)

The movement for separation consumed the energies of two generations in Sindh. From the inception of this idea to its fruition in 1937 (when, by the government act of 1935, Sindh became autonomous) myriad motives surrounded the issue. Speaking of those days, G.M. Syed mentions, "We used to write a lot on the issue of Sindh being a separate nation. But we certainly did not have a deep understanding about it as we do today. Sindh had no link with Bombay in any historical or religious sense. But there was one main reason for the separation: that there were more Maratha or Gujarati people in Bombay. We wanted Sindh as a Muslim majority area" (Syed 1949/ 1996, iv).

Sindh became an autonomous province on 1 April 1936, and irreconcilable differences had been created between its Hindus and Muslims. Commenting on one of the consequences of this moment on our present, Mani Shankar Aiyar remarks,

Malkani and Advani became communalists together in their early youth in Sindh when, in the late '30s the separation of Sindh from the province of Bombay led to a passionate upsurge of Hindu communalism. The socio-religious status of the Hindu community changed from being members of the Hindu-majority composite province of Bombay to a religious minority in the new province of Sindh. The origins of Partition of India lie in this tortured history of this tangled partition of Bombay. (*Telegraph* 2001)

With the achievement of Sindh's autonomy, the Muslim leadership seemed to have reached a pinnacle of political triumph. They had achieved a broad measure of success; they had established close relations with the all-India Muslim leadership; and, they stood to become the new power brokers in the newly autonomous province of Sindh (Jones 2002, 28).

3   The Run up to Partition (1937–1947)

Sindh is a peculiar province, where principles hold no field, nor can anybody be trusted to keep his word or promise. It is a strange place.
                                        —Sardar Vallabhbhai Patel

By this time [1944], there were only two organisations left in Sindh— the League and RSS.
                                        —N.R. Malkani

If the separation of Sindh was a moment of triumph for the Sindhi Muslim, it was also a paradoxical moment that defined both secular nationalism as well as communalism (see Tejani 2002). The government act of 1935 resulting in the formation of provincial governments not only gave the people of Sindh considerable autonomy, but also established a synonymy between religious communities. The communal implications of separate electorates for different religious identities have been a much-discussed issue. However, it is still useful to remember that this phenomenon nurtured in everyday life "the idea that [Indian] society consisted of groups set apart from each other...The result was the flowering of a new communal rhetoric, and ultimately of the Pakistan movement" (Menon 1998/2004, 38). Sindh would become one of the most important regions for not only the Pakistan movement, but the physical reality of Pakistan. We shall return to Sindh's support for Pakistan; for now, let us look at the political developments that took place in the autonomous Sindh of 1937.

FIRST ELECTIONS IN SEPARATE SINDH

In the decade following the separation of Sindh from the Bombay Presidency, the province saw political parties frequently making claims that meant to serve the specific interests of the Hindus and Muslims. However, in effect it was only a rampant making and breaking of governments—the fall of one ministry, the murder of a chief minister and the rise of the Muslim League amidst political rivalries and tensions. The first elections in autonomous Sindh foreshadowed the lack of strong political leadership that would fulfill the dreams of a more self-sufficient Sindh and bring prosperity to the bulk of the rural Muslim poor. In the elections of 1937, a new 60-seat Sindh Legislative Assembly had to be formed. The newly formed parties such as the Sind Azad Party (SAP; formed by Shaikh Abdul Majid Sindhi), the Sindh United Party (SUP; formed by Haroon Abdullah), the Sindh Muslim Party (SMP; formed by Hussain Hidayatullah and Mohammad Ayub Khuhro) emerged as unequal and bickering partners, all claiming to represent the Muslims of Sindh. On the Hindu front, the newly formed Sindh Hindu Sabha (a branch of the All-India Hindu Mahasabha) adopted a protective stance towards the Sindhi Hindus. It claimed to protect Hindu life and property and openly accused the Congress of letting the Hindus down with regard to the issue of the separation of Sindh from the Bombay Presidency. At the same time, there were Hindu members in Sindh who belonged to both the Sabha and Congress, just as there were Muslims who were members of the League as well as other parties. Unlike the Sabha, the Sindh Congress Party (affiliated with the All-India Congress Party) did not have a communal manifesto. In the general elections of February 1937, the Sindh Congress Party initially planned to contest for 20 seats, but had to eventually whittle it down to 15, a figure that included both Hindu and Muslim candidates. The elections concluded with the following results: SUP – 22 seats; Sindh Congress – 7; SMP – 3; SAP – 3; Congress – 8; and the Mahasabha – 11. Besides these, several Hindus and Muslims were returned as independent members. Defying all logic, the governor, Sir Lancelot Graham, invited the Sindh Muslim Party's Hussain Hidayatullah to form the government (see Syed 1949/1996). Ideological and personal differences were kept in abeyance as Hindu politicians along with the independents and other Muslim leaders supported Hidayatullah. Consequently, this gave the SMP 28 seats to the assembly. The Sindh United Party and the Congress who were in the opposition eventually brought his ministry down in a year's time on 22 March 1938. On 23 March 1938, Allah Baksh Soomro, supported by the Sindh United Party and the Congress, formed a new ministry.[1]

Soomro's coalition with the Congress crystallised a 'Muslim' stance against him, represented now by the new opposition that had strong alliances with the Muslim League, in the shape of Hussain Hidayatullah, Mohammad Khuhro, Abdul Gazdar and Abdul Majid Sindhi. This group began a vicious propaganda against Soomro's Hindu loyalties. The League vs Soomro war went on for some months after 1938. At the same time, the All-India Muslim League looked at Sindh as a province with new, unexplored possibilities. Despite its long-standing association with Sindh (where it held its first session), the Muslim League in the 1930s did not have a very firm footing because it had not fired the imagination of Muslim leaders (see Zaidi 1996, 19–46). It gradually began to direct its attention towards local as well as rural concerns to increase its credibility. Ansari's study shows how the League cultivated the pirs (who were much revered in Sindh) to

---

1. Allah Baksh Soomro is remembered fondly by the migrant Sindhi generation as the most 'secular' chief minister of Sindh. He was a Congress loyalist.

draw support from the rural areas (1992). In the process, the Muslim League also created its most successful and controversial leader in Sindh, G.M. Syed.

G.M. Syed

G.M. Syed, the icon of Sindhi identity and nationalism in Pakistan today, fought for the self-determination of Sindh through the Jeay Sindh, a movement initiated in 1973. He made the Sindhis aware of their marginalisation in a Mohajjir (immigrant) and Punjabi-dominated Pakistan. However, prior to Partition, Syed was the mainstay of the Muslim League in Sindh and although his relationship with Mohammad Ali Jinnah (and therefore, the All-India Muslim League) was far from easy, he was a very important figure in local politics from 1939 to 1946 and the prime mover of the Pakistan movement in Sindh.

Born in 1904, Syed was the descendant of a prestigious sajjada-nashin pir who began his political career with the Khilafat conference in his hometown on 17 March 1920. The Khilafat also made him connect with the Congress. "Born in a Muslim family, having its own traditions and sentiments as well as its own past history...I had come under sufistic influence and I was mentally in a receptive mood to welcome the Congress" (1949/1996, 30). He also remarks, "Since there was a great unity between Hindus and Muslims at the time of meetings of the all-India Congress, the Jamanit-I-Ulema-Hind and the Muslim League used to be held at the same city at the same time. I began increasingly to wish to join the intrepid and organised struggle which was gathering pace against British imperialism" (1995, 10).

Syed was the president of the district local board from 1919 to 1921. In 1925, he participated in the Simon Commission and from 1928 onwards, he was involved in the movement for Sindh's separation. It was in 1937, after Sindh's separation, that Syed was elected as a member of the Sindh Legislative Assembly. When Jinnah visited Sindh in 1938, at the invitation of Haji Abdullah Haroon, Syed realised that the Muslim League had merely a communal propaganda and did not have any programme for the emancipation of the people. But he felt that by joining it, he may bring some economic upliftment to the rural masses of Sindh. He had also begun to feel disillusioned with the Congress which came to be perceived only as a 'Hindu' party that did not care about the economic problems of Sindh (which were by and large the lot of Sindh's Muslims). In his letter to Choithram Gidwani (president, Sindh Congress) he said, "It was on Congress that I had pinned all my hopes for a bright future for Sindh [but] I visualise that a parting of ways is at hand" (1995, 23). Syed joined the League and became a bulwark against the Sindh Congress and the independent Hindu group. His chief contribution lay in bringing together the pir and Syed members of the assembly who formed the most influential rural elite. After Syed joined the League, he, "succeeded in raising the Sindh Muslim League membership from 6,000 to 300,000 which came to 25% of the total number of adult Muslims in the province" (1995, 32).

However, the League still needed an icon, a reason for connecting with people. The answer, it felt, lay in bringing down the Soomro ministry and firing the local imagination (Ansari 1992, 118). The outcome was the Manzilgah incident.

Masjid Manzilgah

Manzilgah was the popular name of a group of buildings on the banks of the Indus at Sukkur in northern Sindh. One of the domed buildings in this cluster was under dispute. It was allegedly a mosque during Akbar's reign, but had been out of use since the seventeenth century. After the nineteenth century, the disputed structure lay with the British government. In 1938, the demand to restore the Masjid Manzilgah to the Muslim community for use as a mosque created one of the most divisive moments in the Hindu–Muslim relationship in Sindh (see Khuhro 1998a; Ansari 1992; Jones 2002). In an article aptly titled "Manzilgah: A test-case in Hindu–Muslim relations in Sindh", Khuhro mentions that the Muslims had always wanted to restore the mosque for prayer, but it had never been possible because the complex stood facing Sadh Belo, a place of pilgrimage for the Hindus. When Sindh was part of the Bombay Presidency and the Hindus dominated the political processes in the legislative assembly, the issue of restoring the mosque did not arise. However, in the autonomous Sindh of 1938, the Muslim League found in Manzilgah an opportunity to draw all the Muslims of Sindh to a common and sacrosanct cause, and harness their diversities to create an Islamic solidarity much needed by the League. Although discussions on Manzilgah by Allan Keith Jones and Sarah Ansari do not mention a pre-1939 history of the monument, a recent study attempts to establish the lack of veracity to the claim of the use of Manzilgah as a mosque (see Parwani (a)). On the whole, it does seem likely that the Muslim League raked up an issue hitherto insignificant and unattended to in order to establish its credibility with the masses. In that sense the Manzilgah episode is not unlike the Bharatiya Janata Party's move to 're-establish' the disputed Babri Masjid as a Ram temple in the India of 1992. This incident was not only very significant in consolidating the presence of the Muslim League in Sindh, but also had severe implications and outcomes for the relations between Hindus and Muslims. In the years that culminate in Partition, Manzilgah stands as one more context for the intensifying fears and insecurities of the Hindu community.

When the demand for Manzilgah was made by a group of Sukkur Muslims in 1938, it had the support of the Sindh Muslim League. Apart from an invigorating sense of being (once again) in a province with a Muslim majority, the Sindhi Muslims were also reassured in their demand by the government intervention in the Om Mandli and the Hanuman Mandir case, where a disputed site was restored as a Hindu temple (see Chowdhry 1996; Syed 1949/1996). The demand was placed before the chief minister, Allah Baksh Soomro, who had strong Congress leanings and Hindu support. Soomro vacillated on the issue, which only helped to intensify the demand and also furthered the perception that he was a Hindu stooge. Meanwhile, the Hindus registered their protest against the Manzilgah resolution in the Sindh Assembly. Their fears – part real, part imagined – stemmed from feelings of religious persecution. Hence what should have been entirely between the government and the Muslims of Sukkur became a communal test case and also brought to the fore the political alliances sharply drawn between Soomro and his 'enemies'. Apart from Soomro's deliberate delays, the League's own execution was riddled with differences—where one group believed in achieving this end by democratic means such as petitions and resolutions, the other wished to adopt more radical tactics. A Manzilgah restoration committee came into existence (29 July 1939); it appealed to the Muslim members of the assembly to withdraw their support from the Soomro government if he continued to drag his feet. In the following month, a 'Manzilgah Day' was observed throughout the province, and finally in late September/early October of 1939, the decision to occupy Manzilgah illegally in a passive and non-violent agitation against the Soomro government was made. It is not possible to summarise here the many stages of the Manzilgah resolution from the point of its first draft in 1938 to the illegal occupation by Muslims in the winter of 1939. As satyagrahis began to stream into Manzilgah to offer prayers, Sindh witnessed its most tense months before Partition. The fuel for communal disharmony was also coming from Hindu quarters; they not only resisted the restoration and pressurised Soomro not to give in to the demands, but also organised meetings and distributed pamphlets that whipped up paranoia. The Hindu Mahasabha's role during these pre-Partition years was particularly divisive. On 14 November 1939, the Hindu Mahasabha arranged a conference in Sukkur under the chairmanship of Dr. Moonje who said,

> I know you Hindus in Sind are worried...and you do not know whose turn may come next for you feel that nobody's life is safe. I would address the Muslims and request them to tolerate the Hindus and allow them to live. The idea of retaliation is not good and I would not like to hold out that threat to them...The Muslims have now openly asked for a separate Muslim Federation for themselves. They do not want to live in harmony with the Hindus...They must...either live with Hindus together in India or they must cease altogether. We cannot allow them to break away and form a separate India for themselves. (in Parwani (a))

While the Muslims still observed a calm but collective satyagraha in the premises of Manzilgah, Kanwarram, a Hindu saint revered by Hindus and Muslims alike was murdered allegedly by the Pir of Birchhundi. The link between Kanwarram's assassination and Manzilgah has not been clearly established, but the incident served to fire communal passions further.

Relenting under the pressures that mounted upon him from all directions, Soomro simply let the government crack its whip upon the illegal occupants of Manzilgah. Physical injuries were visited upon the Muslims through lathis and tear gas, and some of their formidable leaders such as Khuhro and Syed were put in prison. According to Hamida Khuhro, the "Hindu press was jubilant at the government crackdown of Muslims on the Muslim occupation of Manzilgah and tactless wounding of Muslim susceptibilities" (1998a, 72). What followed was a Muslim retaliation on the Hindus in Sukkur whose houses were burnt and properties stolen. Many Hindu families fled from Sukkur and moved to 'safer' districts. Although both communities suffered, the Hindus paid heavier prices in terms of loot as well as bloodshed. My interviews with the migrant generation show that the Hindu landowners of Sukkur remember being attacked by peasants who saw this as an opportunity to settle scores. According to a respondent, Tahilram Makhijani, "Muslims never forgave us for Manzilgah. They took their revenge and killed three of my relatives" (personal interview).

In terms of political consequences, the Manzilgah issue brought down the ministry of Allah Baksh Soomro and witnessed the ascendancy of a new government that contained many members of the Muslim League; on 18 March 1940, a new coalition government was formed with Mir Bandeh Ali as the premier. For our purpose, it is important to know that the Sindhi Hindus growing up in those years were witnessing the Muslim League brand of Islam, especially through the Manzilgah issue. Although the Manzilgah riots were restricted to the district of Sukkur, they permeated into the everydayness of Sindhi life.

Support for Pakistan

The decade of the 1940s witnessed a consistent ascendancy of the All-India Muslim League in Sindh despite its occasional squabbles with the provincial League. G.M. Syed, who was a product of a syncretic Sindh, and a political and social activist who had strong ties with the Hindus, spoke a different language now. Amidst the chaos of the Manzilgah incident he is known to have said, "all Hindus shall be driven out of Sindh like the Jews from Germany" (K.R. Malkani 1984, 121). It was in Sindh that the question of Partition was first raised informally in the annual session of the Muslim League held in Karachi in 1938, and Muhammad Ali Jinnah was asked to make Pakistan the official demand of the Muslims of India. The legislative assembly of Sindh passed a resolution supporting the demand for Pakistan in 1942 (Baloch 1982, foreword). This did not mean that the Sindhi politicians were in favour of the Muslim League's demand for Pakistan. Given a choice, the Sindhi Muslims would have preferred an autonomous province. For the Sindhi elite, the situation was one of being placed between the devil and the deep blue sea. They feared Hindu domination under Congress rule and Punjabi domination in the case of Pakistan. In any case, in the end, Sindh opted for Pakistan (Khan 2005, 136). Syed remembers walking through the villages of Sindh and putting up posters saying: "Muslims demand Pakistan. Pakistan means an Islamic state" (Syed 1995, 32).

He also remembers being warned by his friends that he would end up becoming an instrument used in the promotion of a communal agenda. Allah Baksh Soomro's words proved prophetic: "You will get to know that our difficulties will begin after Pakistan has come into being…At present the Hindu trader and money lender's plunder is worrying you but later you will have to face the Punjabi bureaucracy and soldier and the mind of UP…After the creation of this aberration [Pakistan] you will have to struggle to fight its concomitant evils" (Khan 2005, 136). However, as things stood in the decades of the 1930s and 40s in Sindh, it seemed to the Muslim leadership (including Syed) that the Muslims of Sindh would prosper only if Sindh was looked after by a party like the Muslim League. The oppositional voices in this discourse were few and far between.

The separation of Sindh introduced a majority–minority discourse in Sindh since representation and numerical strength came to be closely linked through the electoral processes and the formation of governments.

The first part of this chapter was an effort to understand the changed public sphere through landmark events such as the first elections after separation, the fall and rise of governments, the success of the Muslim League and its first feat, the Manzilgah episode, and finally, Sindh's support of the Pakistan movement. I would like to now focus on the Hindus of Sindh, who experienced new – real and imagined – fears on watching the ascendancy of the Muslim League and found their old organisations inadequate in protecting them. As a consequence of the Muslim–Hindu discourse, in the 1940s we witness, not uniformly, a leaning towards more conservative and aggressive socio-political organisations. The syncretic character of Sindh, which almost always drew from the commonalities of territory and the language and shared cultural symbols, stood slightly shaken (not obliterated). During moments of vulnerability, caused not the least by the increasing success of the Muslim League, the Sindhi Hindus looked to pro-Hindu organisations. While the Muslim League claimed to serve the Muslims, the Congress appeared to disappoint both the Hindus and the Muslims. The discussion below shows how, in the face of the new challenges that confronted the Sindhi Hindus in a separate Sindh, the role of the Congress had begun to recede.

THE SINDHI HINDUS' RUPTURED RELATIONSHIP WITH THE CONGRESS

During the 1930s, the Hindu Mahasabha seized upon the 'betrayal' of the Sindhi Hindus' trust by Congress and reminded them of how the Congress had supported the motion of separation. Congress representatives in Sindh such as Dr. Choithram Gidwani and Tarachand Gajra felt that the Nehru–Gandhi–Patel combine was indifferent to their province. In the years following the separation of

Sindh, when the Sindhi Hindus felt progressively insecure, Gandhi's stand on non-violence made less and less sense to them. In their correspondence with Gandhi in the late 1930s, the Congress leaders report frequent cases of lawlessness. Tarachand Gajra and C.T. Valecha (members of the Sindh Congress Committee) wrote to Gandhi with some sarcasm,

> We trust you received our previous communication, 'A note on the present state of lawlessness in Sindh'. It is a sad story of silent misery that has befallen those who are migrating without any financial aid from the public or the authorities. Elsewhere such things would evoke wide international public support and sympathy. We hope your interest in the province will grow. (in Jotwani 1998, 333)

Gandhi's repeated plea for non-violence seemed to fall on deaf ears, and the Sindhi Hindus were looking for something more 'effective'. In an article in the *Harijan*, Gandhi admits the waning confidence in non-violence among the Sindhi Hindus. After the Manzilgah riots in Sukkur in 1939, he wrote,

> Now the only effective way in which I can help the Sindhis is to show them [the] way of non-violence. But that cannot be learnt in a day. The other way is the way they followed hitherto: armed defence of life and property. God only helps those who help themselves. The Sindhis are no exception. They must learn the art of defending themselves against robbers, raiders and the like. If they do not feel safe and are too weak to defend themselves, they should leave the place which has proved inhospitable to live in. (in Jotwani 1998, 322)

Gandhi's advice to the Sindhi Hindus to equip themselves was well taken, but his suggestion that the Sindhis should undertake a hijrat (exodus) if they could not protect themselves seemed very unfair to the Sindhi Hindu leaders. He received a strong reaction from Gajra to his article "The Sindh Tragedy" which mentioned hijrat as a viable option for the community:

> In your article 'Sindh Tragedy' you have advised the oppressed Hindus of Sindh to perform hijrat if they cannot protect their honour and self-respect by remaining in Sindh. Where do you expect them to go?

Who will provide them the wherewithal in their place of refuge? May
I further ask you if the remedy of hijrat is meant for the Hindus only?
Why do you not advise hijrat to the Mussulamans in the Congress
province who complain loudly of oppression? (in Jotwani 1998, 323)

Gandhi did not respond to this question. At the Congress
headquarters in Delhi, Sindh seemed too far away, its problems small
and peculiar. In his correspondence with Sardar Vallabhbhai Patel,
the journalist M.S.M. Sharma reports that Congress leaders in Sindh
seemed "more Hindu Sabhaites than Congressman," and hastens to
add that, "that could not be helped." Patel responded to this by
expressing his incomprehension, a common response towards Sindh,
"Sindh is a peculiar province. I am not sure I understand it. No
principles seem to work there. It is a strange place" (in Das 1972,
137). Nehru echoes a similar sentiment, but with more negativism in
a letter to Padmaja Naidu, "I do not feel attracted to Sindh. I have
nothing to say about it" (in Anand 1996, 55). The indifference of the
Congress headquarters towards Sindh also found reflection sometimes
in Sindh's own representatives in the Congress. For instance,
Narayandas Malkani mentions in his autobiography that when he
wrote to J.B. Kripalani (president, All-India Congress Committtee)
about the Manzilgah riots, his response was, "I have nothing to say
about Sindh. It is beyond the scope of my office administration. I
have no private perspective on Sindh. Even if I had any, nobody is
going to like it. Glad you wrote to Vallabhbhai. You would be coming
to Ramgadh, but the working committee feels it is futile to advise
Sindhis on anything" (in Malkani 1973, 106).

The shades of indifference towards this religious minority in what
was emerging as a laboratory of the Muslim League seemed no one's
concern, neither before nor during Partition. After the fall of Allah
Baksh Soomro – the last Congress leader who had the potential to
bind together the Hindus and the Muslims – the Congress' failure in
Sindh, now heavily influenced by the Muslim League, was a forgone
conclusion. In a letter to Nichaldas Vazirani, (16 December 1946)
Sardar Patel sadly notes that "I am extremely sorry to see that in Sindh

Congress has purchased bitterness and enmity in the bargain" (in Das 1972, 137).

As old loyalties began to fray at the edges, some Congress members asked their younger brothers or sons to join a pro-Hindu organisation that taught Hindus 'defence' against Muslims.[2] This organisation was the Rashtriya Swayamsewak Sangh.

Rashtriya Swayamsewak Sangh

My discovery of the RSS connection in Sindh was first made in an unsuspected corner: it was one of the many nuggets of memory dominating my father Laxmandas Makhija's narrative about his life. Although my father talked to me about Sindh at home as I grew up, he had never mentioned the RSS. In 2001, when I formally interviewed him to record his experiences of Partition, he mentioned the RSS as one of his most "vivid memories". According to him, "From the age of twelve, the high-point of my life in Sindh was the RSS. I was not really involved in politics in Sindh. Many friends and acquaintances were in the Congress Sewa Dal. Me and my brother were in the Rashtriya Swayamsewak Sangh." It was surprising that if the RSS was an important part of his memories, it had never figured in our conversations at home. However, based on what he had said, I went on to interview his brother, Udhavdas Makhija, who proudly stated,

> I know L.K. Advani from my RSS days. RSS was very pervasive in Sukkur, and since Shikarpur where your father and I lived was in the district of Sukkur, we were strongly influenced by it. We were the

2. According to Jayant Relwani (personal interview), "My father was a strong supporter of the Congress. He had been to jail twice and I remember an occasion when he was ready to hit an Englishman who said something against Gandhi. There was no RSS in his time. But when I was about seventeen, the RSS had arrived in Sindh, around 1942. My father felt that the Congress had let people down, that Gandhi did not stand up for Bhagat Singh and he was generally disappointed. He wanted me to go to the RSS because that was the direction in which Sindh was going (*Hindun jee vichaardhara una paase hui*)." K.R. Malkani mentions that he was asked by his brother Narayandas Malkani, a committed Congress nationalist to join the RSS because, "Congress cannot attract the youth, while the RSS does" (in J. Wadhwani 2004, 1).

true nationalists. The shakha sanchalak [branch manager] used to tell us, "Know yourself and help your kind." They gave us the courage to fight outsiders. My brother-in-law was also with the RSS. At least the RSS bothered about us. What did the Congress haraami [bastards] do? Nothing.

The interviews with the Makhija brothers served as the first link in a chain of conversations with many more Sindhis who had visited the shakhas (branches) in Sindh. My father and my uncle, like the rest of the men in my family, are businessmen from Shikarpur. As many more narratives unfolded in the interviews, it appeared that this aspect of the Sindhi Hindus was not restricted either to businessmen or to Shikarpur. The creation of the story in this chapter has been out of a cloudy and murky past that came to me almost accidentally, as part of the process of understanding history. It grew in importance gradually and nudged its way into this book that meant to record Partition memories and their scarred persistence in the subsequent generations.

Context, emergence and impact

The RSS emerged in the peculiar circumstances of the 1920s which witnessed the Khilafat Movement, the Non-Cooperation Movement and its abandonment by Gandhi, the disenchantment with Gandhi in certain circles and the beginning of Hindu–Muslim riots in Bengal and Maharashtra. Its founder, Dr. Keshav Baliram Hedgewar, viewed the communal rioting that swept across the country as a sign of the weakness of the Hindu community. He felt that the Muslims had an edge over the Hindus because the latter had lost their 'manhood' and collectivity. It was important therefore, to instil a warrior-like pride in the Hindus and forge a Hindu national identity. This was the broad aim of the RSS, which also shared some of its ideology with another organization, the Hindu Mahasabha. The Mahasabha was established in 1915, a decade before the RSS. It was concerned with a variety of Hindu interests such as cow protection, Hindi in the Devanagri script and caste reforms. However, one of the chief differences between the Mahasabha and the RSS was that the latter never sought direct political power, a bone of contention with Veer Savarkar (who was sympathetic to the RSS). The Hindu Mahasabha and the RSS shared a symbiotic, but often conflicting relationship. The RSS was a small provincial organisation based in eastern Maharashtra from 1925 (the year of its inception) to 1932. The Delhi session of the Hindu Mahasabha in 1932 passed a resolution commending the activities of the RSS and emphasising the need to spread its network all over the country. In the same year, Bhai Parmanand, an Arya Samaji, extended a special invitation to Dr. Hedgewar to attend the Karachi session of the Hindu Yuvak Parishad. Dr. Hedgewar seized this opportunity to establish contact with youth groups from Sindh and Punjab. The acceptance of the RSS in Punjab was made easy by the path the Arya Samaj had paved and also by the "growing fears of Muslim paramilitary movements" (Anderson and Damle 1987, 38). The RSS had also earned some goodwill as a refuge for Hindus during riots. In contrast, the success of the RSS in Sindh was considerably slower.

The early efforts of the RSS in Sindh were largely abortive. It appealed mainly to the Marathi-speaking people in Karachi, but not to the native Sindhis. In his book on L.K. Advani, the writer Atmaram Kulkarni describes enticements such as lassi, milk and sweets offered to the Sindhi Hindus in order to get them interested in the RSS (1995, 2–3). Sindh in the early 1930s was by and large peaceful, and although riots did take place in Larkano and Sukkur, they were localised and short-lived affairs. The sporadic fights between Hindus and Muslims over conversion had not created the deep-rooted insecurity necessary for the ideology of the RSS to take root. Hence the early recruits in Sindh were government officials and professionals from Maharashtra and Punjab. A turning point came when a young man named Rajpal Vishwambhar Nath Puri from Sialkot came to Hyderabad, Sindh. Rajpal Puri was an Arya Samaji and an RSS activist in Punjab. He had come to Sindh to take up a teaching job in the Navalram Hirananad Academy. The N.H. Academy hired Rajpal Puri's services as a Sanskrit teacher since Sindh did not have many Sanskrit teachers of its own. This gave Puri an opportunity to teach and influence young Hindu boys whom he could cultivate as his first RSS cadre, and one of the young men trained by him was L.K. Advani, "a gentle face with a beatific smile" (Basu et al 1993, vii), who symbolises Hindu fundamentalism in India since the early 1990s. Despite such a conspicuous example, the presence of the RSS in Sindh and the consequences thereof have largely been ignored as subjects of historical inquiry.[3]

In the initial years, RSS activity was more intense in Karachi and Hyderabad. It was in Karachi that Jhamatmal Wadhwani (who was to later become the secretary of the RSS in Hyderabad) came in contact with the organisation.

> I had thought then that it was good for self-defence—lathi and kathi. After some time, I also got interested in the more intellectual sessions. I learnt that sangathan [unity] is necessary. There is shakti in sangathan [strength in unity]. It helps devotion and dedication. I got a wider vision on why Hindu races were defeated. It was necessary for Sindh to know this because people had converted. From Muhammad bin Qasim to Muhammad Ghazni, Muslims have always defeated us. The Muslims ruled over us for six hundred years. Thanks to the courage of Seth Naoomal that he brought British rule to Sindh and we were relieved. (personal interview)

For Wadhwani, there was no contradiction between his Hindu nationalism and English colonialism. Wadhwani's desire for self-defence must also be seen against the backdrop of the movement for the separation of Sindh and the increasing influence of the League. The success of the RSS in Sindh coincides with this period. The number of RSS shakhas in Sindh increased by the early 1940s. Hence, as Laxmandas Makhija remembers, by 1944, the RSS had spread to many parts of Sindh. He remembers visiting Nawabshah, Larkano and Sukkur for training. "My commitment to the RSS gradually

---

3. Social scientists and political theorists have studied pro-Hindu organisations like the RSS, the BJP, the Vishwa Hindu Parishad (VHP) and the Shiv Sena, and their role in communal politics in India. See Hansen (2001), Kanungo (2002) and Varshney (2002). The two seminal studies on the RSS by Anderson and Damle (1987) and Tapan Basu et al. (1993) have already been mentioned. None of these books discuss the predominance of the RSS in Sindh and any post-Partition implications of the same in Indian politics.

became more serious. During the year 1947, I had graduated to being one of the leaders in my locality in Shikarpur. Day and night we were told that Hinduism had been destroyed; we at the RSS had a calling to salvage it from its endangered existence" (personal interview). Anderson and Damle note how the 'Hinduism in danger' discourse provided the most significant context for the RSS (1987). In some cases, joining the RSS was also a response to specific incidents and occurrences; but in the minds of the young impressionable boys, it enlarged itself into 'defence' against attacks on Hinduism. For instance, in the course of the same interview Laxmandas Makhija mentioned that he "prepared" through the RSS for "an imminent war against Muslims" and also that he wanted to learn to protect himself, for as a young boy, "I was harassed by Muslim boys in my mohalla. I wanted to be physically strong and face them" (personal interview). His brother, Udhavdas Makhija mentions, "We had to learn to defend ourselves. The Muslim used to take our women away. I have never liked them. They are aggressive. We used to call them Hurs."[4]

To come back to Rajpal Puri, his success in Sindh motivated Golvalkar (Hedgewar's successor in the RSS, Maharashtra) to promote him to the post of regional pracharak (those in charge of the dissemination and recruitment of volunteers). Puri had under him Khanchand Gopaldas, a man remembered by all the Hindu ex-

---

4. The Hurs were a fraternity formed under the influential pirs of Sindh. They were, for the most part, from amongst the poor and exploited peasantry of Sindh. They rebelled against foreign rule on the grounds of religious autonomy and robbed the rich (including at times, Hindu banias) on the grounds of economic discrimination (see Ansari 1992; Lambrick,1972). By and large, the Hurs perpetrated looting, and not physical violence. In my interviews with the migrant generation, I have noticed familiarity with the Hur rebellion and an ambivalence regarding its direct relevance to the life of the Sindhi Hindus. It is important to mention the subject here, however briefly, for it has links to fear psychosis and stereotyping among the Hindus (about the Muslims). The word 'Hur' exists in the Sindhi spoken in India, and denotes, 'an aggressive, grabbing person'. I have heard little boys described as Hurs. In Udhavdas Makhija's mind, a specific group, which he had never directly encountered, collapsed into an all-embracing category—the Muslims. The Hur rebellion gave the English authorities in Sindh considerable difficulty. In 1942, the British government in Sindh imposed martial law to quell the Hur rebellion and, the driving force behind the movement, Pir Pagaro, was arrested after great effort.

swayamsewaks of Sindh as a key participant in the Shikarpur Colony bomb case (discussed later). The tense atmosphere of the early 1940s when the government imposed martial law on Sindh lent a touch of romanticism to the activities of the RSS. Rajpal Puri and some of his young companions were arrested for creating 'disturbances' during 1942. When they were freed, their popularity had increased quite a lot (Kulkarni 1995, 17). .

The printed word also complemented the oral information about RSS I had received through interviews. The writer Jayant Relwani begins his article on the presence of the RSS in Sindh by saying "there is a general impression that every Sindhi is a Sanghi, a generalisation not without justification. Every Sindhi male has had a direct or indirect relationship with a shakha." He also mentions that there were 41 shakhas of the RSS in the city of Karachi alone (1996, 87). Jhamatmal Wadhwani mentioned that there were 75 pracharaks in Sindh, and that in every district, every taluka had an RSS volunteer, making in all 450 full-time RSS volunteers (personal interview). According to K.R. Malkani, the RSS had "spread to every nook and corner of Sindh" (1984, 86). Autobiographical accounts by Narayandas Malkani (1973) and Mohan Kalpana also make extensive references to the RSS in Sindh. In addition to sources in the Sindhi language, there is a passing reference to the increase in RSS membership from 1945 and 1948 in areas now part of Pakistan (especially Sindh and the North West Frontier Province (NWFP)), Punjab and Delhi in Anderson and Damle's well-known study of the RSS (1987, 45). Such scattered remarks do not give us reliable information about the numerical subscription to the ideology of the RSS. At the same time, memories of the presence of the RSS in the minds of the migrant generation (who in the 1940s would have been young adolescents) speak something of a formative influence this organisation had begun to possess in the years prior to Partition. It was perhaps a brief but impressionable episode in the lives of the young Sindhi Hindu boys who did not much document their association, but clung to what they perceived as 'RSS' values—the ideals of self-reliance, physical exercise and brotherhood in saffron.

"Once a swayamsewak, always a swayamsewak," smiled Seth Naomal broadly at me. Naomal Samtani lives in Adipur, Kutch (Gujarat) and owns three of the biggest sanitaryware shops there. He hails from the Nawabshah district of Sindh.

> I felt very restless when I moved to this place. While I was putting my best into my business and I have passed on to my sons three sanitaryware shops, I also wanted to see if there were swayamsewaks in Adipur. I was quite sure I'd find them. That sense of bonding only the RSS can give. *Swayamsewak ko ghar pe baithna nahin aata* [an RSS volunteer does not like to rest at home]. He would be restless until he has found his own kind. (personal interview)

When there were hardly any mechanisms for keeping together a community that is geographically and culturally dislocated, the RSS served as one of the few common links. Bound not only by feelings of self-reliance and solidarity and what they perceived as essential RSS values, the Sindhi Hindus also had a shared view of history. They tend to believe that Sufism was a fringe phenomenon and a mild version of Islam created to entice Hindus to Islam (Relwani, Wadhwani, personal interviews). At a broader level, it leads to a view that only Hindus are the rightful inheritors of India and that the Muslim was here on sufferance. The generation that watched the communalised politics in Sindh was that of the adolescent swayamsewaks of the RSS, who formed Sindh's first significant cadre and came to a divided India with that legacy. In India, they have un/consciously transmitted their 'experiences' and ideology to the next generation. From among those succeeding generations have emerged some of the most hardened followers of Hindutva – a form of Hindu fundamentalism – strengthened intellectually by the RSS, politically by the Bharatiya Janata Party and pragmatically by outfits such as the Vishwa Hindu Parishad. To give but a few examples, Maya Kodnani the BJP MLA, claims to have been inspired by her father who was in the RSS (personal interview). Seth Naoomal from Adipur told me that he was the BJP president in Adipur, Kutch, and that his sons were with the BJP (personal interview).

Of the many factors that might be responsible for the Sindhis' preference for a rightwing Hindu political party like the BJP, one is the RSS. Since Sindhis represent a minority, their ideological affiliations have not drawn attention, but an examination of such micro-communities is needed to locate majoritarian politics in local cultures. The detailed discussion on the RSS in this chapter is an attempt to open up the possibility of studying Sindhis in this light, but also with an understanding that the RSS was part of a recent history in the lives of the Sindhi Hindus—a tendency than a trend.

The Shikarpur Colony bomb case

It is important to note that from 1943 to 1947, Golvalkar (fondly remembered as 'Guruji') visited Sindh every year. Incidentally, Gandhi's visits to Sindh had stopped by then. The perception of the Hindus as a religious minority strengthened the hold of the RSS and Golvalkar began drawing crowds. His last visit to Sindh, a week before Partition remains most dramatically etched in the minds of some of the RSS respondents.

> About nine days before independence, the chief of the Sangh organised a seminar in Karachi and took me there as a volunteer. I remember Golvalkar mentioning that that was his last visit to Sindh and that we would have a different rule now, and new dangers to contend with. I stayed back in Karachi and noticed with my own eyes on 14th August that Lord Viceroy Mountbatten was taking Jinnah with him in the car. I came back to Shikarpur and noticed that many Hindus had begun to leave, houses were becoming empty. I went to school and found it closed. I realised that it was not possible to live there any longer. (L. Makhija, personal interview)

Once the Partition of the Indian subcontinent had become a reality, two urgent aims arose in the minds of a particular group of RSS activists in Sindh: to facilitate a smooth evacuation of the Sindhi Hindus who had begun to repose considerable trust in them, and to blow up a few government structures before leaving. They saw the former as a duty and the latter as a legitimate response to the looting and riots supported by the Muslim League. Both aims required arms; a group of twenty-one young men made intense preparations. In Shikarpur Colony, Karachi, the house of one Raibahadur Tolaram became the hideout for this cadre. The house was ostensibly taken over for tutoring students, and this turned out to be perfect camouflage for making bombs. The secret operation proceeded smoothly until the 14th of August, when a powerful bomb accidentally exploded. It blew two swayamsewaks and the house to pieces. The two young men who died were Prabhu Badlani and Vasudev. The local police swooped down on the premises. All but one escaped. He was imprisoned and tortured for several months, until he was exchanged for prisoners of war in 1949. There are contradictory opinions about the precise identity of this prisoner and his connections with the RSS.

The story of the Shikarpur Colony bomb case has come to us through individual accounts as well as lesser known written sources. Among the mainstream studies on the RSS, only one makes a passing reference to the, "manufacturing of bombs in Sindh" (Anderson and Damle 1987, 48). Among lesser known sources, the writer Jayant Relwani refers specifically to the Shikarpur Colony bomb case in an article on the predominance of the RSS in Sindh (1996, 89–90). The case finds a detailed discussion in what claims to be "an authentic and critical biography" of L.K. Advani, president of the BJP and former deputy prime minister of India, by Atmaram Kulkarni (1995). Kulkarni's intention in mentioning the Shikarpur Colony bomb case is to show Advani's participation in it as testimony of his courage. However, Advani's participation has not been confirmed by any other source. An anonymous pamphlet titled *Balidan ki Baldevi Par* provides photographs of the 'martyrs' who died in the explosion at the Shikarpur Colony. Besides these few written references, the Shikarpur Colony bomb case exists as an important episode in the minds of the RSS activists from Sindh who are now in their late 70s and 80s. Fortuitously, I have met at least two members of the group of twenty-one who were involved in the Shikarpur Colony bomb case. The two men are Jhamatmal Wadhwani who lives in Mumbai and Harish Vazirani who lives in Ahmedabad. Wadhwani was one of the key figures in the plot to make bombs for use against the Pakistan government. He remained in Pakistan until 1948 to help people under surveillance after the Shikarpur Colony bomb case. He corroborated the incident, but refused to reveal specifics like names. Wadhwani was the secretary of the RSS in Hyderabad during his involvement in the Shikarpur Colony bomb case. He has continued to be involved in the post-independence avatars and affiliations of the RSS by being an active member of the Jan Sangh and the BJP. L.K. Advani, K.R. Malkani and Jhamatmal Wadhwani are three of the most experienced members of the RSS from Sindh. Harish Vazirani, on the other hand, did not sustain his links with the RSS after coming to India. He is, however, proud of a past that brought him close to the organisation and volunteered information about the Shikarpur Colony bomb case as a context for his unplanned departure from Sindh. He was the first person to lead me into what, while it turned out to be an unsuccessfully conducted operation, remains a concrete testimony of RSS activity during Partition.

* * *

As we bring this chapter to a close, it is important to recapitulate its chief themes because as G.M. Syed remarks of this period (1937– 1947), "During [the] past dozen years or so events have taken place with such breathless succession that even landmarks stand exposed to oblivion and obliteration" (1949/1996, 1). A simplistic rendering of the discussion above would lead one to believe that identities in Sindh were moving from blurred inclusiveness to relative polarisation in the twentieth century. The economic chasm between the Hindus and Muslims of Sindh paved the way for a separate Sindh, which in turn created a majority–minority discourse. The Muslims of Sindh leaned towards the League and the Sindhi Hindus, towards the RSS. Consequently, the road to 'Pakistan' was formed and the Sindhi Hindus, angry and embittered, left Sindh during 1947. While speaking of Sindh and the Sindhis, it is crucial to be aware of the nuances that characterised its socio-political life. While it is true that organisations like the League and RSS correspond with the categories of 'Muslims' and 'Hindus' and appear irreconcilable, there stood, even in moments of division, 'Sindhiness' which drew sustenance from language, culture and Sufi traditions and which is even today the hallmark of Sindh. The province of Sindh, the 'land of pirs', did not/could not change overnight. Its culture now withstood, now submitted to the new challenges of the twentieth century. By and large, the people of Sindh continued to engage in its syncretic ethos. There was, however, an alteration in self-perceptions.

While the discussion on the Shikarpur Colony bomb case tells one kind of story of the time of Partition, Motilal Jotwani's account provided below, is also typical of Sindh. According to Jotwani, the incident helped sustain his interest in Sufi literature:

> It was January 8, and I was barely 12 at that time. Our country had been divided into India and Pakistan on a narrow religious basis on August 14/15, 1947. After the Partition communal frenzy raised its ugly head and cities ran amuck, their streets roaring 'Allaho Akbar' and 'Har Har Mahadev'...We were in Karachi those days, for my father had taken up a teaching job there. We lived in a rented set of two rooms in a building belonging to a devout Muslim. Things were never bad in Sindh before the Partition, for the people bred, and brought up as they were on the Sindhi Sufi soil, lived in peace and harmony. But on the fateful day of January 8, 1948, it looked like the world would come to an abrupt end for us. The rioters were at the gate and demanded of the house owner to quietly hand over all the kafirs (non-believers) in his premises. Huddled along with other members of the family in a small store room of the house, I waited with bated breath for destruction and death. I knew what could happen to us in such circumstances, but my younger brother and sister in the cellar would not quite know that they lurched between life and death. Presently our house-owner [Allahdino] lied to them, saying, "The people you are looking for sailed to India yesterday...The poor creatures couldn't even take along with them their possession...Do you want their belongings?" (1998, v–vi).

Allahdino let the rioters take what they wanted, and spent the rest of the day singing songs of Kabir with the author's father. This kind of incident typifies the attitudes in Sindh where a long-standing tradition of Sufism survived even in the heat of Partition. The Partition narratives in the next chapter provide an opportunity for us to examine this.

4 Leaving Sindh

Sindh remained nervously peaceful. Hindus were leaving, their property either sold or abandoned. Sources of credit dried up as liquid capital was converted into hoondis and bills of exchange that could be hidden in the lining of a coat.

—Roger Pearce

In a Hindi film called *Hey Ram*, two very significant aspects of a Hindu Sindhi's life are concretised through the supporting role of Lalwani (played by Saurabh Shukla). In one of the early scenes of the film, we see Lalwani dancing and singing in an extremely westernised and cosmopolitan club in Karachi. In one of the last scenes we see Lalwani selling papads near a refugee camp in Maharashtra. He is found exchanging furtive looks with an RSS activist. The first scenario refers to the Sindhi Hindus' loss of wealth and status due to Partition, the second to a new affiliation with Hindutva for which also Partition serves as a context. With this chapter, we come very specifically to the Sindhi Hindus' mass migration from Sindh in 1947. This chapter is

about the migrant generation, people who *directly* underwent the
Partition experience. It exists as one of the few records of personal
narratives about Sindh's experience of Partition. Rather sadly, this book
comes late, at a time when people such as Dr. Choithram Gidwani
and Jairamdas Daulatram, who were directly involved in the 'handling'
of Partition problems in Sindh, are lost to us.

The story of Partition in Sindh is about the experience of fear and
displacement, and not so much about violence. Three months after
Partition, Acharya Kripalani (president, Indian National Congress, a
well-known leader from Sindh) visited Sindh and noted that "There
was only a slight exodus of the Hindus and Sikhs from Sindh. It did
not suffer from any virulent fanaticism. To whatever faith the Sindhis
belonged, they were powerfully influenced by Sufi and Vedantic
thoughts. This made for tolerance" (2004, 703). Kamala Patel, who
represented the Indian government in its investigation of the cases of
abducted women during Partition, also testifies to the lack of violence
in Sindh, "There were a few instances," notes Patel, "but nothing like
the Punjab" (1985, 187). The excerpt below captures a precarious
moment of fear, an apprehension of what might happen:

> The radio announced that the nation was divided. Newspapers
> mentioned that the entire province of Sindh had gone to Pakistan.
> Refugees had begun to come into Sindh. The next day we heard that
> five thousand Muslims had come into Hyderabad. Some had been
> put up in the Muslim hostel, while some others lived in the
> neighbourhood of the Salatis. The Muslim hostel was on the street to
> our right. The atmosphere was marked by fear and misgivings, and
> terror gripped our hearts. If this was not enough, some young Muslim
> men got out of the hostel and began to shout slogans, "Hand over
> the beauties of the beautiful Hirabad to us." Our heartbeats raced.
> Young women in every house were being warned. The moment a
> Muslim enters your house, you must shove your fingers in the nearest
> electric plug, turn the switch on and bring an end to your life. Small
> packets of poison were also begin given to them. (My translation;
> Hiranandani 1981/1999, 67– 68)

The Muslims of Sindh were driven by economic need rather than
religious frenzy. The instances of looting and robbery by the Sindhi

Muslims during Partition show that class rather than religious antipathy informed their responses to the Sindhi Hindus. Moreover, all Sindhi Muslims were not fired by Islamisation as is evident in the extract from Sindhi nationalist Ibrahim Joyo's *Save the Sind, Save the Continent* (1947, 57).

> In the Counsels of the Congress as well as those of the League, we the Sindhees, appear as mere chattels to be summarily attached either to a totalitarian Hindustan or to a totalitarian Pakistan. The idea of both Hindu or Muslim nationalism is anathema to us.

Later, for the benefit of the Sindhi Muslims, he adds,

> The Musalmans forgot one thing, that the Hindu trader or moneylender was exploiting them not because he was a Hindu but because he was a trader or a moneylender, and the Hindu clerk in some government office was occupying that position not because he was a Hindu but because when he got in there and that office needed somebody, no Muslim was there in the field.

Until the fateful August of 1947, the Sindhis had not expected to leave. Oral accounts testify to the Sindhi Hindus' surprise at having to leave their homes, and also to their hope that they might be able to go back. By and large, both oral and written accounts point in the direction of the influx of refugees as the chief reason why the Sindhi Hindus left. Adeel Khan asks, "The main question here is to explore why Sindh, one of its more peaceful provinces that was comparatively less affected by communalism, had to suffer the most from the influx of refugees" (2005, 138). The answer may lie in the fact that the incoming refugees were destitute and had arrived after having undergone brutal violence in India. They also had the support of the League-run government that had, without any regard for social order, let them loose in the heart of cities like Karachi and Hyderabad. The refugees were not made to settle outside the city, but were tacitly allowed to occupy any empty property in urban Sindh. Like the Hindus of Godhra in Gujarat (see chapters 5 and 6), the immigrant Muslims waited for the Hindus to leave so that they could occupy their properties. In the riots of 6 January 1948, the incoming refugees created havoc for the Sindhi Hindus in Karachi. Given below is my translation of a brief extract from a story "6 January, 1948" by Thakur Chawla (1998, 46).

It must have been around twelve in the afternoon. The day was 6 January 1948. We heard screeches and screams from our neighbourhood in Karachi. I must [have been] about fifteen or sixteen years old then. I came up to the balcony of our house, and saw daylight looting going on. The spoils were being put in trucks. These were non-Sindhi Muslims, that is Mohajjirs, who were raiding the house of Dr. Premchand. They were hastily filling up trucks with looted objects. Dr. Premchand's house was only four buildings away from my house. It was clear that these were Muslims from UP and Bihar who had immigrated into Sindh. They had come to raid our houses. I ran downstairs. The watchman, who was a bhaiya from Allahabad, was making his dal in a corner, oblivious of all the havoc around him. I scolded him and quickly locked up the iron gate, returned and made him aware of his surroundings and responsibilities. I returned to the building and rounded off all the women from the building and took them to my house. In those fifteen minutes, a cluster of Mohajjirs came to our building. With cries of Allah-Akbar, they tried breaking the iron gate. About seven or eight of us started throwing unwanted things upon them from our balconies and hoped to disperse the crowd. There was a government building across us where many Sindhi Muslims worked. They stood watching the tamasha from their windows.

We had many unwanted objects but they got over. The crowd had reached the ground floor and was breaking the wooden door. It did not take very long for the door to give away, and the crowd rushed in to loot what it could. I tried phoning the police but the telephones lines had been cut off. People who had accompanied me earlier, slipped away to hide in their respective houses. Some escaped to the terrace leaving their precious things available for the Mohajjirs. They entered into our house. There were only three of us left, myself, my cousin Hardasmal (who had bought tickets to go to India) and the watchman. The watchman went and hid himself. Eight of my cousin's suitcases were lying near the door. He fell unconscious. I took the watchman's lathi but could do nothing with it. The Mohajjirs had knives with them. They pounced upon me with fists, lathis, knives. My clothes were smeared with blood. I kept yelling, "police, police," but nobody came to our rescue. Everything was looted. The Mohajjirs went away.

After about two hours, the police came. The wounded ones were taken to hospitals. The next day's newspaper, *Sindh Aabzarvar*, carried news of the riot and also my name among the list of the dead. I was not expected to survive the injuries. But I did.

Meanwhile, all my relatives and family had left Karachi to go to Hindustan. Reluctantly, I also decided to migrate. I did not ever entertain the thought of selling our village houses, lands and wells. However, the building in Karachi where we lived (and rented the rest) and which cost one and a half lakh before the riots was half its price. It had come down to sixty-eight thousand but the government had issued an order that any sales transaction made after 6th January would not be considered legal. I needed a certificate from a collector proving that I had sold my house before 6th January. I went to a Sindhi Muslim collector through a lawyer. He said, "Bania, for once I can lay my hands on you. You give me one thousand and I'll give you the certificate." In this way I sold the building in Karachi, left all the lands and houses in villages and migrated.

The Muslims of Sindh collaborated with the immigrant Muslims if they had old scores to settle, or in some cases, they expressed helplessness in the face of the new power equations that made them feel like 'outsiders' in their own province. In either case, the communal situation in Sindh did not lead to massacres. All the same, the Sindhi Hindus could not help feeling that both their properties and their lives were in danger. The increasing fear among the Sindhi Hindus stemmed from two sources: the immigrant Muslim population from Uttar Pradesh (UP) and Bihar, and the lurking danger of the complicity of the Sindhi Muslims. It is difficult to arrive at a conclusion on the basis of anecdotes, but there are more accounts of cooperation from the Sindhi Muslims than there are instances of communal revenge.

At the same time, Pearce's description of Sindh as "nervously peaceful" (2001, 471) in 1947 aptly captures the uncertain state of the Sindhis who did not know whether they ought to be leaving or not. Sindh's problem was not partition—a physical process of halving land and people; the land was never divided into two. It was precisely this that made the fate of the Sindhi Hindus uncertain. They could continue to stay where they were and there was no question of an exchange of population because almost all Sindhi-speaking people (Hindus and Muslims) lived within the province of Sindh. The Sindhi Hindus were just suddenly on sufferance in an Islamic state. While initially it had seemed that their wings were clipped and their spaces shrunk, the months after August 1947 also brought serious threat to life. Referring to that period, Pearce notes, "This was a time when Sindh was very anxious lest the reports from the Punjab lead to serious rioting. Fourteen Hindus were killed in Karachi, and at once a full curfew was imposed. The riot was really after loot, not blood, and the only body I saw was an Anglo-Indian at the post office killed by a looter" (2001, 470). Sporadic rioting had begun in Sindh, although it never acquired enormous proportions. At the same time, the atmosphere of fear made every random event seem a harbinger of disaster. At what point did the Sindhi Hindus feel 'compelled' to leave their homeland?[1] When did living in Sindh as a religious minority become unbearable? Did the Sindhis see their exodus as a natural consequence of Partition, or did each one respond to his/her own personal impulse?

There are multiple contexts against which the migration of the Sindhi Hindus, their 'decision' to leave may be traced. To start with, one could examine the highly inadequate but common mode of handling these questions by providing a 'riot narrative'. This would mean fixing days and dates on what had grown to be an ambivalent relationship with one's territory. Alternatively, one could provide 'high politics'—the parleys between the Congress and the Muslim League, and the breakdown of communication. One could also examine an altered subject–state relationship, that is, to see how the Sindhi Hindus came to be discriminated against by the state. All three paradigms are used below as modes of entering into the Sindh of 1947.

1. It has been estimated that out of the one million and four hundred thousand Hindus who lived in Sindh in 1947, about a million and a quarter had come over to India leaving behind the remaining in various parts of the province, especially in the Thar Parker district and other urban areas of Sindh (Thakur 1959/1997, 30).

RIOT NARRATIVES

In narratives of this nature, riots are seen as illustrations of 'how bad things were', as lapses into primitive madness. Inasmuch as riots are overt expressions of violence, they do serve to define intense moments. They become defining moments in popular memory, to be reckoned with, whenever necessary, to show how the conflicting communities (in this case, Hindus and Muslims) cannot live together. They provide justification for dividing nations along the lines of religion, but provide a false sense of continuity. For instance, the memories of 'communal riots' (an Indian expression for riots between Hindus and Muslims) occludes the significant periods of the so-called 'peace'. The cracks that form during these periods of peace make the recurrence of riots a possibility, and the riots in turn may create more cracks. As far as Sindh is concerned, there was some breach of confidence in the period of 'peace' when Hindus and Muslims went their separate ways on the issue of Sindh's dissociation from the Bombay Presidency, when the Arya Samaj went on the offensive, when the Hindus began to blatantly practise untouchability, and when the Sindhi Muslims occupied the Manzilgah. Commenting on the nature of peace, Roger Pearce remarks, "Below a peaceful surface there was always a danger of sudden violence" (2001, 47). On the other hand, Sindh was relatively calm in what was a turbulent period during Partition. Pearce, who has commented on the misleading nature of peace, also noted that he hardly saw blood in Sindh during Partition. The Sindh riots were few and not very intense, but they acquired a large significance in the minds of some Hindus because of the pre-Partition context and also the new fears caused by what was happening in Punjab. However sporadic, the post-Partition riots in Sindh are important for they tell not stories of violence but of insecurities caused by a gradual breach of confidence and also of economic disparities.

On the face of it, Sindh had exactly three instances of riots. It is possible to begin our riot narrative with the Quetta riots on the night of the 20 August, when a quarrel took place between some Pathans and Muslims over the question of the hoisting of the flag. This developed into a "general riot followed by arson and loot" (Anand 1996, 27–28). The second instance is that of the unrest in the Nawabshah district where, in September 1947, refugees from the East Punjab province migrated. A train containing Hindus from Punjab passing through Nawabshah was attacked and looted by non-Sindhi refugees. The next stage in this riot narrative is the 17th of December 1947, when twenty-seven people were killed in the city of Hyderabad. The trouble, notes Anand, "was not from Sindhi Muslims," but "some Sindhi Muslims did take advantage of the situation" (1996, 47). The last episode of rioting was the infamous riot of 6 January 1948, which as the respondent Harish Vazirani claims was, "state-sponsored, like the Modi riots in Gujarat" (personal interview). The 6 January riots were limited to the city of Karachi, but sent waves of fear among the Hindus to whom it was crystal clear that the Pakistan government wanted them to go. During these riots it seemed that all forces had conspired against the Hindus who were simply not wanted in the new Pakistan. Although evacuation (largely unorganised) had begun by then, this was when Gandhi told Narayandas Malkani, "Ask the Sindhis to leave now" (N. Malkani 1973, 139).

The written accounts on Partition are uniform in their view that the riots in Sindh were never intense and that they acquired significance through fear and not through actual instances of physical injury. Sindhi sociologists from India such as U.T. Thakur, Subhadra Anand and J.B. Kripalani ascribe the sources of these riots to external circumstances (mainly the Punjab effect and the influx of Muslim refugees from India), and not as a consequence of hatred between the Hindus and the Muslims of Sindh. Rioting in Sindh did not start in the immediate period before or during Partition. Anand notes that there was some 'participation' from the Sindhi Muslims if the Hindu in question was resented. Riots in such situations became a way of settling old scores (1996, 47). This could imply that the integrated relationships between the Hindus and the Muslims of Sindh withstood the violence of the times and did not succumb to a Punjab-like situation. It could also mean that Partition memory and scholarship on Sindh has not reckoned with the internal disharmony within the province, but has ascribed the 'blame' to an outsider. Interestingly, my conversations with Sindhi Muslims also testify to a similar response. One thing is clear: the predominant reason for any chasm between the Sindhi Hindus and the Sindhi Muslims was economic. Hence, even the resentment among the Sindhi Muslims did not go beyond looting. The Sindhi Hindus knew this and yet they feared that under the changed circumstances of a divided India, the property-grabbing (which was bad enough) might extend to violence on the body. It may be concluded that the Sindh riots had a strong economic context to them as far as the 'perpetrators' were concerned, and a psychological one as far as their 'victims' were concerned.

INTERSTATE PARLEYS AND DIALOGUE

Another plausible mode of tracing the reasons why the Sindhi Hindus left Sindh entails an examination of interstate parleys and dialogue, and their subsequent breakdown. On 2 June 1947, in a leaders' conference held at the viceroy's house, the Partition scheme was discussed. Among the ten salient points, which included guidelines on how Punjab and Bengal were to be divided, the North West Frontier Province (NWFP) and Sindh were also included. It was decided that in the absence of a legislative assembly, the NWFP would have a referendum. The Sindh Legislative Assembly was to decide which part of India it would join. In the case of Baluchistan, it was to be decided by the viceroy in consultation with the Indian parties. While all this may seem equally uniform or arbitrary, the arrangement for the Hindu minority of Sindh was particularly unfair compared with those for NWFP and Baluchistan. Sindh did have a legislative assembly, no doubt, but the province of Sindh was under the political ministry of the Muslim League. In effect therefore, the Muslim League in Sindh, which obviously chose to belong to Pakistan, muffled the voice of the Hindu minority. Thus, unlike Punjab and Bengal, Sindh was not divided or partitioned. It simply went to Pakistan. The Hindus of Sindh were not given a chance to retain even the Hindu-dominated parts of Sindh such as Thar Parker which was contiguous with

Rajasthan. A similar situation had arisen with respect to Sylhet in Assam, but the choice of plebiscite was given to its inhabitants (Kripalani 2004, 682).

In August 1947 when India and Pakistan were formed, very few Sindhi Hindus had considered leaving Sindh. The interstate agreement between India and Pakistan had not made provision for the exodus of the Sindhi Hindus who, though a religious minority, could continue to live in Pakistan as equal citizens. However, this was a matter of faith, a fragile affair given the circumstances of Partition. The discussion below shows how the Sindhi Hindus felt that the Pakistan government was not interested in fulfilling its promise of safeguarding its minorities and that the Indian government had little time to follow this up. Although Gandhi was concerned about this issue, his voice was drowned in the immediate problems of refugees and the riots.

As Muslim immigrants from Bombay and Kathiawar, Bihar and UP began to pour into Sindh, the Pakistan government was further put to the test. The Congress leaders asked for a common minority plan to protect themselves against 'invading' immigrants who began to riot and occupy properties illegally. The local Congress leaders made several petitions to the Governor of Sindh, Ghulam Hussain Hidayatullah, to bring the rioters to book, but in vain. The common minority plan would also include Hindu participation in the judiciary and the corporation, and also in the selection of the flag for the nation in which they meant to live. However, the minorities' complaints made little difference. Consequently, the executive committee of the Sindh Minorities Association passed a resolution on 16 September 1947 and registered an emphatic protest against the terrorist activities tacitly approved by the state (Anand 1996, 32). The evacuation procedure in Sindh continued to be flagrantly ignored. The Hindus did not leave Sindh immediately, so there was no evacuee property that the refugees could occupy straight away. Resentment against the Hindu affluence found expression in the forcible eviction of Hindu occupants from their houses. There was also the fear that the average Sindhi Muslim, who by and large did not suffer from religious fanaticism, would lose his balance in the communal frenzy (Kripalani 2004, 705).

In fact, some felt that the Sindhi Muslim was already complicit in the looting and although he had not been violent so far, it was not worth taking chances. Thus, terrified of their future and frustrated by the government, the Hindus began to leave sporadically. Meanwhile, the old guard of the Sindh government comprising figures such as Muhammad Ayub Khuhro, G.M. Syed and Illah Bux witnessed the atrocities upon the Hindus, but they represented waning power; the new reins lay with leaders like Jinnah and Liaquat Ali, the architects of Pakistan. The Hindus were caught between a well-meaning but ineffectual Sindhi Muslim population and Pakistan's undemocratic League government. Their position remained at best ambivalent, and with the Indian government showing hardly any interest, they became victims of the state in both India and Pakistan. Neither their local Congress leaders (who in fact were the first to run away, jibes Harish Jethmalani in a personal interview), nor those representing the Sindh government helped them. In his many speeches during Partition, Nehru made no reference to Sindh (Anand 1996, 55). The Sindhis knew that they had only themselves to rely upon.

Although the journey of the Sindhi Hindus was uneventful, their departure was made painful by the behaviour of the National Muslim Guard, the 'army' of the Muslim League. Much against interstate treaties, the National Guard would rob the Hindus of their possessions—money, jewellery and furniture. The account of a departing Sindhi Hindu, Sitaldas Khemani, narrated by Roger Pearce captures one such humiliating experience. It has been quoted at length here to demonstrate the nature of the 'peaceful' departure:

> Sitaldas Khemani came with his family from Jacobabad where he had stayed in his post as Administrator till the last minute, almost beyond. He came with his wife and children; they had left everything behind except one small suitcase each. They spent the night with us, and we gave them two blankets, because it would be cold on the deck. I went with them to the docks to see them off. On the quay there were scenes that made me ashamed. There were police, but they did nothing, and the subedar told me he dared not interfere; there were such tensions, such bitterness and envy, that any attempt to bring order

might lead to a massacre. So I stood by Sitaldas and his family, and at least no one dared attack him. Soon they went on board in tears and we saw them no more. For a time I watched the looting. The looters were khaksars, so-called patriots tolerated by the Pakistan government and so unwillingly, by Sindh. (2001, 471)

ALTERED SUBJECT–STATE RELATIONSHIP

We now move to the third paradigm—an altered subject–state relationship manifest in economic discrimination, which, in the case of the Sindhi Hindus, is very significant. Historically, the relationship between the Hindus of Sindh and the Muslim League had been far from happy. However, in the pre-Partition economy the Sindhi Hindus were less vulnerable, as they were protected by a 'neutral' government and also by their own economic and political standing. The mere fact of being a religious minority in an Islamic state could not have been a sufficient deterrent to living in Sindh. Save a spell of eighty odd years (from 1854 to 1935 when Sindh was a part of the Bombay Presidency), the Sindhi Hindus had almost always lived under Muslim political domination. They had not only lived, but also flourished in economic terms. Undoubtedly, they faced certain forms of political subjection especially through the prohibition on owning land, on taking out processions and the imposition of arbitrary punishments and (occasionally) conversions. However, the fact that they had chosen not to move despite being able to do so indicates the confidence they had in the system. It is crucial to remember that for a mercantile community like the Hindus of Sindh, an opportunity to grow economically played a very substantial role in their decisions. This aspect of their lives was threatened under the new dispensation called Pakistan. Anand provides several instances of economic discrimination. The discussion below is based upon her research.

Over a month before Partition, in July 1947, Dr. Choithram Gidwani (president of the Sindh Provincial Congress Committee) alluded to the 'injustices' against the Hindus. He said, "Our industries have been strangled, the education of our children seriously jeopardized, and our joint share in Government usurped" (Anand 1996, 23). Gidwani was referring to a systematic disempowerment of the Hindus from industry, trade, the judiciary, education and several crucial positions of power, which they had always dominated. For instance, the town of Karachi had six designated city magistrates for the criminal court and four additional city magistrates. Of these posts, four were held by Muslims and two by Hindus; the city magistrate however, was always a Hindu. As discussed in the previous chapter, the Hindus had both education and economic power and they controlled almost the entire bureaucratic network.[2] After Partition, the post of the city magistrate was scrapped, and then reinstated with a Muslim incumbent. If this serves as an instance of disempowerment from within the government machinery, the case of the Karachi Bus Service serves to show discrimination in trade. A bastion of the Hindus, the Karachi Bus Service was a large firm that ran public buses in Karachi. In the months after 1947, the Hindus' licenses to run these buses were cancelled, although some Muslim firms could continue to do so. Anand also enumerates instances where land belonging to Hindu trusts was quietly requisitioned for building houses for immigrants from Bihar. Furthermore, the Karachi Municipal Corporation, another stronghold of the Hindus, was reduced to being a subordinate department of the government. Its powers were curtailed, especially over ownership of land and it was also deprived of police assistance in demolishing illegal constructions.

The foregoing discussion on the three paradigms is aimed at 'explaining' the Sindhi Hindus' exodus from Sindh. Needless to say, none of the paradigms operated in isolation; they perhaps reinforced each other and overlapped. The following letters from Jairamdas

2. By desiring a Muslim government, the Sindhi Muslims had hoped to dislodge the Hindus from power so that they could occupy these positions. Given the levels of dispossession among a large majority of Sindhi Muslims, this cannot but be justified. However, it is a historical irony that neither the Hindus nor the Muslims of Sindh profited from the creation of Pakistan. Power remains with the immigrant generations of Muslims who had moved from UP and Punjab. Both economic and political standing continue to be inaccessible to Sindhi Muslims even today.

Daulatram written to Sardar Vallabhbhai Patel show the quick deterioration of Sindh:

> 11 Sept 1947
>
> My dear Vallabhbhai,
> I have been receiving letters and telegrams about the worsening situation in Sind. Migration on an increased scale in the usual unorganized way is rapidly progressing. I think adequate anticipatory arrangements for organized evacuation under military guard would avoid great misery. I hope it will be possible for you to give them a little time. I can realize the pressure under which the government of India has to deal with trying situations in so many directions simultaneously. I hope you will include Sind also in the arrangement being made for the Punjab refugees and the refugees from Sind might be included in the allotments of refugees to be made for different provinces. This would prevent unnecessary distress and discontent. (in Das 1972, 360).

Jairamdas followed this letter up with a telegram dated 19 September 1947 (eight days after the above letter) that had a more urgent note:

> Several thousand waiting at Hyderabad station anxious to leave Sind. Despite three trains carrying daily four thousand passengers number of remaining passengers continue swelling. Attitude of military civil authorities police and national guard extremely hostile subjecting passengers to various humiliations. (372)

In the last letter of that period, dated 24 September 1947, Jairamdas concludes,

> Hindus apprehend if they are not rescued in time they would be subjected to two alternatives—Islam or Death. (373)

It is useful to examine the erratic pattern of the Hindu exodus from Sindh as given below.

The Sindhi Hindus left sporadically from August 1947 – the month of Partition – up to 1951. U.T. Thakur's research on their evacuation shows the following pattern:

Table 1: Pattern of Sindhi Hindu Exodus from Sindh

Pattern of evacuation	Number of evacuees
November 1947	246,000
December 1947	140,000
1 Jan – 15 Feb 1948	180,000*
1 Feb – 18 March 1948	94,000
March 1948	100,000
April 1948	41,000
May 1948	51,000
June 1948	20,000
1949	27,000
1950	9100
1951	644

* The sharp rise is attributed to the 6 January riots.
Source: Thakur 1959/1997, 29–30.

The geographical location of Sindh and the modes of travel demand special attention for they also determined to a very great extent the non-violent experience of the Sindhi Hindus. First of all, the metaphor of trains used extensively in Partition narratives does not carry an experiential charge for the Sindhis who by and large managed to come to India by sea from Karachi. Travelling by sea was safe; it did not allow the opportunities for perpetrating violence that the stopping of trains did. Those who found Karachi far and expensive (until 1948, when arrangements were made for bringing the poor by country craft) travelled by trains. They boarded the train from either Hyderabad (Sindh) or Mirpur Khas and came safely into Rajasthan, bypassing the violent Punjab. A large majority of Sindhis could travel by sea—boarding ships from Karachi and coming either to Bombay or to the Kathiawari ports in Gujarat. Since Sindh in its entirety went to Pakistan, the most familiar visual image of kafilas – long columns of people walking in opposite directions and killing each other in the process – also does not apply to this province, which did not have any kafilas.

So far I have tried to capture the external side of the Sindh Partition story, a narrative built upon the sociological accounts of U.T. Thakur and Subhadra Anand (the only two Sindhi scholars who have written on the subject of the Hindu exodus from Sindh). The following section is concerned with the psychological side, and hence it foregrounds personal narratives. It provides first-person accounts by members of the first generation of migrants to India and also those of Sindhi Muslims residing in Sindh who shared their memories of the Hindus' migration. In order to provide continuity in the personal voice, my analysis is not interspersed in this section, but follows the accounts. Thus, print and people compensate and contradict, and provide us with what can be seen as a version of the Sindhi story of migration, built through memory.

Dr. S. Karamchand

Dr. Karamchand lives in a Sindhi colony called the Kanwarram Colony in Vadodara. The colony has a series of narrow lanes running into each other, dotted on either side by houses of people who formerly lived as refugees in Harni and Outram camps. You can also see vendors selling Sindhi food—papads, pickles and pakodas. In one such lane, outside a small clinic, Dr. Karamchand practises as a retired medical practitioner. He sits on a chair and waits to examine any patient from the colony. He charges only Rs. 5, regardless of the ailment. It is easy to see that the minimal fees are to maintain the patient's dignity and are not profit for Dr. Karamchand, whose gentleness and capacity for service permeate even his account of Sindh.

I was born in Karachi on 1st April 1917. My father was a station master. I studied in N.J. High School and acquired matriculation. Sindh in those days was a part of the Bombay Presidency. I had stood first in the entire Bombay Presidency and took admission in the medical college in Hyderabad. There was no university in Sindh [in] those days, so we used to go to Bombay to appear for the final examination. I stood first even in my medical examination. I joined as a medical doctor with the government and began to be posted at various urban and rural places in Sindh—Jacobabad, Berar, Hyderabad. That was in 1939.

I have very happy memories of my life in Sindh. Since I was a doctor I used to meet all kinds of people, rich and poor, and treat Hindus and Muslims. How much love I received from them...It's all very sad, but I have made service my goal even after Partition.

I had a friend called Noor Mohammed Shaikh. He held an important position in the Karachi Municipal Corporation. His father was a well-known pir in Sindh. Noor Mohammed and I were very close. When I was transferred to a village called Bhria in Nawabshah, Noor Mohammed told me to visit a Sayyid there who had severe pain in his stomach but nobody had provided relief to him. I examined the Sayyid and knew that he had a problem with his kidneys. I prescribed medicine for him. Within a few days, he felt much better. I became the apple of his eyes and my reputation spread among many pir families of Sindh. The pirs would simply not let go of me. Noor's father treated me as his own son and the Sayyid I had cured was so fond of me I can't tell you. During Partition I saw many people leaving, but I had no courage to leave. How was I going to inform Sayyid sahib? Would he let me go, I wondered. But in any case, medical services were essential services, so I would not have even been easily given the permission to leave. But when the 6th January riots took place, my father said we must absolutely leave. I was worried about informing my Muslim friends and patients that I had decided to go. I told my pir that I had to go to Karachi to see my family off. The D.J. Sind College in Karachi functioned as a refugees-in-transit camp. I wished to go there; my family was waiting for me there. Two of my brothers had already left. They were in Gujarat. The pir sent a couple of his murids [followers] for my protection. Times were really bad; the National Muslim Guard was terrifying. Frankly I went to Karachi trembling in fear, but I also felt that my Sindhi Muslim companions would protect me from harm. Would they have the power to [do] that, I wondered. They did stand by me. Along the way, the Guard stopped us and asked my Sindhi Muslim friends, "*Murgha hai kya? De do haemin.*" [Is that a catch? Give it to us.] My guardians told them I was a noble doctor, very helpful to them. They immediately apologised. Once when I was going from one village to another at night, a similar thing had happened. There were a bunch of Hurs on camels. They stopped me to take any valuables from me. Their fight was with the British, not with people like us. But if they saw a rich Hindu, it angered them. I told them I was a doctor and they immediately let me go. I have not had any negative experience from the Sindhis, in fact I received tremendous love and respect.

Rochiram Thawani

I was familiar with the name of Rochiram Thawani. He and his family had played an active role in the nationalist campaigns in Sindh and every account of that period refers to the Thawanis as the Nehrus of Sindh. Thawani has also been a teacher to some of the most well-known Sindhi writers. He lives in Nagpur.

I was born in Halani in the district of Nawabshah in the year 1916. I do not remember the date of my birth. I studied in Sindh from my primary school to college. In 1935, I happened to be in Quetta to take up a job as a teacher. The same year the notorious earthquake took place in Quetta and I lost my siblings. I was buried under the debris and presumed dead. Local newspapers also declared me to be dead. But somehow I had been pulled back to life. So from a very early stage, death was never fearful to me. My father was also like that. He had been to prison several times. We amils put 'bhai' to denote a senior, respectable person. I suppose you also do that in Gujarat. My father's name was Bhai Satchitanand. He was in government service but he must have hardly worked for four or six years with the government. During Non-cooperation, he quit government service and responded to Gandhi's call for freedom. I too did the same thing, but became a teacher. Like RSS-wallahs, I paid close attention to children. I had organised padayatras [political campaigns undertaken by walking] for eight days to establish intimacy with children and gradually make them patriotic. I used to tell them about Bankimchandra's *Anandmath* and the first war of independence. The British government found my activities objectionable and pressurised the management of my school to throw me out. The management persuaded me to resign, but my contact with students continued. Kirat Babani and Naari Gosani were my students.

When migration began from Nawabshah I got very worried. What were the arrangements for these people who were leaving? The collector Masud in Nawabshah (whom everyone from that district remembers) was very cruel. He was largely responsible for an early migration process in Nawabshah. A fanatic Punjabi he was. But the Congress believed (rightly or wrongly) that the Sindhis should be able to live in Sindh. All of us believed that. Perhaps we were naïve. But really speaking, had there been no Muslims from Bihar or UP, we would not have left. Dr. Choithram Gidwani was very anxious about the Hindus. He wanted at least a hundred Hindus to be in the army so that people were safe. Anyhow, we avoided leaving immediately. In fact, we even joined the procession on 14 August 1947 to celebrate Pakistan. They began to shout slogans like "*Hans hans ke liya Pakistan, lad lad ke lenge Hindustan.*" [Laughing, we acquired Pakistan; forcibly, we will acquire India.] We quit the procession.

On 24th August, a Hindu Sikh was murdered in broad daylight in the main bazaar. I rushed to Delhi. I informed the leaders there and was told that Hindu Sikhs should evacuate, but the rest can live. In September, Sindhi Sikhs left from Nawabshah to go to Mirpur Khas. There was a station called Shahpur Chaker where all the Sindhi Sikhs were murdered. Again I rushed, this time to inform the Pakistan government, but no one believed me. My social and political life was confined to Nawabshah. Other volunteers and I told the people there that we would help them leave by November. I left in December 1947.

When I look back I feel happy with what I did for the people there. But I also feel somewhat wistful that Sindhis were so embittered by Congress. I think that Jan Sangh took good care of the Sindhis, so they have obviously moved towards them after the '60s. I would have been incomplete without Gandhi and Congress.

Gangaram Samrat

I went to see Gangaram Samrat in his house at Kubernagar Camp with very high expectations. He was known to be one of the most knowledgeable men of Sindh—not only among Indian Sindhis but also Sindhis in Pakistan. He spoke authoritatively on the Indus civilisation, and had written several works on the Aryan origins of the Indus Valley inhabitants (Shudh Ramayan *1989;* Naon Chachnamo – Bhayankar Dhokho *1991;* Sindh Sagar *1995).*

I was also told that Gangaram Samrat held provocative views, that his anti-Islamic writings in Sindh were banned and that he had been banished from Sindh. I came to a small house with just one room and a kitchen. Gangaram Samrat lived there with his son and daughter-in-law. As long as he was alive (he passed away a month after his interview with me), Gangaram Samrat ran a printing press in Sindhi which barely met its costs. Partition may not have brought an end to his writing, but it certainly ruined his economic life. The signs of poverty around him were unmistakable. However, the spirit of an opinionated, blunt and individualistic man lived in a frail body that seemed ready to release his spirit. Neither an interview nor a conversation was possible with Gangaram Samrat. Spurred by a single question on what he did in Sindh, he gave me a rambling account of his life and views, not necessarily in response to my questions. Since he stood before me as an important source of history and as a writer whose books were influential in Sindh, and since he held views unarticulated by most Sindhis, I have provided his disjointed narrative.

I lived in Jillo Dadu, same place as G.M. Syed. Syed and I used to write to each other quite regularly. I advised him to support Benazir Bhutto; she is a Sindhi after all. I have letters of G.M. Syed with me. I will show them to you some day. Now he is dead, but he was crying a lot in his last days. He regretted giving Sindh away to the wolves. At that time they were all carried away. They thought once the Hindus are gone, they would become zamindars. Some hope. The Punjabis have not given them anything. I am not saying we Hindus gave them everything. I think we are responsible for Hindustan–Pakistan. We treated the Muslims like untouchables and obviously they wanted us to go. They became Muslims because we practiced caste with them. I am strongly against caste. I am an Arya Samaji, I believe in the Aryan dharma. Hindus are foolish; they will quickly lose their religion whenever they see anything new. They had no business chasing that bearded Nanak and forgetting their own Aryan dharma. But who understands? I am writing a history of Aryan Sindh. Only an Arya Samaji can write pure history. You know people used to read my books in Sindh; even now the Sindhis there place orders for my books. Have you seen *Aryavrat*? It was banned in Sindh. I write against Islam, but not against Muslims. I have very close relations with Muslims who would read my books and say we don't like them but it doesn't matter. I did not leave Sindh when everybody else was leaving. I left in 1952. I was thirty-one then.

I used to be a very successful teacher and almost every student I taught stood first in the district. The headmaster of the school, Muhammad Urs, was my student. I wanted to quit the country when one student whom I had taught failed.

In any case, they were also keen on throwing me out. After *Aryavrat* appeared, they wanted to arrest me. It was my Muslim friends who managed to get me an income tax certificate. I needed that certificate because the Pakistan government had started a permit system. You could not leave overnight without clearing your papers, without the government giving you a 'No Objection' certificate. How was I to manage all that? I was never very rich.   But my Muslim friends managed to arrange everything for me. These people in Ahmedabad blame the Muslims for Partition. I don't; I blame the likes of them.

Udhavdas Makhija

Udhavdas Makhija is my uncle, my father's brother. He is a retired businessman. Along with my father, he had started a small hosiery workshop in Ahmedabad in the 1950s. We call him 'dada'. I had always found Dada a foppish person; his passion for Hindi cinema, his compulsive habit of comparing every young woman with a Bollywood heroine—basically, his treatment of real life as an echo of Bollywood both irritated and amused me. Prior to this project, I had not known that he had been an active RSS trainer or that he held an irrational dislike for Muslims. While these were surprising elements in my interview with him, there was also a recognisable element of Hindi cinema even in his Partition account.

I was born in 1926 in Shikarpur. My father died when I was hardly ten. I have no memory of playing anything or with anyone. I would come back from school and leave to earn money. By the time of Partition I had begun to earn Rs. 40 a month. My mother was very particular about that. She said boys have to be constantly earning. I used to study in a school meant only for Hindu boys. There was no question of having Muslim companions. I have never liked Muslims. Good that we came here during Partition. They would have made life miserable for us. They used to say, "All this belongs to us. We will take everything from you." We used to call them Hurs. They used to abduct our women.

For about four years I lived in Karachi. My maternal uncle took me there and I used to work in a grocery store. I gave up studies at the age of twelve, I think. Once again I came to Shikarpur and lived there up to the age of seventeen. My father had left us a big house but hardly any money. He was in the money-lending business in Afghanistan. He would go to Tashkent and Bukhara, but after the Russian Revolution he had to give up that business. He had put by enough money to lend to Muslim neighbours who would mortgage their jewels and precious things with him. I remember an occasion when my father had a very bitter fight with my eldest brother who then walked out of the house. But he also took with him small knick-knacks and precious things that Muslims had left with my father as mortgage. My father was quite worried. I don't know what happened then. Perhaps it was because of this that my father gave up the money-lending business (we used to call it soodkhori). But he was a much-respected man. Ours was a Muslim locality and each time my father left home by a horse-cart they would do salaam to him. Muslim haaris used to keep coming to our house to give small agricultural gifts like watermelons or vegetables. My father used to tell us that they had such respect for him because he was helpful to them. In his last days, my father had got into the habit of playing with his money. He began to buy shares and do speculative business. He must have lost money there. After his death, we used to earn money from renting our property to Hindus and Muslims. Life went on this way.

When people began to talk about Partition, we in the RSS knew that it was not going to be safe. I left for Karachi as soon as the Pakistan government took over on 14th August. My sister Bhagwani's husband Thakoredas was in Karachi. He had told me that I should go to him and he would take me to India. He was also in the RSS. In fact, there was a point when I was appointed as a shikshak [teacher/trainer] and I had to train him, among a group of eleven people! I remember feeling embarrassed. How could I train my brother-in-law? But anyway. He came to fetch me from Shikarpur. My mother was there with your father. But I left because I had people to take care of me. She was not planning to come at that time.

We took a train from Shikarpur to Karachi. It used to cost six rupees and it was a twelve-hour journey. When we got down at Karachi, the atmosphere was very tense. Hindus were being killed everywhere. We still had to inquire about when we would be able to take a ship and therefore [had to] stay in Karachi until we got a place on some ship. Thakoredas gave me a Muslim cap to wear.

There was a Noorjahan and Dilip Kumar film playing at Radhe Talkies. It was *Jugnu*. We thought a cinema hall is a safe place and it would help us forget about the danger. So we went and watched the film. I did not really enjoy the film, I was really very scared. But I was equally scared of going outside. There were slogans everywhere. Somehow we managed to reach one relative's house. That was the most fearful evening of my life.

Since we were among the early ones to leave, we could immediately get the tickets to go by ship. The fare was ninety-six rupees that day, although it should have been only nineteen rupees. They had hiked it up like a cinema ticket! I did not have any money with me. Thakoredas advised me to pay a bribe of five rupees to the guard and somehow sneak my way in. I did that. But I was hounded almost all the time. I had to keep hiding so that the officers didn't catch me.

When the ship disembarked at Bombay, I was hugely relieved. An old mate Buddho Advani met me there; he took me to Masjid Bunder where my old friend Pratap was staying in a tent. I was thrilled to see him, and we spent many hours together.

Tilli Mulchandani
My family has known Tilli maasi for over thirty years. My family thinks of her as an old wise woman with clairvoyant powers. I remember feeling resentful about carrying messages to her because she lived in Wadaj Camp, a Sindhi locality which always appeared dirty. Now even Maasi has moved out of her camp home, and lives in a large bungalow with her three sons and their families. Maasi leaves home once a day to hear the Guru Granth Sahib at the Sindhi darbar in Wadaj. She is almost eighty years old but has very clear

*memories of pre-Partition Sindh. She lived in rural Sindh and her
narrative serves as a very important source of rural and gender
sociology in Sindh.*

I grew up in a village Dabhro, near Tharu Shah. I was brought up by
my maami. My mother's brother, that is, my maami's husband, died
at a young age of twenty-one. My maami did not remarry. She lived
all alone with her mother-in-law, that is, my naani. My mother gave
me away to her so that she could have a little child for company. I
studied in a school upto teen patti, it would be equivalent to fifth
standard for you. I used to walk to school and carried with me a
mango and roti. We would walk through a small stream and go to
school. There were both Hindu and Muslim schools I think, but I
can only remember one girl from those days.

That was a lot of education. After all we were in a village with
not more than twenty houses. There was a legend about the village.
It was born out of a woman who had survived a flood. Every other
house had perished in the flood but one woman had survived. My
maama used to be a zamindar. To be a zamindar was a very big
thing in those times. We had a very big house, cows and buffaloes,
and milk and ghee. I know how to draw milk from a cow. Muslims
used to invite us to their weddings. We would bring uncooked food
from them and cook at home. Food was so good and healthy. We
used to buy a goat for hardly some annas and have such good
mutton and fish. In Sindh, people used to eat all that food. Now
they have stopped.

In Sindh even dacoits came with notice! They were called the
Hurs. They would send a note saying we would come on this day
and keep things ready for us. The Hurs would even be fed and
given away some gold, or money, or produce from the fields. But
the zamindars had enough, they were very rich.

The haaris used to till our lands and give us half the share from
the produce. They would take some and the rest went to the
Jungshahi station where it was sold. The Muslims had no brains at
all. They used to be scared of us and never dared do anything to us.
They became like lions later when Muslims from here went and
instigated them. I remember we used to have Pathans from Quetta
and Baluchistan who would sell almonds and raisins to us. Then
there were [Hindu] Sindhis who came on donkeys and sold us cloth.

Nobody was poor in Sindh. Even the poorest Sindhi woman had at least a thin gold bangle on her arm. Muslim women used to carry thick rotis and curds for their husbands. My maami and I would embroider things for them which they would sell. I used to make very nice chaadars [thick cloth used as veils]. Women used those chaadars to keep their faces covered. We also had to do that. We were allowed to show only one eye, this tradition was called 'akhdi'. If you did not cover your face properly, the panchayat penalised you. We never went out of the house. Even now, you can see I hardly go out of the house. Women do not observe purdah anymore though. Times have changed. I remember Chandru master's song:

> *Dissi rang duniya ajab ilahi*
> *Sas rahi sabr mein*
> *Nuhan mare manyayi*
> *Kan jiyare judai*
> *Hikdi chai chapan*
> *Bi bidi bharai*
> *Halandiyun hotel vatun*
> *Basi bharan, chai, chutney*
> *Lemon soda.*

New shades of the world emerge
The mother-in-law lived in restraint
Daughter-in-law put her foot down
They live on their own
They go visit restaurants
Drink tea and light bidis,
Tea, chutney, lemon soda.

I remember having a glimpse of Chandru Master in Sindh. I heard him again in Ulhasnagar. There were radios even in our time in Sindh. I don't remember listening to the radio, but the Hindu families used to invite Muslim singers who would sing songs of Sasui Punnu and Umar Marvi. Muslims were very good singers. We used to listen to their Sufi songs also. Some Hindus were Sufi bhagat [mystics]. But in Sindh there were fewer darbars and temples than I see here. Also in Sindh, we did the ritual of *akho payan*, worshipping water, a tribute to Darya Shah. And once a year, for cheti chand, people gathered at Daryakhan goth. But there were not many cheti chand

[Sindhi new year] processions. Guru Nanak was worshipped more than anybody else, even Jhulelal is an avatar of Guru Nanak. There was a small place where Guru Granth Sahib was placed. We would go there and read a bit every evening. Every woman knew Gurmukhi.

When people began to talk about Hindustan–Pakistan, my naani sent me off to my mother's. She said it was unsafe to have a young girl in the house. I must have been sixteen or seventeen then. So I went and stayed with my parents and two other sisters in Moryo. It was in Moryo that I got engaged. I began to live with my in-laws in Kandiaro. My father-in-law had a kothi, a big grocery store in Karachi. Nand's father [the husband] was studying when we got married. I must have lived in Sindh for barely six months after my marriage. People in villages were feeling very scared. They said Gandhi and Nehru had differences and now we would have to go. From the village of Moryo, we took a train to Hyderabad. There were many of us from the same village. We came to Hyderabad and stayed there for many days. We saw Muslims breaking the doors of Hindus' houses. The Muslims from here were very aggressive. Sindhi Muslims were not very aggressive. They were misled by Muslims from here. In Sindh, the Muslims used to be scared of us, now it is the contrary, we are scared of them.

We waited in Hyderabad. Free train services had not yet begun. We left quite early before those things began or even the riots began. We did not see any Hindus getting killed, but later there were very bad riots in Karachi. My father-in-law's uncle never came to this country. He just got lost. But we had no problems at all. In fact, we left with all the gold we had. Once it was decided that we would have to leave, we started selling our utensils and big valuables to the haaris. The haaris wanted to buy them, but they soon realised that we would have to leave everything for free. So they stopped paying.

We left without my father-in-law. He brought whatever money he could. I remember wearing five kurtas on myself! I had a salwar made of silver. I wore that as well. My father-in-law came dressed as a Muslim.

Ladi Goplani
Ladi Goplani (called Amma) lives in Bhavnagar. Her memories of

*Partition and especially the process of resettlement are fairly distinct,
although she was too young to understand what was happening.
Amma is in her late sixties now. She hardly ever leaves home except
to go to a gurudwara in the evenings. She came to Bhavnagar at
the age of eight or nine, and has hardly visited any other part of
India. Amma uses the collective pronoun perhaps to refer to herself
and her sisters who were all married at the same time.*

I don't know my age. In our times, people did not celebrate birthdays
so we never came to know our age. Moreover, Sindhi girls do not
have horoscopes. I must be in my sixties, although illnesses make
me look older. We are from Khairpur Riyasat. We were never sent to
school. Our elders said that girls became too clever by going to
school. So we were all taught Gurmukhi at home. I have also taught
Gurmukhi to all my daughters.

We regularly read the *Sukhmani* which had Guru Nanak's
teachings in Gurmukhi. Our midwives were Muslims; my maid here
is also a Muslim. But we never accepted cooked food from Muslims.
They would invite us to their homes and weddings, but we would
be given uncooked food. Our family believed strongly in Guru Nanak;
men from our house used to do gurbani at gurudwaras, so they
were vegetarians. Not all Sindhis were vegetarians—our family was
somewhat exceptional.

I married at a very young age. When people began to talk about
Hindustan-Pakistan our elders got me and my sisters married off.
We were three sisters and we were married into the same family
which had three boys. My father feared that the Muslims would
abduct his daughters. My husband must have been four or five
years older than me. He was studying when we married. Even at a
young age I had so much maryada [shame]. I used to keep my head
covered up to my neck. We would never talk to men, only nod. My
husband's mother was not alive, so we did not [have] a mother-in-
law who would explain some things to us. My husband was also
young and since we were not supposed to 'talk' to men, we never
really knew what happened during Hindustan-Pakistan. We were
put in a bus from Khairpur which brought us to Karachi. We came
fully prepared with our *Gitas* and *Sukhmanis*. We were told that
Muslims were driving Hindus away and if we did not go, we would
have to live with humiliation. So each one came to protect his or her

izzat [honour], our religion. There is no question of resentment or bitterness. There are Hindus who still live there, but those who felt strongly about their religion, left. I have no bitter memories of Muslims or even a negative thought towards them. Nothing happened to us, although we were very afraid. There were some who went through violent times. But we had a dignified departure.

We boarded a ship at Karachi. It must have been around Holi. We came to Nayabunder in Gujarat. We were given tents to stay. Women were given spinning wheels to spin khadi and earn money. My husband had to suddenly assume a lot of responsibility. He had hardly worked, but now he needed to. We did not have any problems on the way, but all said and done, we were not rich people in Sindh either. My husband became a fruit vendor. We Sindhis do not believe in doing jobs for someone. As they say *naukri aa tokri* [to be employed is to carry garbage].

Gena Nawani

Gena lives all alone in a Sindhi colony in Adipur. Most of the inhabitants of the colony moved to Adipur after having spent some unsuccessful years in places like Bantwa and Junagadh in Saurashtra. Some of the most poor and rural Sindhis settled down in Saurashtra. Gena is also very poor. She has also lost most of her relatives. She moves about all alone, visiting peoples' houses and taking up small jobs for them.

I was eleven years old when we came to Hindustan. I was married off at the age of nine. I must have been sitting on my mother's lap when I got married. My natal home was in Khair goth. I did not go to school. My brother died at a young age when I was in school. My mother said, "*Vidya phire nathi.*" [Education has been not been auspicious for us.] On the day of my wedding, I was going around prancing thinking it was my sister's marriage. I was distributing sweets. My father perched me on his shoulders and cried. Our Muslim neighbours were also crying.

My father-in-law had a grocery store. There was 'control' on jaggery, but my brother-in-law had stocked it illegally. He was selling it secretly. Someone informed the police and my brother-in-law was imprisoned. My father-in-law was very angry. He said let the rest of the family leave, those two fellows can join us later. My father-in-law wore a Jinnah cap and brought us by train. We looked like Muslim women anyway. We took a train from Mirpur Khas and came to Marwad. We had no problem during the journey. It was a safe journey. But some of us were neither peaceful in Sindh nor here. Others have made a lot of money here. My son died, I lost my husband. Your fate will follow you, it does not matter whether you live here or there.

Draupadi Nathani

Draupadi Nathani lives in Ahmedabad. She is in her late seventies. Her husband and sons are engaged in the textiles business, while she and the women of the family look after the home. In terms of her beliefs and lifestyle, Draupadi does not show a marked transition from being a small-town, pre-Partition Sindhi to an urban, post-Partition Sindhi. As we shall see, her narrative reflects gender conceptions more strongly than any 'traumatic' account of Partition.

We are from Tando Adam. We belong to the bhaiband caste. We are more conservative than Shikarpuris. My father used to tell me that other women live freely, but we must have purdah. Now women go around freely, not a shred of restraint. How would people tell whether you are talking to your father or father-in-law? There is no adab [decorum] left now. I remember a day when my husband and I were in Hyderabad. My husband said let's go to a movie. My father-in-law found out and he was so angry.

I was sixteen years old when Partition happened. My father-in-law was a zamindar. Muslims tilled our land. My father was a grocer, he did wholesale business in grains. Muslim neighbours were weeping when we left. They used to sit on the floor. I married in 1942 and left in August 1947. For a month we stayed with my sister-in-law. I had a twelve-month-old baby. Then we took a free train from Mirpur Khas. We were carrying a bag of clothes and utensils and I had covered my arms with all the gold bangles I possessed. They inspected every bit at the station and took away everything but my gold. Since we lived like Muslim women, I had my face covered and there was not a part of my body they could see.

We came to the Looni Station in Rajasthan and lived in tents. We had free supplies of food. My maama [mother's brother] had left before we did. He had told us that Ajmer and Beawar were good places. We lived for five years in Ajmer. We lived off our gold. We never lived in camps. We bought Muslims' houses in Ajmer. I am proud to say that. In the five years we spent in Ajmer, we suffered a lot because our men could not do business successfully.

We came to Ahmedabad in 1953.There were empty houses available. We wanted to live with the Gujaratis although we knew they are strictly vegetarians. But we wanted to live peacefully, not with gossiping Sindhis. We didn't want to be considered dirty. We had told our Gujarati neighbours that we were Brahmins. We told them we had left our lands and big houses, that we were the sethias [rich upper classes] of Sindh. They respected us. After coming to Gujarat, I stopped wearing salwar kurta. Our neighbours said we looked like Muslims, so I began to wear saris.

Our men started a restaurant. They found it very difficult to learn the ropes of business. Our restaurant ran into massive losses. They were landowners after all. Finally when they bought a cloth shop at Revdi Bazaar, things improved for us. Recently our shop got burnt. People say Muslims took their revenge; my sons say it was a short circuit problem. I don't know. My sons do a lot of business with Muslims. I feel Muslims in Sindh were khandaani [of respectable families] but Muslims here are so violent.

I have six children, of whom the first three were in Sindh Modern High School, but the rest went to Gujarati medium. They don't even speak Sindhi. My grandchildren go to English medium schools.

We used to visit the gurudwara earlier. Now we do cheti chand. Sometimes I feel bad that I have abandoned the Guru. My entire family believes in Jhulelal.

Lata Badlani

She lives alone in a well-furnished apartment in Ahmedabad. She has a circle of elitist, non-Sindhi friends who visit a club in the mornings. Lata also goes to a satsang [a gathering to listen to spiritual discourse] in the evening, which is also her contact with other Sindhis in Ahmedabad. She finds it difficult to relate with the Sindhis of Ahmedabad, who have by and large, come from a rural and conservative background. Her narration was in English.

I don't see why you need to talk to me about Sindhis. I don't know too many Sindhis myself. You must tell me what have you found out. But I will tell you whatever I can remember.

We are amils from Hyderabad. My husband was from Larkano. During Partition, I was a married woman. I had studied in the Indian Girls School and later at D.J. Sindh College.

I came in the October of 1947. My father got us, all the women of the house, with him. My husband joined us later. He was a deputy collector so he could not leave immediately. He joined us in Udaipur. Mr. Sukhadia, the rehabilitation minister in Rajasthan was a good friend of my husband's. Except [for] a few months of uncertainty about my husband's job, we had no problem in resettling. Which is why I feel my experience is not going to be useful to you. But anyways...We came with royal treatment. There was first a jeep that brought my father-in-law and other women of the house to the station. It was funny and ironic—we had Muslim bodyguards to protect us from Muslims!

Then we took a train from Hyderabad. The train before ours was looted. My brother had got wind of it. He dressed like a Muslim and got my mother off that train on time.

We were very friendly with Muslims there. Of course we would be prevented from going into Muslim slums but apart from that there has not been any negative experience or perception. Even here my husband and H.K. Khan were both [in] high position[s]. We stayed away from politics.

PARTITION AS A HETEROGENEOUS EXPERIENCE

In the various voices we hear above, Partition is mediated by class, gender and, of course, personal experience. For instance, Dr. Karamchand's profession as a doctor structured his relationship with Hindus and Muslims, and positioned him as a healer. His service-minded temperament and what may have been seen as his 'healing powers' raised his interaction with his patients to a non-religious and non-sectarian plane. His work took him to both urban and rural places and exposed him to different strata of Sindhi society. Despite comprehensive interaction with the Sindhi Muslims he does not make any judgments about them, whereas Udhavdas Makhija collapses all Muslims into Hurs and casually concludes that they are not to be trusted. Did Udhavdas Makhija's prejudice come from his being a moneylender's son, from his lack of interaction with Muslims, or from his being a member of the RSS? The two perceptions (Dr. Karamchand's and Udhavdas Makhija's) are startlingly different; however, they meet on the grounds of fear. Both felt enough fear to leave, although one left soon after Partition and the other waited until things appeared genuinely bad. Dr. Karamchand shows an ability to separate his experience from the fear surrounding him, whereas Udhavdas Makhija tends to generalise, without accounting for his own experience. The two accounts also point to two very important phenomena of Sindh—one economic, the other spiritual. Dr. Karamchand's reverence for the Sufi pirs he treated and the love he received from them speak of a tradition of tolerance, while Udhavdas Makhija's suspicion and fear of the Muslim comes from the economic context of land-holding cum money-lending. Udhavdas Makhija's identity as a bania determined perhaps not only his reception of Partition but also the lack of nostalgia he feels for Sindh. Meanwhile, Gangaram Samrat represents the enigmatic side of Partition. Despite his vitriolic writings, he did not leave Sindh during Partition. He waited for five years after Partition and left perhaps when he had no choice but to leave. His identity as a staunch Arya Samaji did not contradict his stay in what had become an Islamic state. In fact, he had fond memories of his village and Muslim friends. On the other hand, the writer Kirat Babani who worked closely with Muslims and participated in campaigns against peasant exploitation was forced to leave immediately after Partition. On what basis did the state decide that a socialist was more dangerous than a staunch Arya Samaji? When the destinies of nations coincide with individual desires and when they do not are also aspects of Partition scrutiny. It is also significant that Gangaram Samrat blames not the Muslims, but the Hindus for Partition—for having forgotten the Vedic definition of religion and become ritualistic and casteist. This made the so-called untouchables seek refuge in Islam and thereby left Hinduism weak and unorganised. Samrat's articulations may appear outlandish, but they point to a need for us to have a nuanced approach even to the discourse on religious fundamentalism. Unlike the three men quoted so far, Rochiram Thawani's account betrays a public side to Partition. Thawani's account provides insights into the helplessness of being a Congress worker in Sindh who was faced with distrust from his own people and lack of support from the top brass of the Congress in Delhi. The closing lines of Thawani's narrative sum up the Sindhi community's affiliation with hardcore Hindu fundamentalist organisations like the Jan Sangh. Sadly enough, Thawani also participates in that shift, theoretically at least.

In the section on women, we learn more about the patriarchal and feudal aspects of Sindh than the historical and political event of Partition. This is not to say that women do not have a sense of history, but that they were not involved in the nitty-gritty of historical details. They have participated in 'Hindustan–Pakistan' without very often knowing the month and year. Their narratives do not provide the details of leaving and travelling which become central in the men's experiences. It is clear that the men were the ones deciding and/or implementing those decisions. Very significantly, the women do not see themselves as individuals undergoing the Partition experience. Women use language differently. The use of the plural 'we' in the women's narratives shows how intertwined their selves were with their family collective. At the same time, Partition impinged on their individual lives in very serious and irrevocable ways. For instance, we heard from the rural women that that they were married off the moment their parents heard of Partition. With their heads covered and lips sealed, they seem to have followed and not noticed the details. The fear that the Muslims would abduct the women left no possibilities of letting them out of a prison whose walls were further enclosed. Kamala Patel's work on the recuperation and rehabilitation of women from Sindh testifies to their relative safety compared with that of the women from Punjab (1985). However, we also notice in the interviews references to hasty marriages owing to fear. The larger and enduring implications of such marriages for the women themselves and the subsequent generations must also be studied in the context of Partition. Another aspect of interest is that even Partition was class conscious; so that unlike Tilli, Ladi, Gena or Draupadi, Lata Badlani came with "royal treatment". Her sense of physical displacement was mitigated by her class privileges, which provided her family with immediate support and prestige even in India. Living in an elitist, isolated world and also belonging to a negligible minority of westernised Sindhis, Lata Badlani's experience does not represent the common Sindhi experience of Gujarat. However, it provides an insight into the role class plays in shaping the Partition experience. Also quite significant, is the fact that hers was the only interview in English from among this generation.

The 'fact' of Partition registered differently with different people. With some it was a moment's flash, while for some others it was a slow and reluctant foreboding. For instance, Nirmal Vaswani, a young boy of ten did not 'understand' Partition, "All I remember is travelling with my parents by ship. I had a small alarm clock with me. It began to ring and the guards pounced upon us. My parents felt very scared and they immediately gave the clock away. I realised something was seriously wrong then" (personal interview). On the other hand, Laxmandas Makhija mentions that he had gone to Karachi to attend Guru Golvalkar's last address to the followers of the RSS. During that meeting, the Sindhi Hindus were told that that was the last time they were meeting in Sindh. "Guruji addressed us a week before Partition. At the end of the week I saw Lord Mountbatten taking Mohammed Ali Jinnah with him in a car. I came back to Shikarpur. The next morning I went to my school and saw a lock there. I knew then that Partition was final. We are not talking of temporary things here," says Makhija, whose involvement in the RSS at a young age made him politically savvy (personal interview). Similarly, Jhamatmal Wadhwani (member of the first cadre of the RSS in Sindh) was also prepared. According to him, "the Sindhi Muslim wanted us to go. He was no different from other Muslims during Partition. There was no violent incident because we were warned by Guruji. Guruji came to Sindh on 5th August so we left soon" (personal interview). Wadhwani's affiliation with a pro-Hindu organisation makes him reconstruct memory in a different way compared to the accounts we have heard so far. In his memory the specific experience of the Sindhi Muslims collapses with a generalised view of 'all Muslims are violent'. Radha Lilani who is in her late eighties and lives in Kalol asked me suspiciously why I wanted to ask her questions about Sindh. She explained that her fear came from seeing, "humans slaughtered like sheep and goats around me" (personal interview). She could not remember who these people were and where she saw them. Whether the violence she thought she witnessed actually happened, or her fear blurred the boundaries between the real and unreal is difficult to judge. It is equally difficult to know if the ideology of Wadhwani made him 'receive' certain experiences of the Sindhi Muslims, or whether was he able to 'perceive' things clearly because he could saw them at close quarters. Thus Partition differed not only in modes of reception, but was also constructed differently in memory. In the process of recognising personal feeling as an important focus of investigation, I have attempted to present both real and imagined fears. By and large, a common thread that ties together the diverse narratives of Sindh is the absence of instances of conflict with the Sindhi Muslims on a day to day basis. The Sindhi Hindus were taken by surprise and were afraid of what they perceived as the new arrogance of the Sindhi Muslims. However, very few (if any) can cite instances of suffering at the hands of the Sindhi Muslims. According to Anand's sociological research, despite threats to life, property, livelihood, freedom and self-respect, the Hindus were again and again told by the Muslims as well as by some of the Hindus to stay on (1996, 51). In cases where the Sindhi Muslims were worried about the safety of the Hindus, they urged them to leave for their own good. Ram Jethmalani, the Supreme Court lawyer recalls his poignant parting from his friend and partner Allahbaksh Karimbaksh Brohi. Until the riots in Karachi, Brohi was confident that his friend Ram would not have to leave Sindh because the Sindhi Muslim was a "genial, god-fearing creature, greatly influenced by Sufism and that violence was not part of his nature". However, it was Brohi who advised his friend Jethmalani to leave and said, "It is time for you to go. I can no longer ensure your safety. You are too precious a friend for me to take a risk" (Gera 2002, 32).

When people left (if they did), depended largely upon the equations they shared with their contexts. For instance, a rural Hindu zamindar is more likely to have been compelled to leave by his changing equation with the Muslim peasants whom he could no longer control. On the other hand, an urban businessman in Karachi or Hyderabad may have simply felt threatened by the competition in business posed by the new immigrants. The choice of staying simply did not exist for political activists and people with controversial backgrounds. The writer Kirat Babani said to me, "They had to literally throw me into a ship. You think I would have ever left Sindh?" (personal interview). Kirat Babani subscribed to a communist ideology. He was actively involved (along with other Hindu and Muslim activists) in self-determination movements for the peasants. The same lack of choice perhaps existed for women who were never asked to stay or leave, but were merely told to follow. It must also be noted that about three million Sindhi Hindus still live in Pakistan, and for some of them, migration is still not over. A respondent, Banni Jambha who now lives in Adipur, mentioned to me that she came to India twenty-three years ago. "I used to live in Adalpur, district Sukkur. Our men were zamindars. During Partition we did not come because there was nothing the matter with villages. Riots were in cities. But gradually we felt fear, so we moved to Sukkur town. When our children went to school, we waited with bated breath. We saw that Sindhis had done so well for themselves here in India, so we came here. But to be a Sindhi here or there is the same—rubbish bins, that's what we are" (personal interview). Another respondent, Bhugromal Advani who runs a small provisions store in Surat, moved to India in 1989. According to him, "Our women had a miserable life there. They could not go out of the house and we constantly lived in fear of their abduction. Our relatives are here, so we thought it's still not too late to start a life here" (personal interview).

During my visit to Pakistan, I had the opportunity to ask some Sindhi Hindus who continue to live there why they had never migrated to India. In one case the answer was very simple. Brij Jesrani, an engineer from Karachi told me that he grew up in a small village, Kundkot. "My father tells me that during Partition there used to be buses taking the Hindus from rural Sindh to Karachi and from then on they would leave for India. My father's bus did not come in the first two or three weeks and soon he ceased to have the desire to leave." He has no memory of any violence he witnessed or experienced in rural Sindh. "Meanwhile, I grew up as a citizen of Pakistan, and although I am a member of a religious minority here, I have been drawn by the larger identity of Sindhiness. My friends are Hindus and Muslims, both. In fact, when I first visited India and happened to visit a gathering of Sindhis there, I missed hearing a Muslim name" (personal interview). The ease with which Brij Jesrani spoke was missing in an interview with another respondent* in Karachi, Mulchand Dasani, who said,

> We were zamindars. We sold everything and were about to leave when some Muslims from the village came and told us, "We will look after you. Don't go away." In any case, we had hardly any cash with us. Some years went by without much trouble. But during the 1971 war, we felt we were being observed. I was put in prison under false charges of espionage. My brother migrated since then and now lives in Ujjain. We Hindus here continue to feel this is not our country. The thought of leaving has been niggling our consciousness. You forget some times, but the moment something happens to Muslims in India, we feel scared. We had a hard time during Babri Masjid. We have made a mistake by not going. (personal interview)

The presence of fear even during the interview was palpable and I realised that although my question about why some Sindhi Hindus had not migrated to India referred to their past, it was not isolated from their present in Pakistan. Willy-nilly, I did not probe too deep and frequently into this past of the Sindhi Hindus and thereby avoided what might be seen as an infringement on contemporary politics in Pakistan. However, it was easier to meet Sindhi Muslims who had vivid memories of the Sindhi Hindus' departure during Partition.

Amar Jaleel
A regular columnist for the Dawn *and former academician, Amar Jaleel is in his late sixties. He lives with his wife in Karachi. A*

---

* Name changed to safeguard privacy.

courageous and controversial writer, Amar Jaleel betrayed tremendous pain and anger while talking about Partition. While listening to him in his house at Clifton in Karachi, I could not help feeling the futility of dividing nations and along with it, tearing people away from each other.

I have been thinking of the dilemma of Partition and where did it all go wrong. Perhaps it all went wrong between 1940 and 1947. So many things happened then, including G.M. Syed who went around putting up posters in favour of Pakistan. He said we will protect the minorities in an Islamic nation. As if that's possible. The Muslims cannot build a democratic nation, they live with water-tight compartments. They can't coexist with differences. And what did our G.M. Syed do, really? I am sure the Sindhi Muslims don't like to admit these things about him. But he was also after power.

What had the Hindus not given to Sindh? Hospitals, reading rooms, libraries. I used to live in Shikarpur and it was like New York. There was not a thing you could not find in its dhakka bazaar. How enterprising that community was, and see how all they left has gone to seed. We have not even been able to create anything, nor preserve what they left. The greatest loss of Pakistan was Sindh. How would people ever piece it together?

I was ten years old during Partition and yet I don't know how I remember everything. Perhaps children suddenly grew up faster those days. I remember my classmates saying to me one day, "We are going with baba and amma." I used to study in Ratan Talao School and I had two close friends, Indra and Arjun. They were the children of the owner of Imperial Cinema. They were both so beautiful. They would come in a buggy. They went away. I remember Sushil in my school. He was hit by a ball one day although we were not allowed to bring balls to school. He had a swollen cheek. I could not even say goodbye to him. I am told he is a doctor in India. And then one day, I heard that my school had been burnt. What had my school done to anyone? How many things will you take away from us? I have still not found answers to those questions. It's as if a part of me has been amputated. It's a polio. Next year I will be seventy and this fire will go with me to my grave or the tower of silence, wherever people choose to bury me.

Khalique Jonejo

Khalique Jonejo was a government employee who gave up his job to devote time and energy to the Jeay Sindh Mahaz, one of Sindh's movements for self-determination in the post-Partition state of Pakistan. As member of an organisation that asserts the history and identity of the Sindhi-speaking people, Jonejo believes that commonalities of shared culture and land are far stronger than religious differences between the Hindu and Muslim Sindhis. G.M. Syed, who after his differences with the League launched the Jeay Sindh movement, propounded this ideology. By drawing the solidarity of all Sindhi-speaking people, the Jeay Sindh sets the 'Sindhis' apart from the 'Muslims', by which they mean Urdu- and Punjabi-speaking Muslims who occupy the power centre in Pakistan.

Jonejo lives in Karachi where he divides his time between socio-political activism and practice of law. He extends generous help and hospitality to anyone with an emotional bond for Sindh. Activists like him believe that the solidarity between Sindhis across the borders is one way of improving the political and economic marginalisation of Sindh.

The migration of the Hindu Sindhis from Sindh is much regretted by us. We carry a burden of guilt—of having collaborated with the new powers to cause this migration. I don't think that guilt can be washed away. When people like you come here, we try to do whatever we can to assuage that guilt. I know there is no reason to feel guilty. The Sindhi Muslims were not violent to the Hindu Sindhis. And as far as I know, there were hardly any riots in Sindh. The riots happened once the Muslims of India came into Sindh. The riots in Sindh were premeditated. The Muslim refugees also came with a lot of anger and bitterness and greed for a better life. They knew that as long as the Hindus were around, they would not have the chance to become rich. The main reason was economic, not religious. The Muslims who considered themselves oppressed in India came here for better opportunities.

This is not to exonerate Muslims Sindhis like us from blame. To a certain extent, we must take responsibility. Our own leader G.M. Syed was involved in an anti-Hindu agenda through the Muslim League. But even there, the main reason was economic and not religious. Well-meaning people like him took some emotional decisions.

The Hindus should have also been more responsible. After all, they were urban and well-educated people who need not have left in such fear and hurry. Now both communities across the borders are paying for their mistakes. We have become refugees in our own nation, because we never received what the Hindus left behind. The influx of refugees that came into Sindh has alienated us from our land to the extent that our existence is at stake. Try and imagine, now the governments are talking of about opening up the old railway line from Rajasthan to Sindh. All kinds of people will come into Sindh and we Sindhi-speaking people would be rendered a minority community. The Hindus who went away have also paid prices. When I visited India some years ago, my friends were saying we have done very well for ourselves. But we have still not found acceptance. They were saying we are also Mohajjirs, we only have money, no social status.

[I had visited Jonejo along with Salam Dharejo, a young activist associated with a Labour Institute in Pakistan. Salam is from rural Sindh and has watched at close quarters the poverty and exploitation of the labour class, the haaris. Salam comes with a sharpened understanding of the exploitative structures in Sindh, and refuses to believe in an unproblematic Hindu–Muslim unity before Partition. While I was talking to Jonejo, he intervened.]

Salam Dharejo's intervention: There are two perspectives on the Hindu and Muslim relationship in pre-1947 Sindh. The first one is about the Sufi tolerance of the Sindhis and the harmonious relationship between Hindus and Muslims. As a part of this perspective, the blame for making the banias leave rests upon the 'outsider'—the Muslim who came from India during Partition. The other perspective is that the Hindu–Muslim relationship was rife with social and economic discrimination. I remember my grandfather telling me that when he visited Hindu shops he would be given the lowest seat to sit. The Hindus considered Muslims as untouchables; 'mlechh' is what they called them. They also exploited the illiterate Muslims to the fullest. Partition was a result of such socio-economic inequalities. In this second perspective, the blame does not lie outside because Partition is then an evolution of certain processes from within. Which of these views do you subscribe to?

Jonejo's response: The so-called hierarchies between the Hindus and Muslims were differences of class and demography rather than religion. The Hindu shopkeeper would give respect to the wadero of a village, talk to him and lend him money. Yes, his rate of interest may have been high, but the relationship was not without human concern. The discrimination your grandfather experienced would be the same as any poor person visiting a rich one, regardless of religion. There were some Hindus, especially the RSS types who were like this. But they were a negligible group—like salt in flour.

At the same time, the Hindu Sindhis shared the culture of Sindh and its land with us. They did not have contempt for us, which the Urdu-dominated Muslim of Pakistan does. I just wish that the remaining Hindu Sindhis in Pakistan would not go away and showed greater affiliation with their land and culture. Migration is still on.[3]

Nuruddin Sarki

Jonejo's senior colleague Nuruddin Sarki, who was an assistant professor at the Islamia Arts College, Karachi, has a less glowing picture of the Hindu–Muslim relationship before Partition. Sarki, who is now an advocate, was a member of the Muslim League during the 1940s. He is in his early eighties and lives in Karachi.

We were told that Pakistan was for poor Muslims. But later we realised that the League had created Pakistan to support its own kind and made use of us. We felt Jinnah had betrayed us. We began a 'Sindh for Sindhis' movement. *[As he looks back upon the moments of cleavage between the Hindus and Muslims in Sindh, Sarki feels that]* it began after the separation of Sindh from the Bombay Presidency. Initially, the Hindus and Muslims worked towards the separation together but there came a point when the Hindu Mahasabha and

3. The mention of ongoing migration in Jonejo's interview refers to the district of Thar Parker. During Partition, Thar Parker had remained isolated from the main currents in the larger cities of Karachi and Hyderabad. Its rural and predominantly Hindu population did not have much to do with the influx of refugees who were looking at cities to settle down. However, the successive generations in Thar Parker feel divided between India and Pakistan. The desire to live amongst Sindhi Hindus in India, away from what they perceive as a lawless state, is in conflict with the fear of starting lives all over again.

the League members would not even see eye to eye in the assembly sessions. No, things were not ideal. I remember Pir Muhammad Ali Rashdi's book also mentioning that even a respectable member like him would be given water in a separate utensil. I have a feeling those things began in the '40s. During 1938, I lived in a boarding school along with other Hindu students and I don't remember any discrimination. Initially, we began to see at the railway station that there was Hindu paani and Muslim paani, but that was not a matter of conflict. One accepted that as a matter of course. However, in 1946 one thing began—the RSS shakhas. Hindus would swirl their lathis this way and that. I remember RSS shakhas in Larkano, Shikarpur, Sukkur and Hyderabad. On seeing the Hindus do this, we also felt the need to arm ourselves. I must tell you about another issue—in 1939, the issue of the Sukkur Barrage. The government had borrowed a large loan to build the barrage. In order to redeem the loan, the government levied heavy taxes upon the people who lived near the barrage. This affected the Muslim zamindars who lived near that area. However, the Congress supported the cause initially, but backed out later. These things brought the situation to such a degree of polarity that after 1940, the League and the Congress could not function together.

On 6 January 1948, I was in Karachi when the riots happened. There was curfew everywhere. There were transit camps. I remember we did not get dinner on that day. The local Sindhis had no role in this. I also remember Hindu Sindhis who joined the Pakistan procession and welcomed it. The writer Gobind Malhi was dressed in a sherwani and Jinnah cap. The Communist Party supported the Pakistan movement. The Hindu intellectuals tried their best to support Pakistan, but things didn't work out that way. In interior Sindh, life was peaceful even during Partition. The Muslim League had brought one of its favoured officers to the Nawabshah zilla, his name was Masud. He had incited the haaris to protest against the Hindu zamindars. Lachman Komal Bhatia remembers that his father was locked up by Masud in the name of the haari committee.

If you ask me whether Partition could have been avoided, I feel it was avoidable. Yes, there were economic and social tensions between Hindus and Muslims, but it did not call for Partition. The Cabinet Mission proposal was accepted by both the Congress and the Muslim

League. Partition was not even in the picture. I think Nehru made some irresponsible statements during that period and invited Partition. Even the so-called exploitative Hindu bania was a nice man. I remember my neighbourhood. It was almost entirely Muslim with only one Hindu shopkeeper. He would welcome his Muslim customers, offer them hukka and or chana-bugda [gram seeds used as offering]. He would be very hospitable and then ask, "Saiin, what do you need?" He would sell things, and of course, also say, "Pay whenever you can."

[Sarki also related to me an incident about G.M. Syed, which again throws light on the Jeay Sindh's burden of guilt.]

When Syed visited India in the early 70s and met the well-known writer Kirat Babani, he asked if Baldev Gajra knew that Syed was in the country. He was told by Babani that Gajra had refused to meet Syed. Finally, when they did meet, Gajra refused to shake hands with him. He told Syed, "Your hands are covered with the blood of Hindu Sindhis." Syed's reply to this was, "If twenty-five years are enough for capital punishment, I have suffered for twenty-five years. Do I still not deserve forgiveness?"

The harmlessness of the Sindhi Muslim, his vulnerability to the new forces of the League and his relative exoneration in comparison with the refugee Muslims who inundated the cities of Karachi and Hyderabad are some of the familiar motifs in the Partition narratives from across the border as well. Apart from an insight into the economic and political dynamics of the period, talking to some Sindhi Muslims in Pakistan also brought up poignant moments when as adolescents they had seen their playmates suddenly depart. A noted writer and lawyer, Siraj Ul Haq Memon, mentioned, "Luckily or unluckily, most of my friends were Hindus. It was the saddest day for Sindhi Muslims when our Hindu brothers left. I was only a boy of fourteen then and I lived in Hyderabad. It was such torture for me. I went to see my Hindu friends off at the border" (personal interview). Memon added, "There were rabble rousers in both communities. But I think the elders of both communities played a very positive role in not letting animosities breed."

By and large, Sindhi Muslims remember the departure of the Sindhi Hindus with sadness. Their memory of the Sindhi Hindus has acquired a tinge of wistfulness and glory. The Sindhi Muslim's unhappy relationship with the nation state may also have played a role in his relatively unproblematised memory of the Sindhi Hindus and Partition. The Sindhi Hindus, on the other hand, tend to engage with Partition in a compartmentalised manner—a chapter in his/her past, now best left behind. Despite pain and nostalgia, there is an overall reluctance in the Sindhi Hindus' narratives to dwell on emotional moments. Is the pragmatic and mercantile bania not allowing sentimentality to surface? Have the concerns with resettlement in India numbed memories and emotions? Perhaps the last question can be answered when we see the Sindhi Hindus' struggle with resettlement. Meanwhile, a significant commonness (with a few exceptions) in the narratives on both sides of the border is the near-total absence of hatred and violence.

5 Refugees in India: Nirvasit in Gujarat

"Congress*wallah's* necks should be broken
Those men have done us injustice."
Pounding the clothes on the river bank,
Pohu's mother curses.
"They gifted Sindh to those *jats*,
Terrible conditions thrust upon us.
Even Jinnah did not care,"
Pohu's mother curses.
"*Yari pir* will teach them a lesson,
Lal *saeen's* stick will fall on their heads. Giving us
A kilo of *atto*, they tossed us in the camps,"
Pohu's mother curses.
"Cut off from our land,
Thrown in this good-for-nothing place.
Those ice-cold *muaas*, no feeling in their bones,"
Pohu's mother curses.

"Look at the rations those *muaas* give us.

Selling our ornaments, we make ends meet.

Yet they say: 'Such good care we take of you!'"

Pohu's mother curses.

—Parsram Zia

When the Sindhis left the shores of Sindh, dressed in two to three layers of clothes, unsuccessfully hiding their money from the hawk-eyed National Muslim Guard, they did not know where they were going and what they would do once they got there.[1] Only a few privileged ones knew their destinations and had alternative employment. Some managed to bribe Pakistani officers at the docks and brought jewellery with them. However, a large majority felt more vulnerable with money and decided to safeguard their bodies instead. With their houses locked and the keys given to their Muslim neighbours and friends, they left, hoping to return. During 1947, some managed to sell their possessions at throwaway prices. In 1948, even such choices were not available. After 6 January 1948, the Pakistan government prohibited desperate liquidation and sale of land and property without ancillary clearance certificates. Once in India, the migrants could put in claims for what they had left behind, but the procedures were long and the compensation poor. The claims barely

1. On both sides of the border, there was 'official' support to check what the migrants were carrying with them. This extract from a letter dated 17 September 1947 shows that the Indian government may not have been free of that 'concern'.

> The Police Commissioner has reported to me that silver in large quantities is leaving Junagadh by rail which dealers from here carry with them. He suggests that the question of such exports of precious metals from Junagadh may be considered from all view points. He further stated that his information is that Gondal does not allow Muslims to take any precious metals or other moveable property out of Gondal limits. Not only Gondal but other states are reported to have restricted the movement of precious metals out of their limits. We have information that the present policy of the Pakistan and Indian dominions is not to hamper the refugees when they carry their personal effects with them and they are not subject to any examination. We may adopt the same policy in respect of ornaments but I am not sure that in respect of dealers carrying precious metals for business purposes we should be as liberal.
> (Junagadh Record Office (JRO), Gujarat State Archives (GSA))

managed to meet the tangible losses of farms and houses; the intangible losses remained unnoticed. In Narayan Bharti's much-acclaimed story, "The Claim", Joharmal, a Sindhi refugee, says to the refugee officer, "I have left the whole of Sind in Pakistan. I am now putting in the claim for the whole of Sind, it should be given back to me. The proof of that claim is that Joharmal is a Sindhi, his language is Sindhi and his culture is Sindhi" (1998, 219).

THE IRONY OF ARRIVAL

Leaving behind homes, land and shops, the rich traders and zamindars of Sindh boarded trains and ships empty-handed, like migrant labourers, thankful to have escaped unscathed. Once in India, their poverty and dependence dawned upon them acutely but they had neither the time nor the luxury to entertain thoughts of going back. Distracted and caught up in their immediate concerns, they did not know whether to search for missing relatives, to earn a living, or simply to swallow their pride and live as refugees. When I asked my uncle, Udhavdas Makhija, whether he tried to look for his friends and family as soon as he landed in Bombay, he said, "Silly, who had the time?"

At the same time, however, Bhawanwari, a mother of four sons wrote to the Maharaja of Baroda (on 13 October 1948) simultaneously requesting the location of her lost children and asking for some money:

> I am a poor lady whose four sons have been lost in the past political disturbances and yet I have no news of them. They are somewhere in India but exactly it is not known where they are. I am giving you their names so that you can please find them. I am also sending you numbers of certain cash certificates I had bought in Sindh. If you can kindly issue new certificates from India, I will have some money with me. (Baroda State Archives (BSA))

While people were displaced and depressed, they blamed (like Pohu's mother) different circumstances for their suffering. My father, Laxmandas Makhija, unequivocally mentioned in his interview that the Sindhi Muslims had treated the departing Hindus well. They were weeping when he left with his mother, although he did have some humiliating experiences with the National Guard. However, once he came to India, the specific memory of Sindhi Muslims had receded and he merely wanted to kill some Muslim and take his revenge. The account was told to me with sad amusement.

> When we were shifted to the Ahmednagar Camp, my brother and I felt we must carry out our project of killing at least one Muslim. [Laughs.] After all, we had freshly emerged from the philosophy of Hindutva. We took huge knives with us one day and set out to kill a Muslim or two. We looked for a Muslim tongawallah! We did find a Muslim tongawallah (God save him); he behaved with us very kindly. Our hearts softened. We got down at a vegetable market and thought of getting hold of a rascal Muslim. In the meanwhile, some Marathas suspected our motives and warned us in the bazaar. We got scared and gave up. Over the years as we got more and more involved in business, we moved away from such feelings of anger and indignation. We didn't forget them, just moved far away from them. (personal interview)

Very often, among the Sindhis, the moment of arrival possessed a tragic irony far greater than the moment of departure. The Sindhi story of Partition does not privilege the 'day of departure', although there are dramatic instances of people escaping disguised as Muslims. It was the hostility of the local population upon arriving in India that gives the Sindhis some of the most excruciating memories of this period.

> We waited in Hyderabad for three months before we could get tickets. Finally we left Hyderabad—eleven families together. The train brought us to Marwar. People there did not let us get down at the Marwar junction. So we were taken to Barmer, or rather the desert-like outskirts of Barmer. We lived in a single tent. We were given free food but we felt too scared to eat. After the way the locals had behaved with us, we didn't know what to expect. We cooked our own food. One day, when the dust storms were blowing and we could hardly see, one of the children fell into a sizzling kadhai [large frying pan]. Those were the worst days of life. (R. Lilani, personal interview)

The owner of the most well-known chain of sweet shops in Ahmedabad said to me,

> I am so embarrassed about giving you details about how I was treated on coming here. First of all, there was the embarrassment about fleeing Sindh when we, Congress workers, were needed the most. But I already told you about those circumstances. And when we came by train to Rajasthan, we first landed in Barmer and then moved to Ajmer. I remember going with my wife to a tea stall in Ajmer. The chaiwallah gave me a cup of tea, but just when I was putting that cup down along with others he shouted at me for 'polluting' other cups. Untouchability?! In Sindh, we did not do that to *anyone,* and the Jains and Oswals considered us low castes here? (Rochwani, personal interview).

The feeling of humiliation was far more common among the Sindhis who came to Rajasthan or Gujarat than among those who came to Bombay. The strongly vegetarian Hindus of Gujarat and Rajasthan treated the Sindhis with suspicion because they came from an Islamic province, ate meat and drank liquor. In parts of Rajasthan, the locals gave the Sindhis food in a humiliating manner, making them feel like untouchables. In parts of both Gujarat and Rajasthan, Sindhis were not allowed to disembark or enter into the heart of the cities. Bombay, on the other hand, responded with far more understanding. Anand's study (1996, 66) shows how in the initial stages, the local population in Bombay showed sympathy for the refugees and formed independent voluntary committees to provide relief. Dr. T.R. Nanavane, chairman of the Bombay Provisional Volunteer Board, issued an appeal to all institutions and individuals to help accommodate the refugees and provide assistance. Many public and private organisations (the Asbestos Cement Workers Union, the Mahila Mandal, Devidayal and Sons, Mangaldas Verma, etc.) responded to this call. Later though, there were tensions in Bombay too between the local population and the Sindhis. The local residents feared that the Sindhis would add to the burden of Bombay. This is when Acharya Kripalani reminded them that the Sindhis were an enterprising community and that their exodus from Pakistan had brought its economy to a standstill. Moreover, he added, "We cannot consider evacuees aliens, nor can we afford to consider them a nuisance. This is a very perverted approach. We cannot claim any merit for ourselves simply because we happen to be born or reside in that portion of India which has not been divided" (in Anand 1996, 70).

Gujarat, incidentally, has no record of help from non-governmental or individual sources. In fact, in some of the letters received by Sardar Vallabhbhai Patel during 1948, there is a litany of complaints about how the Sindhis have intruded upon Gujarati life and created dirt and disruption. The placatory tone of the letter below is a response to the complaint that the Sindhis only look after themselves but not the Gujaratis of Karachi who also had to repatriate:[2]

> I received your letter dated 21st. What you say does appear true, 'these days regional feelings are on the rise.' I feel that Sindhis have gone through a lot in recent times, seeing as what happened to Sindh. It is understandable that the Sindhi leaders would be sympathetic [to their own community]. If the assumption is that Gujaratis will manage anywhere else in India, it does not lead us to conclude that Sindhis leaders are provincial. It would not be proper to think that consideration for Sindhis is also injustice towards Gujaratis. The Sindhis have to leave a lot behind them, it is natural for Sindhis leaders to be considerate… (Patel 1975, 139)

The trauma caused by the uncertainty of their destination and livelihood, and by the hostility of the local population was also sometimes accompanied by the recognition of one's own weaknesses.

As refugees, the Sindhis fought for limited resources and sometimes engaged in stealing. The realisation that their own community members in the camps could not be trusted was shocking to the Sindhi refugees. The account below captures an early moment in this change:

> We locked our houses and gave [the] keys to the Muslim midwives. We thought we'd go back. We had a child with us who looked like a Sikh because his head had not been shaved. He was also wearing a

2. See Jaisinghbhai's *Gujarat no Rajkiya ane Sanskriti Itihas* (1977), which states that during Partition, 116,173 Sindhis and 200,000 Gujaratis from Sindh migrated into Gujarat. What we see in Sardar Patel's correspondance is these people competing for refugee resources.

kada [a thick bangle worn as a mark of Sikh identity]. Some Muslims kidnapped this child, but the wadero of our village was very helpful. He offered refuge and also managed to get the child back.

We took a train from Hyderabad. It brought us to Pali, then to Ratlam. We got down there, fearing what the responses of the locals would be like. There were dust storms and scorpions around our tents. Scorpions would creep into our food. So from there we moved to Devlali Camp in Maharashtra and felt relieved to have arrived among our own people. We reached quite late. There were hardly any rooms left. We all slept in one small room. We did not know that Sindhis had begun to steal. Our trunk was stolen. We had no clothes left. (P. Motwani, personal interview)

The Sindhis were also not coming as victims of Partition to a place that was rightfully theirs on this side of the border.[3] They were not a population in exchange, but unwanted immigrants, the burden of whose resettlement fell largely on four Indian states—Maharashtra, Gujarat, Madhya Pradesh and Rajasthan. When the Sindhis first started to come to India in 1947, they boarded ships and came directly to the port of Bombay; after hearing about the experiences of Punjab and its trains filled with corpses, the Sindhis felt terrified of boarding trains and the sea route from Karachi to Bombay provided the most direct and safe mode of travelling. Hence, we find the first rush of migrants in Bombay. Anand's study provides a detailed account of the influx of refugees in Bombay and the number of camps and kinds of arrangements made for them. People who did not manage to board ships or lived too far from Karachi took the Jodhpur Railways train that left from Hyderabad and Mirpur Khas and arrived at Pali and Marwar in Rajasthan. From 1948 onwards, arrangements for bringing

3. Sarah Ansari comments, "In contrast, Muslims leaving India for Pakistan perceived themselves to be migrating to a place of refuge which 'belonged' to them as 'Pakistanis' just as much as it did to the Muslims who already lived there. They presumed themselves to be there not by kind humanitarian invitation but by right, and those who received them were equally expected to be bound by duty to make that reception as positive as possible." (2005, 10). The Sindhi writer Amar Jaleel told me in an interview, "The Muslims who came here [Sindh] behaved as if they had brought true the dream of Pakistan. They claim, *'Kurbaniyaan de de kar aaye hain Pakistan ke liye'* (We made sacrifices to come and build Pakistan)."

refugees were more streamlined because people were leaving in very large numbers. The burden of rehabilitation had been laid largely on Bombay. It was at this stage that the three ports of Kathiawar – Navlakhi, Okha and Veraval – were opened for receiving the refugees from Sindh. These ports were also directly linked to Karachi and the distance between them and Karachi was shorter compared to Bombay. During 1948, the Government of India arranged for multiple steamers and country crafts to bring the Sindhis to the ports of Gujarat. Thus three places – Gujarat, Rajasthan and Bombay – served as direct destinations for the Sindhi arrival in India. However, these three destinations were only the beginning of a series of migrations and re-migrations as people got pushed around from one camp to another. For instance, people coming to Rajasthan by train were sent to transit camps in Ratlam, Ahmedabad and further. Alternatively, a refugee from Mulund Camp would be asked to leave on the closing of the camp there and be sent off to another in Madhya Pradesh. In addition to being transferred in groups, the Sindhis also made individual choices to go to places that held personal or business promise.

According to U.T. Thakur, over 452,800 Sindhis were living in refugee camps in 1948 (1959/1997, 31). Built at a 'safe' distance from the heart of the cities, a hundred camps (or rather erstwhile army barracks constructed for prisoners of war during the world wars) housed the Sindhis from 1947 to almost 1949. The Bombay government set up camps away from the big cities so that the angry refugees did not excite the general mass of the population with their horror tales, a mistake that Karachi had made. The story of staying in refugee camps in India hinges on a set of common problems faced by the Sindhis. Quarrels over the limited resources of water and food, scramble for employment, unhygienic living conditions and consequent infections and epidemics—all of these angered and frustrated the Sindhis living in the camps. The graphic picture provided below by the writer Bhagwan Atlani holds true for any camp in India:

> Refugee Camp. Women pulling each other's hair for filling water from
> a single tap, swarms of flies outside latrines, drops of water leaking
> from the barrack roofs, gunny sacks held up as curtains with children

sleeping behind them but watching parents, rationed grains on a skewed weighing-scale, a register with more names than people in the camp, sacks of wheat and rice grains bound from godowns to camps, 25% cut on amounts allocated for refugees...(1998, 131).

A gamut of issues forms the refugee history in post-Partition India. The state archives show letters asking for loans, or requesting an increase in the amount, or asking to be absorbed in government offices or be made permanent. There are letters about the use and abuse of relief and power in the camps. There are complaints about discrepancies between state policies and their implementation for refugee welfare, between the amount sanctioned and that actually disbursed as dole, and so on. Such complaints occurred everywhere, evoking bitter interactions between refugee authorities and camp inhabitants. In the context of Gujarat, as we shall see later, such letters also show deep prejudices against Sindhis. Meanwhile, correspondence between refugees and the state, provincial and central departments of rehabilitation, and letters of protest documented in newspapers provide insights into a crucial aspect of Partition history and serve, in Urvashi Butalia's words, as "An Archive with a Difference" (2001, 209). Given below are letters written by Sindhi refugees in Gujarat to the Government of India:

1. Baroda
   10 July 1948

   The Assistant Secretary, Government of India, New Delhi
   Ref No. 23-GCRD, 16 June 1948

   Sir,
   I have the honour to state that my application dated 6th May in continuation with the claim of my property lost in Hyderabad has been forwarded to the Chief Secretary, Baroda by your good self.
   I have already placed my circumstances to the Government. I want to give education to my children and in these hard days how can one refugee maintain? I request you that my property claim for 7,775/- should kindly be settled immediately so that I may establish myself here in Baroda. I am supplied by the Government free ration. I have no business at present and no property to sell off. I have to pay house

rent of Rs. 40/ per month and to meet with my expenses I need money for starting business so that I can establish myself. We have sold off my wife and children's ornaments. My son sends some money, but it is not possible to pull on with life without business.

I therefore humbly request your honour to settle my claim of my property immediately for which I will pray God for your long life and prosperity.

Jay Hind,
I beg to remain, Sir, your obedient servant
Tikamdas Dharamdas.

(BSA)

2. Luddoo Puttkaloomal
Navsari, Refugee Camp No. 196
Lunsikui, Navsari
19 January 1949

The Officer-in-charge
Refugee Department
Government of India
New Delhi

Respected Sir,
I the undersigned most humbly beg to pray as under—
I have come here at Navsari with three families out of which some ladies and children of other families whose husbands are yet in Pakistan (Jacobabad, Sindh). Here I could not get the residence for the said families and yet some families are to come and the ladies are crying here without their husbands and children. Even we cannot get the Ration cards for food-stuff and it is advised that we should apply to your honour. After you issue us the permit cards, we would be able to get the residence and food ration cards. Until then we shall have to starve. Other members of some families still in Pakistan shall have to take poison if no convenience and facilities will be given to us in Baroda state.

In your service,
Luddoo Puttkaloomal

(BSA)

The Sindhis lived in camps until they could manage on their own—this meant a period of anything from a few months to two years. From 1 July 1949, doles were available only to children and the disabled. The well-known Supreme Court lawyer Ram Jethamalani mentions how shocked he was to see his family living in the Ulhasnagar Camp, but he soon managed to take them away because he found quick employment in India. Laxmandas Makhija remembers living in camps for a year:

> When we came to the land of Hindustan, we were sent to a refugee camp near Ahmednagar in a special train. We were given free food, clothes, soaps for some time. Later on, an order was issued that that camp had to be shut down. We had to go to Vithalwadi near Kalyan. We left once again. Once again we had free clothes, free electricity for almost a year. In the meanwhile, proud Sindhis felt that the free facilities will not last forever and even if they did, it did not become them to keep using those. People started looking for employment, I was one of them. My mother also asked me to go and look for work and stop living off free gifts. (personal interview)

Such challenges were fewer for those with privilege—people who could fly from Karachi to Bombay or Delhi and more or less go directly to new positions without having to stay in camps. People in prestigious government positions found it easier to rehabilitate because the government had schemes for absorbing them. The educated elite of Sindh, the amils, went to big cities like Bombay and Delhi and remained relatively fortified by their class privilege. By and large, such continuities were rare because a large portion of the population was in business and trade. Meanwhile, zamindars were seen frying pakodas in Sindhi camps or peddling wares. In the initial years, the Sindhis would spot their acquaintances in trains selling sweets, biscuits or papads. Students had to discontinue education and sell wares. Laxmandas Makhija's memory of this period is poignant:

> I remember spotting a friend of mine as a ticket collector at Boribundar Station and I felt very bad about my wanderings. If only I had finished my education, or at least carried my certificates…I had by then heard of Punjab University's efforts to allow Partition children to resume

education. However, I had hardly 5 rupees in my pocket. From about 1947 to 1953, that was the maximum amount of money I enjoyed after slogging every day. I wrote to my brother in Amritsar requesting him to lend me two hundred rupees so that I could resume my studies. He wrote back saying he didn't have any. (personal interview)

Equally sad was the story of a school teacher who became a fruit seller because Sindhi schools had not yet come into existence. Here is his daughter's account:

My family lived in a tent in Sabarmati, Ahmedabad. From there we were sent to the Kubernagar Camp in the same city. My father began to draw a handcart and sell fruit. His own father used to run a small restaurant in Sindh. He wanted his son, that is, my father, to have an education. When my father became a teacher, there was great joy in the family. They thought we had turned into an educated family now. But in Kubernagar there was not a single Sindhi school. It was not the township it is today. So he started selling fruit. When the competition got fierce, my father took us to live in the nearby town of Kalol. There were only Gujaratis in Kalol, but my father, a teacher of Sindhi, said we cannot fill our stomachs with Sindhiness. (Gurbani, personal interview)

Pragmatic concerns took precedence over everything else and Sindhi men dotted the landscape of west India now selling sweets, now cloth and now fruits. Their women helped them in making papads and pickles (Ulhasnagar Camp, Maharashtra) or spinning khadi (Bhavnagar and Kutiyana, Gujarat). The children gave up their education to help their parents and learnt brisk business at an early age. These children would grow to become a strong entrepreneurial community that would never look back at its roots or communicate to the next generation to do so. In order to survive, the Sindhis sold what they could. In Surat, they managed to buy rationed grains and sell them at a higher price, illegally, of course. In Bombay and Ahmedabad they took advantage of the textile mills and bought subsidised cloth pieces, which they sold on pavements as 'cutpieces'. The cutpiece market at Grant Road and Khar in Bombay generates millions today, but its origins go back to a bunch of desperate and ingenious Sindhis refugees. As long as their wares were sold, the Sindhis persevered. If certain things were indigenously produced, the Sindhis ensured that they made them. For instance, the Sindhis brought the markets of hosiery and fruit in Gujarat into existence. In their desperation to earn money, the Sindhis cut margins and sold at a lower profit—evoking in the process tremendous resentment and distrust from local businessmen. They also captured businesses that were hitherto run by Muslims. A case in point are the bakery shops in Godhra which were earlier the property of the Muslims who left for Pakistan in 1947, and are now owned almost entirely by the Sindhis. In Ahmedabad, the hotel business, once a Muslim turf, is now with the Sindhis. They tried the quickest possible means of earning money and of learning the ropes of the local business and the local language without intruding upon the social space of the local communities. At the same time, intrusions in economic spaces are not without social implications. When, in Gujarat, one mercantile community nudged its way into the space of the other, the repercussions were quite negative. The economic resentment was also overlaid by social revulsion, caused by the perception of Sindhis as intruders from Pakistan and a non-vegetarian community in a predominantly vegetarian state. A series of negative stereotypes about Sindhis that cut across many communities in India acquired a further edge, given Gujarat's peculiar socio-economic complexion. We shall look at the issue of Sindhi and Gujarati dynamics in the next chapter. For now, let us turn to the general and specific contexts that brought the Sindhis to Gujarat.

GUJARAT: CONTEXTS OF MIGRATION

Gujarat was a destination for both direct and indirect migration. The movement towards Gujarat happened gradually and sporadically, so that the census figures of 1951 show Maharashtra as having the highest Sindhi population (Thakur 1959/1997, 33). However, the census figures of 1991 show more Sindhis in Gujarat than in Maharashtra, with the figures at 704,088 and 618,696 respectively. Some of the difference may be accounted for by the fact that parts of Gujarat were earlier in Bombay and because Gujarat was not a linguistic state in the 1950s. The difference can also be accounted for by the gradual gravitation of the Sindhis, for reasons of business, to cities like Baroda and Ahmedabad, and also by the development of Gandhidham.

It is useful to mention here the broad and general reasons behind the Sindhi presence in Gujarat, before we turn to the specific contexts of migration in Gujarat. Apart from the physical contiguity between Gujarat and Sindh which made both sea and land travel possible, there is also a shared cultural history between Saurashtra and Kutch on one hand and Sindh on the other. The ethnic origins of the Lohanas of Sindh, Kutch and Kathiawar overlap (Thakur 1959/1997, 58). Also, Sindh and Kutch are bound in a long-standing history of invasions and refuge, where Muslim invasions in Sindh caused the Sindhis to take refuge in Kutch, while the Kutchis sought refuge in Sindh during earthquakes. For instance, King Ra Khengar sought refuge in Sindh when Muhammad bin Tughlaq invaded Kutch (Jaisinghbhai 1977, 36). Similarly, in the fifteenth century when Muhammad Begda fought the Sumra and Sodha tribes to rescue Muslims from their torment in Sindh, some Hindus took refuge in Kutch. Thus, the geographical and cultural boundaries between Kutch and Sindh have always been porous. This is evident from the fact that about 300,000 Sindhi-speaking Muslims live in the Banni region of Kutch. The commonality of cultural history between Sindh and Kutch may have served as an invisible background for the Sindhis' decision to come to Gujarat.

Moreover, Sindh and Gujarat shared trade transactions. Khambat was a significant port and it was the highest producer of cloth and textiles. Sindh used to get its cloth and rice from Khambat (Jaisinghbhai 1977, 293). The merchants of Sindh have also had trade links with the ports of Surat. According to Govindram Nihalani (citizen of Surat, member of the Sindhi Panchayat), his ancestors had come to Surat in 1919 and were engaged in the zari (brocade) business. Finally, both Sindhis and Gujaratis are two of the most successful South Asian entrepreneurial communities in the world. Of all the states available to the Sindhis after Partition, Gujarat was the most attractive for the business-minded Sindhi. The mercantile Sindhi (who it must be remembered formed the largest section of the community) was drawn to its robust trading history and textile mills, while the more educated and industrialist Sindhi went to metropolitan cities like Bombay and Delhi. Besides historical familiarity and practical considerations, the Sindhis also came to Gujarat because in 1948, it was a state that undertook the responsibility of the rehabilitation of the Sindhis in multiple ways. During 1947, the central government of India had entrusted Bombay with the responsibility of accommodating the refugees from Sindh. Neither the Hindus of Sindh nor the governments had expected a mass exodus; hence, preparations for rehabilitating the Sindhis took shape only in 1948. It seemed clear in 1948 that Bombay alone could not undertake all the responsibility and that neighbouring states such as Madhya Pradesh, Rajasthan and Gujarat must share the task.

Baroda

On 20 October 1947, the Maharaja of Baroda received a letter from Mr. F.D. Vaswani from Karachi, Sindh:

Sir,

The vicious communal atmosphere has made it impossible for any Sindhi Hindu to be certain about this future which he finds simply dark and dismal. Many Hindus have to cut short their careers and their fortunes outside Sind. It is against this background that I venture to present this application of mine for your kind perusal and action. I am double graduate of the Bombay University having qualified in B.A. L.L.B. in the latter of which I secured second class. I have also kept term for M.A. course. I have been a keen and enthusiastic student through my school and college, and the certificates will show that...I have been taking keen interest in extra-curricular activities in my school and college life.

I am 26 years of age and am at present having a flourishing practice at the Bar for the last 18 months which I am obliged to interrupt for insecurity of person and property.

I belong to a high class Hindu family. My father has remained the Secretary of the Social Service League and the Sind Hindu Association. In recognition of his public services he was awarded a Gold medal on behalf of the Social Service League of Sind.

I will be obliged if you find me any suitable employment in any department under your control.

Awaiting to hear from you…

(BSA)

Many such individuals wrote to the Maharaja of Baroda for help during 1947–48, and by and large, the refugee department in the Baroda state tried its best to respond to them. The telegram sent by the central government states the desperate need for provincial governments in undertaking the responsibility for rehabilitating the Sindhi Hindus:

From
State Sind
New Delhi
12 January 1948
No. 89-G (R)

His Excellency,
Dewan Saheb
Baroda State

Situation of non-Muslims in Sind has suddenly deteriorated and reports from HI command Karachi state large scale evacuation unavoidable. Total number nine to ten lakhs of whom greater proportion in Upper Sind. It will take some time to finalise arrangements with Pakistan for evacuation through Government machinery but two outlets available namely from Karachi by sea and from Hyderabad by rail. Arrangements being made for reception of refugees from Karachi at Bombay. Refugees from Hyderabad by rail will reach Marwar. There may be about one lakh of these during next four to six weeks. Absolutely imperative take emergent measures for reception of refugees at Marwar and for their temporary care and shelter for two or three months in nearby Indian states. Government of India would be most grateful if you can make immediate arrangements for sheltering twenty thousand. It is requested that your agreement may be communicated with least possible delay so that we can make further incidental arrangements for reception of refugees at Marwar and transport by rail to your state. Jodhpur Jaipur Bikaner Udaipur Indore and Baroda also being addressed. Please also telegraph names of stations to which trains are to be routed. Government of India willing to reimburse expenditure that may be incurred on temporary care and shelter for this period and will also make arrangements for food stuffs but request your Government should help with medical sanitary and other incidental camp arrangements.

(BSA)

The Dewan of Baroda responded generously and offered to rehabilitate 20,000 refugees from Sindh without any reimbursement from the government. As a consequence, the district of Baroda witnessed the emergence of ten camps in Outram, Harni, Bechrajee, Navsari, Billimora, Vyara, Sidhpur, Dabhoi, Okha, Petlad and Sankheda. This provides us with one instance of a systematic effort at rehabilitation.

The Baroda State Archives show a range of interactions between Sindhi refugees and the relief and rehabilitation department at Baroda. This interaction took the form of letters of complaint and/or request, newspaper articles and responses. The relief and rehabilitation department at Baroda covered a large number of regions in Gujarat, save some parts of Saurashtra, Kutch and Godhra. The Sindhi refugees' official interaction with the Baroda department (which was also the most organised of all rehabilitation departments in Gujarat) provides an insight into certain tensions between them and the relief authorities. It also brings out the poignancy of being a refugee. For instance, the laconic note below belies fears of the deepest kind:

To
The District Magistrate
Mehsana

Respected Sir,
I, Narumal Shambhumal, inhabitant of Sind, presently residing in

Sidhpur, beg to apply for the safety and information of my family members, residing in Tundo Bago, place Khadtarro, District Hyderabad. It is learnt that, now a days they are much troubled by Mahomedans and specially few are enforced to change their religious ideas which are to them even more than their lives. By all these news we are worrying about their lives.

(undated letter, BSA)

A substantial number of letters in the same department reveal bitter quarrels between the refugees and the authorities, and also throw light on the prejudices about Sindhis in Gujarat. For instance, examine the tone of distrust in the refugee officer's report below. The report is in response to an application made by Nihalchand H. Mahtani of Sindh (on 30 January 1948) for resuming the maintenance of Rs. 152 that he used to receive from his son before Partition.

He [Nihalchand Mahtani] states that his son who was trading in Manila (Philippines) used to send to the applicant his maintenance expenses. During war, he could not send money to him for obvious reasons. He approached the Government of India who used to pay Rs. 152/- a month for his maintenance. This allowance was continued to him from 1941 to 1945. Owing to the partition of the country, he states that the subsidy has been stopped.

The applicant left Hyderabad (Sindh) on 17th December and came to Baroda with family member[s] on 4th January 1948. He requests that some amount may be given to him as maintenance allowance since his condition is very bad and it would not be possible for him to carry on.

The refugee officer's observations sharply point out the discourse of distrust:

How could it be that an Indian is interned in Manila—unless he may have committed an offence against the state of the Philippines.
(Report by the refugee officer submitted to the Refugee Minister, Baroda, 11 March 1948, BSA)

The distrustful tone in the above letter seems to lack grounds. However, there are other exchanges where the issue of right and wrong becomes grey. In an application made by three people who ask to be shifted to the Kalyan Camp, it is difficult to know what the real reasons are and whether the report below has accurate observations. Here are both accounts:

> Copy of the application dated 19-1-49 from Shri Ludimal Alumal Tanumal of Navsari Refugee Camp, Navsari Nos. 196, 195 and 198 respectively we beg to request your honour as under—

> We have applied one application to your honour and again have to request that there is mosquitoes which are biting us seriously and my wife is sick and spent 50–55 rupees and medical treatment is going on and there is one child of 4 months is sick and have to sit for a whole night and there is a crowd of 1100 men in one camp and they have left the camp for the very reason and only 40 persons are there. Half in Andheri camp and half number in Kalyani camp is filled up by the camp refugees of Navsari. They are getting their rations. I have been to Kalyani (two men) in the camp no. 3 and 5. The camp officer refused to let me enter because ration is stopped for new persons. I returned for the very same reason to Navsari. At present I Ludu Kalumal is becoming sick and I am old and I have no one to look after me and my son is underage. So I beg to request your honour that you must order to the effect that we may be entered at Kalyani camp.

The Refugee Officer's report on the application states:

> All three applicants Shri Ladumal, Acharmal Balumal, Alumal Tanumal are related to one another and are at present staying in Navsari, outside the refugee camp in a rented house for the last one month and a half. In their application it seems that they have misrepresented and exaggerated the actual facts in order to achieve their end of getting free rations and free railway facilities to go to Kalyan Camp. Free rations are only given to those refugee families who stay in the Camps. No facilities can be given to those who stay outside the camp. The applicants inspite of their staying outside the camps require free ration and all other facilities.

>   The Navsari District being a damp area the trouble of mosquitoes and other insects is a general complaint not only of the camp people but of other people of the town too. Just about a month ago, the

nuisance of bugs, mosquitoes, fleas and other insects was acute. It would be pointed out here at this stage that the refugees themselves are mainly responsible for increasing this nuisance as they never keep their rooms and blocks clean inspite of repeated instructions. They use vacant rooms, bath-rooms, open space, road as latrines and urinals even though separate arrangements are specially provided for. They were requested to cover their floor with cow dung coating which was supplied to every room but none of them availed of it.

As the climate of Navsari, they say, is not suitable, to them, many of the refugees go to Kalyan and other camps without informing the camp officer. The refugees, if they take up to labour, work and stick to one place, they would soon be rehabilitated and will have no difficulty for their absorption. But as these people have no liking for any labour they move from one place to another for a suitable and comfortable life. It would be seen from the application itself that their aim is to go to Kalyan camp with all the members of their families and their claim for their credit notes for free railway facilities.

(BSA)

The use of phrases like 'these people' and general references to 'free' things, unclean ways and idle lives to describe all refugees indistinguishably is common and betrays prejudices. It is undeniable that the circumvention of laws and rules to make quick money was common among the refugees. For instance, the selling of rationed grains received in camps at a higher price in the open market, or showing more members in a family than actually existed, or indulging in nefarious activities, has been recorded in refugee documents. The frustration, anxiety and the greed of the refugees, and the exasperation of the authorities who felt they had more than met the needs of the migrants were perhaps common to all departments. The case of a refugee, Mr. Verumal is relevant here. According to the letters exchanged between the refugee officer and the Maharaja of Baroda, Verumal was found guilty of black marketing and was consequently expelled from the camp. The circumstances of Mr. Verumal's conflict with the refugee officer in charge are not known to us. However, when Mr. Verumal asked for a public inquiry against the refugee officer, the refugee minister wrote to the maharaja. His report is telling:

His Excellency
15 July 1948

Respected Sir,

This is with reference to a letter written by Mr. Verumal asking for
public inquiry against the refugee officer. The refugee officer found
this "preposterous and unjustifiable" and requests the Maharaja not
to take it seriously because Sindhïs do not deserve sympathy or
courtesy. Verumals are found in all places where Sindhis are spread
up. Allegations could be made—as those making them may gain cheap
popularity in their own circle, and are secure against any Government
action against them as they are privileged refugees. In spite of ourselves,
we have to be considerate towards them. Your Excellency has heard
bitter complaints about their insolence from almost all parts wherever
they have been. It is time that in Baroda men like Verumal are either
silenced or are completely disregarded. Your Excellency will excuse
me but I believe that men like Mr. Verumal do not deserve the extreme
courtesy you have been showing them. The Sindhis everywhere have
gone out control and have become turbulent. Turbulence and
impertinence are temperamental with them.

(BSA)

Saurashtra

Compared to Baroda, the refugee influx in Saurashtra was less
systematic, but the logistical convenience of Gujarat lay in its coastal
belt, which made it possible for the Sindhis to board ships from Karachi
and land at any of the three ports of Veraval, Navlakhi and Okha, in
Saurashtra. The Sindhis began moving to Saurashtra before the
arrangements for rehabilitation were formally handed over to the
provincial governments in 1948.

A respondent, Harish Vazirani, mentioned earlier in the context
of the RSS, said that he boarded an Okha-bound ship from Karachi,
"A relative of mine had moved to Rajkot a hundred years ago and I
knew his family would be able to help me. However, once I reached
Rajkot from Okha, I did not bother to look for them. I found an

empty evacuee house. I merely broke the lock and occupied it"
(personal interview). We shall return to the issue of evacuee houses,
an important aspect of refugee rehabilitation in Gujarat, later. For
now, it is important to note that sporadic migration to Saurashtra had
begun in 1947. It has been recorded in the Baroda State Archives that
the states of Bhavnagar and Jamnagar were taking 10,000 refugees
each in September 1947. The earliest reference to the influx of refugees
in Saurashtra State is found in this letter:

For the sake of speed and secrecy

OFFICIAL
AND URGENT

The influx of refugees in Junagadh State has started and they are
coming in large numbers, from different Hindu States. About 40
refugees have no food or a place to live in Junagadh. I don't know
about other cities of this State so far.

A Refugee Committee to be presided over by a sympathetic and
energetic officer should be formed immediately to start a refugee camp
and to avoid danger of peace, public health and sanitation etc. We are
already in the midst of this cholera season.

D. S.

10/9/47   Commissioner of Police
                                                  Junagadh state

(JRO, GSA)

However, it was in mid-February 1948 that twelve camps, with
the capacity to accommodate 32,000 refugees from Sindh, were
opened. The numbers exceeded expectations. A telegram dated 23
October 1948, mentions that 150,000 refugees had arrived at Okha.
In such a situation, the burden was shared between the states of Baroda
and Saurashtra; Saurashtra arranged for several temporary
accommodations. The *Annual Administrative Report* of the state of
Saurashtra (1950, 68) provides the following list of places where relief
and rehabilitation were made available:

1. Women's Home, Junagadh
2. Infirmary at Kutiyana

3. Infirmary at Bantwa

4. Jamnagar Camp

5. Palitana Camp

The poor conditions of relief, especially accommodation, incurred the severe displeasure of the refugees. In at least one instance, the Gujarati newspaper *Sansar Samachar* reported this (12 December 1948). A copy of a summarised translation of the article was found in the refugee files at the Gujarat State Archives (see Relwani 2002, 67–80).

Under the headline, "**Sindhis are not accorded a good treatment on the port of Okha—The authorities of the Post and Telegraph refused to send their wires**" the *Sansar Samachar* publishes the following report:

Rajkot, 12 December 1948 (From our representative): There are no adequate arrangements for the Sindhi refugees coming to Okha by steamers. The people coming here from Okha are complaining that the officers in charge of the Okha port and the contractors in charge of food behave in unmannerly way towards the Sindhi refugees who are fed with the food prepared two or even three days before. There are only ten or twelve tents for the refugees, the rest have to sleep in the open in this wintry cold, with the result those poor children and the aged persons are benumbed by cold and have been the victims of the various diseases. If anybody dares to make complaints the fellow is suppressed and bullied to the extent of using the Military for the purpose. Is it a crime to make reasonable demands? Other complaints made by the refugees are also painful. Some esteemed and educated persons wanted to acquaint the Indian government, the Saurashtriya Government and the Baroda Government with the above facts by sending telegrams but to their great astonishment the postal authorities refused point-blank to send their wires. The Indian government should make inquiries about the matter.

The historian and refugee officer Shambhuprasad Desai testifies to the poor conditions of reception in Veraval and Junagadh in Saurashtra. Speaking of his direct involvement in these two places, Desai mentions that the Sindhis came to Saurashtra much against the will of the local population. The grounds of opposition were both social and economic. The local Gujaratis did not want the Sindhis to occupy the evacuee properties left behind by the Memons of Junagadh who had preferred to go to Pakistan once it was decided that Junagadh would have to merge with independent India. The local Gujaratis resented the government's decision to allocate the evacuee property to the Sindhis. They also disliked the Sindhis who to them, looked like Muslims and ate meat. They made a representation to Desai to oppose the Sindhi incursion in Kutiyana and Veraval. However, in his capacity as the custodian of evacuee property and refugee officer, Desai ignored the local sentiments against the incoming Sindhis. He took charge of the abandoned houses and sealed the belongings left by the Muslims. In the absence of local support and labour, says Desai, he could not manage makeshift arrangements for helping the Sindhis.

Local resistance under similar circumstances occurred in Bhavnagar, when on 13 March 1948 a steamer with migrants from Sindh arrived on the Jhuna bunder of Bhavnagar. They were provided accommodation in godowns of grain. Manubhai Bhatt, a Gandhian social activist from Bhavnagar, was put in charge of organising voluntary services. In his interview with the writer Jayant Relwani, Bhatt noted,

> The refugees were in a terrible state. They were full of anger. Each family was given a mere 10 feet space in the godowns and there were hundred such families. The picture of so many families living in a cellar like that was beyond imagination. What was surprising for us and even for the refugees was how different they looked from us. Their clothes, manners, appearance was a lot like Muslims. In fact they were not even used to thinking of themselves as Hindus, it must have occurred to them during partition that they were of a different religion. They seemed to have blended so much with the majority of the Muslim population in Sindh. The women could not stop saying, *Allah knows* every now and then, while the men would say *khuda khe khabar.* (in Relwani 1996, 177)

The refugees from Bhavnagar were asked to go to Palitana, but they did not want to. According to Bhatt, "We had to forcibly send them to Palitana. We threatened to discontinue their rations" (178). Meanwhile, the government of Saurashtra made efforts to rehabilitate them by giving them small plots of land where they could start business.

However, their shops encroached upon the Muslim spaces, leading to communal disturbances, especially in an area called Aamba chowk. The situation in Saurashtra, especially Junagadh, was particularly volatile because once the princely state of Junagadh was merged with the Indian nation state, there was a considerable out-migration of Muslims along with an in-migration of the Sindhis from West Pakistan. From the archival material obtained from Junagadh Record Office it also appears that for a brief period, Muslims from neighbouring states like Rajasthan and Madhya Pradesh poured into Junagadh, because under a Muslim ruler, it was more 'secure'. While communal tension was causing one kind of imbalance, the local Gujarati businessmen went on a protest march against the Sindhis and issued public notices asking for their evacuation. Incidentally, one of the organisations helping the Sindhis in a big way at this time was the RSS. According to Bhatt, "We tried not to encourage help from the RSS because it led to further instigation of the Sindhis who were anyway vulnerable then. But they were the only ones to offer help, the Congress workers were hardly in sight" (185).

The Government of India reached an agreement with Karachi between 10 and 13 January, 1949. According to this agreement, "No decisions have yet been taken about agricultural property. The urban immoveable property of refugees is now permitted to be exchanged or sold, but such exchanges or sales will have to be registered with the Custodian. Certificate is given by the rehabilitation commissioner or any authority only after obtaining the consent of this ministry" (Letter from the Ministry of Relief and Rehabilitation to the State of Baroda, 19 January 1949, BSA).

The Problem of Evacuee Properties

The percentage of Muslim population in the princely states of Junagadh, Bantwa, Kutiyana and Godhra was large. During Partition and also after the merger of Junagadh in 1948, a large number of Muslims from Junagadh left for Pakistan, leaving behind their properties. These evacuee properties were a strong attraction to the

Sindhis. The procedure of requisitioning evacuee properties to refugees on either side of the border was slow and complicated. We noticed how the immigrant Muslims in Sindh created threatening situations so that the Hindus would leave their properties and flee. In a similar way, the Sindhis in Saurashtra forcibly acquired Muslim evacuee houses. On 28 February 1948, around twenty thousand Hindus from Sindh arrived in Junagadh, hoping to claim the properties left behind by the Muslims after Junagadh's merger with the Indian nation state.

After the riots of 6 January 1948 in Karachi, the Indian government had also managed to provide free transportation through country crafts for bringing rural and poor Sindhis to Saurashtra. Both the anger about their displacement and the desperate need for housing found a common target in the Muslims of Saurashtra. As Patel noted in his correspondence with Nehru, "The refugees are undoubtedly bitter and disillusioned. We cannot ignore this fact. There is plenty of explosive material in them. We have always to bear this in mind. Extremism is bound to be popular among them. This should be a warning to us" (in Das 1974, 204).

In another letter he testified to the forcible occupation of houses, which had both class and communal dimensions, "Thank you for your letter dated 17 November 1947 regarding a report, which we have received about communal riots in Rajkot and Junagadh state. It seems that yesterday some trouble was created by refugees at Rajkot and they occupied houses of Muslims who had left for Pakistan" (481).

Chandra Asrani from Bantwa responds on a more personal note:

> We are from Lower Sindh. Our men were peasants. We lived in villages and never even visited Karachi or Hyderabad. Women in our families draw their veils up to their waists. I don't think my father-in-law even knew what I looked like.
>
> We were brought to Bhavnagar by country craft. From there we came to Bantwa. There were Muslim evacuee houses. I can't remember how, but we managed to live in one.... I remember a woman used to visit our house and quietly walk up to one corner of the house and cry. We, women of the house, called her privately and asked her. She told us that her husband was killed in that corner. (personal interview)

Meanwhile, the *Annual Administrative Report* of the Saurashtra State (1950, 70) shows the following as the allocation of houses, shops and industrial concerns of the evacuees in Saurashtra:

Evacuee houses: 199

Evacuee shops: 540

Evacuee industrial establishments: 36

The foregoing discussion highlighted some of the issues of resettlement faced by the Sindhis in Saurashtra State. The combination of social disapproval from the mainstream Hindu population, and the economic competition with both Hindus and Muslims created bitterness among the Sindhis. Some of the manifestations of this bitterness can be seen in the references to 'communal tensions' in parts of Junagadh and Rajkot. There were a number of issues handled by the cluster of the princely states in Saurashtra that I have not dealt with here, and are worthy of further examination. We now turn our attention to the Sindhi resettlement in Godhra which also shows a history of heartburn.

Godhra

Parts of Bombay that included the districts of Godhra and Dahod (now in Gujarat) also beckoned to the Sindhis due to the availability of evacuee Muslim properties. Migrants to Godhra came from two different directions and socio-economic strata. Of the 15,000 Sindhis who live in Godhra, a majority are from lower Sindh, the region of Lar. Peasants and fishermen by vocation, the Laris are considered, among Sindhis, the most coarse and poor group. The second group, a smaller one, albeit more powerful in terms of political representation, are the people from upper Sindh, from the regions of Larkano and Shikarpur. The Laris came to Godhra by first disembarking at the Navlakhi port in Saurashtra. They were taken to the Katni Camp near Jabalpur. Once that camp closed down, they were sent to Godhra. This smaller group, says Tahilram Makhijani (a member of an influential Congress family), was aware of the properties but we "waited for our claims to come through and then bought them. My brother,

Arjandas Makhijani was a well-known Gandhian in Sindh." After the 6th January riots, other Sindhi leaders advised him to leave. "Another associate of Gandhi, Dr. Valechha, got us free passes for travelling. We came from Karachi by ship. We came to Bombay. We were taken by train to the Pimpri Camp near Pune. My brother Arjandas stayed back in Bombay to ask where we should settle. He was advised by Choithram Gidwani and Nanak Motwani that *'Gujarat thado mulk aa.'* (Gujarat is a peaceful nation.) We are also merchants." He scouted around in Godhra and noticed that there was a lot of evacuee property. "That is how we came to Godhra" (personal interview).

A large number of Muslims from Godhra, whose houses and shops were located in the heart of the city, had not yet left. Apparently, after the vicious riots of 1948 between the Sindhi Hindus and Muslims, many of the Muslims from Godhra left and those properties are now occupied by the Sindhis.[4] It is difficult to know whether the Sindhis initiated the riots (which took place because the Muslims had unfurled the Pakistan flag), or subsequently, with support from the local collector, they managed to drive the Muslims out. It is clear however, that the communal history of Godhra with its notorious series of riots between the Ghanchi Muslims and the Lari Sindhis has, at its roots, the issue of evacuee property. Another respondent, Harish Jethmalani (a lawyer from Vadodara) confirms this claim by saying, "The reputation of the Godhra Sindhis had spread to other parts of Gujarat. The Sindhi aggression against Muslims was seen as a special gift the Sindhis brought with them to Gujarat. The Maharaja of Baroda wanted us to also put the Muslims of Baroda in their place. We were in Harni and Outram camps, but the maharaja wanted us to have townships next to Muslim colonies so that they remain under control" (personal interview). Whether the assumptions communicated on behalf of the maharaja have any grounds is a different matter; what is important and disturbing here is the new self-definition of the Sindhis. Ironically, the roots of this communalised self-definition lie not in a 'traumatic

---

4. This calls for a comparison with the "refugee crisis that accompanied the demographic restructuring of Karachi in 1947–1948" studied by Sarah Ansari (2005).

and violent' Partition experience, but in the circumstances of resettlement.

Ahmedabad and Surat

In addition to Baroda and Saurashtra, the city of Ahmedabad also accommodated a large number of Sindhis by providing transit camps and tents. In 1947–48, the camp of Kubernagar in Ahmedabad (now the second largest Sindhi township in India) could accommodate 100,000 Sindhis. It is difficult to know how many Sindhis live in Kubernagar now, but they must form the largest component of the 400,000 strong Sindhi population in the city of Ahmedabad.[5] Apart from Kubernagar, Ahmedabad had relief camps in the areas of Wadaj, Sabarmati and Maninagar. The city of Ahmedabad was a transit point for Sindhis who were sent there when camps in Rajasthan or Madhya Pradesh had to be shut down. Apart from such collective movements, there has also been individual migration to Gujarat in the hope of better business prospects because Gujarat has a long-standing tradition of trade. Similarly, the Ramnagar Camp in Surat was also made available to the Sindhis when the Devlali Camp in Maharashtra closed down in 1950. About six hundred families came to Surat as a part of this collective migration. The Dhanna Silk Mills of Surat, established by a Sindhi businessman, Dhannamal Assandas, in the early twentieth century, also drew individual Sindhis to Surat. As Surat became more and more industrialised from 1960 onwards, it drew Sindhis from other parts of the country. At present, its Sindhi population is estimated to be 50,000.

Kutch

The most unique event in the history of Sindhi migration and rehabilitation occurred in the region of Kutch in Gujarat. Bhai Pratap,

5. Kubernagar is Ahmedabad's equivalent of the Ulhasnagar Camp in Kalyan, Maharashtra.

a well-known businessman and national activist from Sindh, requested the Indian government to provide a region (if not a linguistic state) where displaced Sindhis could live as a single community and preserve their identity. His concern was both immediate and long term, in that he wished to make opportunities of livelihood available to the Sindhis and also to provide a means of maintaining their collective identity. Gandhi responded to this request and urged the Maharrao of Kutch to come forward and help rehabilitate the Sindhis in Kutch. The maharao granted 15,000 acres of land near the port of Kandla for the purpose of building a new township, which came to be called Gandhidham. On the basis of this offer, Bhai Pratap founded the Sindhu Resettlement Corporation (SRC, a non-governmental organisation) whose main aims were to build the new township of Gandhidham, wherein plots of land were allotted to shareholders on easy terms, and to undertake or aid industrial, commercial and other public utility projects.

Unfortunately, the project became a reality only during 1952 and by then most Sindhis were scattered in different parts of India. As Laxmandas Makhija says, "It was late in the day—the desire to live together had gone. People were scattered in different parts of the country and had resettled with great difficulty. Who would have wanted another uprooting? After all, people cannot live by sentiment alone. There are circumstantial reasons why people settle down in any place. If your family and business is in Madras for instance, you are not likely to feel motivated to go to Adipur or Gandhidham" (personal interview). Resistance also came from the hostile conditions of Kutch, a region of dry wilderness with no industry, vegetation or urbanisation. However, Bhai Pratap did not give up easily and came up with ingenious methods of luring Sindhis to Gandhidham. These included sending well-known Sindhi singers such as Master Chander and nationalist poets like Hundraj Dukhayal to relief camps to urge displaced Sindhis to come to Gandhidham. Composed by Hundraj Dukhayal and sung by Master Chander, this song shows how Kutch was being projected as the new Sindhi nation:

Pyaaro pyaaro Gandhidham
Desh asanjo, vesh asanjo
Hik jahiri aahe raunak
Hik jahiri aahe rahini
Hik jahiri aahe dharti.

Our beloved Gandhidham
Our nation, our clothes
The same spectacle
The same lifestyle
The same earth.

Bhai Pratap had visualised Gandhidham as a settler colony, where Sindhis could start earning money by killing scorpions or even clearing bushes and eventually build the township it is today. He managed to bring people who had not found any means of livelihood elsewhere in India to Gandhiham. Ramchand Gehani, the manager of SRC, recalls, "I moved in 1952. We first went to Jaipur, and then to Ajmer. Nothing seemed to work for us. Finally someone brought my father here. This place is predominantly Lari, the most rural and poor group from Sindh" (personal interview). Hence, Gandhidham became the destination of the poor. As one of its inhabitants, Nirmal Vaswani (former correspondent, *Times of India*, Kutch) says, "We were given enticing details to bring us here. Bhai had two good propagandists – Hasanand Jadugar and Master Chander – they used to compose fast 'rap' songs and attract people. We were told that there are mango trees on each side of [the] roads. [The] majority of [the] people who came to Gandhidham had no return fare. People who had money returned; those who didn't, stayed back and made do with [a] small income" (personal interview).

The people of Gandhidham do not see themselves as refugees, but as early settlers who created opportunities not only for themselves but also for others. The development projects executed by the SRC and the subsequent establishment of the Kandla port in 1965, have now made Gandhidham and its township Adipur, a region with the largest Sindhi population in Gujarat. This context of the Sindhi presence in

Gujarat is different from the rest, since it is perhaps the only example of the Sindhi community's own attempt at rehabilitation, without depending on state help.

THE END OF THE CAMP EPISODE

On 21 May 1948, the assistant secretary to the Ministry of States, Government of India, sent the following letter to provincial governments handling relief and rehabilitation.

> Sir,
> As you are doubtless aware there are about 10 lacs of refugees who are in relief camps in various Provinces and States in the Indian Dominion. These camps have now been in existence for several months past and it is not known for how long these camps will continue. There are already visible signs of demoralization of refugees in these camps. In order to arrest any further deterioration it is considered necessary to take immediate steps for the rehabilitation of these refugees...
> (BSA)

During the same year, Narayandas Malkani, an insider of the community, also noticed the signs of degradation. He mentions in his autobiography:

> I was the Director of Rehabilitation and visited Sindhi camps everywhere in 1948—Rajkot, Delhi and Jaipur. Sindhis had become lazy. They engaged in stealing and their domestic quarrels [were] increasing. They had got used to free things. The line dividing right and wrong had disappeared. With no panchayats and no social control, our culture was gone. The camp life caused a rupture in us and Sindhis have become a quarrelsome community. I had to make them evacuate camps. It was an unpleasant task. (1973, 157)

The refugees' camps were officially closed in 1949. Towards the end of 1948, only the disabled and the old, and/or children were given doles. The rest had to look out for themselves, which the Sindhis did much better than any other migrant community. In Gujarat, they resented the fact that they continued to be called nirvasit (the homeless) for at least a decade more. In other states they were called sharnarthi (refugees), which also evoked images of dependence and being at the mercy of those who gave them shelter. The next few decades would find the Sindhis trying to live down these labels, inventing new ones like purusharthi (hard-working, those making an effort) to suggest success and self-reliance. Apart from the ways in which their identity as refugees shaped the perceptions of others, it also created new cleavages in the community by separating those who lived in camps from those who did not. I remember an offensive word from my childhood – campi – which meant 'a typical Sindhi' or 'a coarse, unrefined Sindhi'. It marked a different class to which we, living in the posh areas of Ahmedabad, did not belong. For people who continue to live in camps turned townships in cities like Ahmedabad and Surat, condescension comes from all quarters of their community. Just as people from the Ulhasnagar Camp left and moved to Bombay, those from Ramnagar in Surat went to posh areas like City Light, those from Kubernagar moved to Navrangpura in Ahmedabad—the movement out of the camp has been a movement towards upward mobility. It also has been a concurrent movement away from a certain brand of Sindhiness—an identifiable and un-likeable Sindhiness. Upwardly mobile Sindhis reject it, and in the process reject their own past and history.

However, this process is not very intense in one region where there were neither camps nor negative connotations to the word nirvasit— Kutch, which is like rural Sindh with its porous religious boundaries and isolation from main centres. Lying next to the vast desert of the Rann of Kutch, there are the villages of Banni, a region that may well have been in rural Sindh. Its Sindhi-speaking Muslims – the Mutwas and Sodhas – have been living there for over four hundred years. They not only speak Sindhi like the Sindhi Hindus but also share with the diasporic Sindhis, a love for Sufi pirs like Shah Abdul Latif and Sachal Sarmast. The Institute of Sindhology in Adipur, Kutch, serves as a locus now for literature of the diasporic and post-Partition Sindhis as well as the Sindhi-speaking Muslims. When you stand on the border of the Rann of Kutch and gaze as far as your eyes can see, it feels as though your sight can touch the Sindhis in the villages of Pakistan. The movement between Sindhis across both sides of the borders was physical and cultural once; now it is only cultural. However, it is easy to see how of all the places in Gujarat that the Sindhis settled down in, Kutch does serve as the most natural habitat.

In the centre of Adipur stands a temple to a god who came into existence in 1950. His name is Nirvasiteshwar or God of the refugees. His temple is part of a circular complex that includes the temples of all gods revered by the Sindhi Hindus. The entire complex is called Sadh Belo, a holy place of pilgrimage for the Sindhi Hindus in Sukkur, Sindh. The Sindhis of Kutch acknowledge their history as refugees by invoking a god of refugees who stands as a product of not some remote mythology, but a set of historical circumstances. He is the Kutchi Sindhis' acknowledgement of migrancy, misery and success.

6   Stigma in Gujarat

When I refused to speak Hungarian anymore, my parents co-operated.
                              —Daughter of a Holocaust survivor, Epstein

The opposition to and abhorrence of meat-eating that existed in Gujarat among the Jains and Vaishnavas were to be seen nowhere else in India or outside in such strength.

                                                              —M.K. Gandhi

Not many of the younger generation can speak Sindhi and the readiness with which they integrate with other communities will, in the foreseeable future, make them a relic of the past

                                                              —Khushwant Singh

Although the suffering of the Sindhis is nowhere close to the Jewish experience, there are similarities between these two communities. Both enjoy the reputation of being successful trading and money-lending communities; both have suffered displacement on religious grounds and have achieved remarkable success as minority communities everywhere in the world; and finally, both communities evoke distrust and dislike. After fifty-seven years of resettlement in Gujarat, the Sindhis form one of its most affluent business communities. They dominate several forms of trade and business. The Sindhis own bakeries, provisions stores, consumer goods stores and readymade garments stores. They also own hotels and cinema halls in Gujarat. The Sindhis travel in sleek cars, wear diamond rings and build huge houses. They proudly declare that there is not a single Sindhi beggar anywhere in India. Of course, they too have their poor, but these are never below the state's definition of the poverty line. The Sindhis are model migrants, who seem to show no traces of trauma. In fact, many claim to have done much better after Partition than before. For a young Sindhi, there is a lot to feel proud about, especially in light of the knowledge of how her dispossessed grandparents re-established themselves and how her parents took that establishment further and have given to her stability and wealth—and all of this, within a span of fifty-odd years. This is the objective, incontrovertible reality of the Sindhis in Gujarat, as perhaps anywhere else in India.

However, the subjective world of a post-Partition Sindhi – in Gujarat, at least – is marked by a sense of discomfort. The Sindhi migrant refuses to speak her language and her parents cooperate with her in shedding not only her language, but also her Sindhi identity. This process has been gradual, beginning with a modification of external appearance and food habits and moving towards a relinquishing of an entire past and world view. It has sometimes been conscious, sometimes not, and each generation has contributed to the dissolution of the historical Sindhi identity. Speaking of this, Dr. Prakash Vazirani, a leading cardiologist in the city of Ahmedabad says,

> There was pride in being a Sindhi for the first generation. The[ir] struggles…affected us also, but we did not get their pride. I am talking about my generation, born in the 1940s and 1950s. In the third generation, there is clearly a stigma. My children grew up in a Gujarati culture where certain negative aspects of Sindhiness got highlighted. My generation did not help correct those perceptions or offer them a more positive side to our history, because we hardly bothered with it.

As a result, our children reject Sindhiness which they think is characterised by coarseness, garish clothes, loud voices, and lack of education. The media has also contributed to this feeling. I don't know if these exist in other parts of India, I am only talking of Gujarat. (personal interview)

In her sociological study, Subhadra Anand outlines the many aspects of Indian Sindhis and demonstrates the disintegration of and ruptures in Sindhi identity. Her study is restricted to the Sindhis of Bombay whose customs, rituals and community structures constitute Anand's focus. My attempt here is not sociological; my purpose is not to attempt to outline the various ingredients that make up what we call 'identity' and study them in a clinical framework. I merely wish, in this chapter, to provide a range of voices across age and space that speak of how they feel about being Sindhi, the negative perceptions of the Sindhi identity they carry, and their means of coping with them. The tone of such voices, their strident confidence and poignant ambivalences provide a glimpse of the experiential world of the Sindhis in Gujarat.

An Unwanted Identity

As a Sindhi growing up in Gujarat in the 1970s and 1980s, I had an acute feeling of being in the wrong community, one that did not value education, or respect women. Its men seemed too mercenary, and the women too preoccupied with the kitchen. The boys barely waited to acquire a minimum level of education before they started earning money at cloth shops, while the girls waited to marry. The marriages entailed (as did my sisters') crude discussions on '*deti–leti*' (the Sindhi way of referring to dowry). There seemed no sophistication of either manners or mind. People did not study, so they did not speak English. They were oblivious to the finer aspects of life such as music and literature. They somehow appeared dirty, and everybody said so. It is difficult to say how many of these perceptions were my own and how many came as a result of internalising things that I had (over)heard in my very English-medium school. I squirmed at the thought of hearing in school once again, a relatively innocuous phrase, "*Sindhi saiin, papad khain, papad kaccha, pet mein bachha.*" (A Sindhi man eats a papad that had not been roasted fully; it becomes a baby in his stomach.) The so-called joke is directed at the widespread use of papad in Sindhi cuisine as well as the physical appearance of Sindhis. I realised much later that what had seemed like a personal and unique experience was not unique at all. For instance, shades of a similar discomfort can be heard in the voice of the journalist Jyoti Punwani in her short article on "A Return to Roots":

> Growing up as a Sindhi in a convent school in Mumbai was no incentive to discover one's roots. The constant taunts of "Sindhi Chor", "Made in Ulhasnagar, not USA", "Papadkhav", were enough to make you wish you had been born in any other community. The Hong Kong printed shirts, gaudy nylons, sleeveless blouses and plunging necklines, dyed hair, mounds of jewellery and loud ways which characterized Sindhis made you keep a healthy distance from your own community. (2002b, 6)

Here too, it is difficult to say whether what Punwani disliked came entirely from within or without. However, what gets created out of this blend of perceptions is an identity you do not want; it feels burdensome and is undesirable. Unlike the case of the Dalits, there is no historical reason for the stigma, and yet there is nothing that makes you feel proud. Given the absence of history, territory and stories that could make you feel connected to a more coherent past, all you see is a present in which this identity evokes dislike and/or mockery. It is both a historical and experiential process, a gradual erosion of comfort in an identity that underwent change and stigma due to displacement.

The nature of Sindhi stereotypes is unremitting, uncompensated by any positive feedback from any quarter. In the best-selling author Shobha De's novel, *Sultry Days*, the protagonist Nisha's mother complains to her daughter about how her (Nisha's) father was unfaithful to her and what made it worse, according to her, was that he was doing it for a Sindhi. The passage below is quoted at some length to draw attention to De's use of the negativism that exists with regard to Sindhis in an upper class family of Mumbai:

...a Sindhi woman! Can you imagine? A Sindhi! Someone from his office – a divorcee. Those are the worst types. Ruin their own marriage first and then ruin someone else's. But what I can't get over is, how could he fall for a Sindhi? You know how he feels about them. He always used to say Sindhis have no class. That they are crude and lacking in taste. You remember the holiday in Goa two years ago? Remember what the women were wearing—shiny clothes with broad plastic belts. And high heels in the sand! Remember, how we laughed? Especially Papa. (1994, 54–55).

In another recent novel, Shashi Deshpande's *Moving On*, the mother is contemptuous of her daughter Manjari's relationship with Shyam, a Sindhi. In a collection of short stories written by a Sindhi writer in English, a granddaughter asks her grandmother, "Nani, nani, all my friends make fun of Sindhis....Why? Why do they make mean digs about our entrepreneurship, like 'guess what Neil Armstrong found on the moon? A Sindhi shop selling American flags, wholesale?'" (Wadhwani 2001, 52). Such jokes may be perceived as indirect compliments to the proverbial salesmanship of a Sindhi who can sell ice to the Eskimos. However, the Sindhi who smarts under them knows that they are intended to point out the shrewdness (and as is the case below, the dirtiness) of the Sindhis:

> One Sindhi is a currency racket.
> Two Sindhis is a *papad* factory.
> Three Sindhis is a duplicate goods shop.
> Four Sindhis is a lot of gas around (yeech!).
> (http://www.asianjoke.com/Indian/my_india.htm)

The examples illustrate the negative perceptions that exist about the Sindhis. These perceptions have permeated through all the states of India. The case of Gujarat, however, seems slightly different. The sense of discomfort among the Sindhis of Gujarat acquires a special edge—there is almost a sense of stigma. This seems to originate from two sources: economic competition and social differentiation. The economic factor stems from the fact that the Sindhis began life in Gujarat as traders. In doing so, they offered direct competition to the established mercantile class who deeply resented this. The mercantile class in Gujarat consists largely of the Jains and Vaishnavs—predominantly vegetarian communities. The non-vegetarianism of the Sindhis accounted for the second factor of social discrimination. Although these factors seem distinct, my field study shows a bewildering extent of the intertwining of the two, so that often they become indistinguishable.

Economic resentment, social dislike

Gujarat divides its psychological world between those who are 'like Gujaratis' and those who are not. The Sindhis occupy a peripheral zone by being neither 'proper' Hindus of Gujarat nor the *others* (such as Christians and Muslims). Coming from a region that is now in Pakistan, speaking in a language vastly different from Gujarati, writing in an Arabic script, frequently spouting 'Allah' and 'Khuda' in their conversation, wearing clothes very like those sported by the Muslims, not observing caste distinctions—the Sindhis in 1948 appeared to the people of Gujarat as 'half-Muslims'. The people of Gujarat knew that the Sindhis had left everything behind in Sindh and escaped to India because they were a Hindu minority in a Muslim province. However, the Islamic influence upon the Sindhis; the pluralistic, atypical Hindu practices; and their blithe indifference to ritual purity made the (Hindu) Gujaratis wonder if the Sindhis were Hindus like them. Some traces of this bewilderment perhaps persist even today.

A common perception of the Sindhis in the eyes of the Gujaratis is that they are 'dirty'. Phrases such as, *'Sindhi to gobra'* (Sindhis are dirty) and *'Sindhi to ganda'* (also, Sindhis are dirty) point to unclean manners. Whether or not Sindhi standards of cleanliness were genuinely low because in the initial years of resettlement they lived under squalid circumstances, or because they did not believe in the ideology of pollution is not the issue here. Such stereotypes helped the Hindu and Jain Gujaratis legitimise distance, while creating in the Sindhis' minds, a 'justifiable' reason for that distance. On grounds of cleanliness and non-vegetarianism, the Sindhis are not sold homes in localities dominated by Jains and Vaishnavs. The Jain–Vaishnav combine is both economically and culturally influential; it determines the 'purity' of the state and by consequence, its social segregations. Their impact is particularly visible in cities like Ahmedabad, Surat and Vadodara where urban trade is mostly in their hands. At the same time, to lesser or greater extents, such negative perceptions permeate almost all parts of Gujarat.

In Surat, Parshram Advani, owner of a successful cloth mill and a first generation migrant told me, "We first came to Udaipur, but because of shortage of water we moved to Gujarat. In Udaipur, the Marwaris used to maintain separate utensils for us because they thought we were untouchables. When we came to Gujarat, people here thought we were Muslims! [Laughs.] For the first thirty years, they would keep their distance from us and not let us anywhere near them socially. Now things have changed. They have also realised that we don't eat non-vegetarian food." When I asked him whether they turned vegetarian under pressure, he replied, "Some of our own satsangs also prevent us, so why blame the Gujaratis alone. We don't feel like it anymore, why create problems?" (personal interview). In Rajkot, I met the Belanis, a well-educated couple. Mr. Belani had worked in a bank in Rajkot and was preparing to move to his new job in Mumbai. I asked them if Sindhis could buy houses in any locality and they replied, "Not too many." Mr. Belani clarified that Sindhi women used to be over-occupied with sewing and embroidery in the early days and perhaps they did not pay enough attention towards cleanliness. Mrs. Belani added to this by saying, "You see we were influenced by Muslim culture, so Sindhis were non-vegetarians. That is why the Gujaratis don't feel comfortable selling them houses" (personal interview). It is interesting to note how even a well-educated, upwardly mobile Sindhi couple seems to have internalised this sense of stigma.

In the city of Ahmedabad, the Sindhis live away from the social and psychological lives of the Hindu Gujaratis. Although they may, on rare occasions, manage to stay in Gujarati-dominated colonies, they must comply with the Hindu Gujarati's norms of vegetarianism for eligibility to live there. When in the late 1980s my parents were looking for a new house, I was shocked to find that Sindhis were not allowed to reside in certain localities. Unlike my family, Naraindas Bhurani was willing to give up his non-vegetarianism and after some effort he has managed to find a house in a newly made cosmopolitan building. A Jain builder told him that even if he were willing to make an exception in his building, the other occupants would object. "I don't think the point is only about non-vegetarianism," says Bhurani. "That is a minor adjustment that we must make to respect their sentiments. What bothers me is that the Gujarati believes every Sindhi is dishonest and that the Sindhi would not stop at anything. It is true that many of us cut corners and did 'adjustments'. But the Gujaratis also do it, why don't they admit that? Also, we worked hard, harder than them. They live with all kinds of hang-ups like can't travel here, can't do that, can't eat with this one and that one—we had no such taboos. A businessman cannot afford to be picky" (personal interview). Born in 1947, Bhurani grew up in the area of Naroda Patiya where Sindhis, lower middle class Patels and Muslims live adjacent to each other. He began his career as an auto-rickshaw driver at the age of sixteen, with practically no education. Presently, he is the owner of a successful business of hosiery, an industry initiated and dominated by the Sindhis. Bhurani speaks in Gujarati with his son Sunil who said, "They are jealous of us. I have heard things like, '*Tame Sindhao Pakistani chho* (You Sindhis are Pakistanis). Why did you have to come here?' They still think of us as outsiders and Pakistanis" (personal interview). Sunil is in his mid-twenties. He studied in an English-medium school but interacted only with Gujaratis. He does not speak any Sindhi.

Although the brunt of the negative perceptions was directed at the first generation, the pressure to resettle gave them little time to be bothered. In the first twenty years, they were too busy making ends meet and living in a self-enclosed world of either Sindhi townships or cheap chawls (low end housing in narrow and congested buildings). Udhavdas Makhija who started his business on a pavement with less than one hundred rupees as a first generation migrant, has now retired from one of the most well-known firms manufacturing brassieres in Gujarat. He moved from a camp to a chawl and eventually to an apartment complex that is exclusively Sindhi. According to him, "Of course there was jealousy, but it didn't matter. Who had the time to bother with it?" (personal interview).

It was the second generation that began to sense this discrimination and began to be affected. Shankarlal Ahuja, the owner of the chain of bakeries that produce 'Super Bread' has felt a tangible sense of exclusion. I met Ahuja in an elite club in Ahmedabad of which he has been a member and where he has spent every evening for over twenty years. "It was only in the last few years that I have been able to make friends here. They were not ready to give me membership in this club. They kept inventing excuses. I used to sit by myself, smoke and play cards. Nobody would come up to me and talk to me. Things have changed now" (personal interview). Ahuja's father was a grain merchant in Sukkur. He came to India with practically no money and spent the initial few years in Baroda. In 1951, his father received a claim of Rs. 2000 from the rehabilitation department as compensation for his property in Pakistan. He set up a shoe shop where father and son began to work very hard. They not only sold shoes, but also made them themselves. It mattered little to them that traditionally Hindus avoid touching leather because leather is considered 'polluting' (hence, caste Hindus leave that business to the so-called lower castes or Muslims). Ahuja became a distributor for the Bata Shoe Company. He also started a bread factory, which now has outlets in every city of Gujarat.

As mentioned earlier, the Sindhi settlers in the urban areas of Gujarat were largely traders coming to a mercantile state. Hungry for survival, no job seemed too menial and no work enough for them. They made inroads into the wholesale and retail trade of Gujarat, offering tough competition to the already well-established, Gujarati-dominated businesses. They made do with low margins, thereby undercutting the business of the locals. They had no inhibitions, religious or otherwise, about working odd hours of the day and night. In a hurry to make ends meet and recover all that they had left behind, the Sindhis adopted whatever means they could. They created tremendous economic resentment and distrust, exemplified in the popular proverb, "If you see a Sindhi and a snake, kill the Sindhi first."[1] Although an intertwining of commerce and ethics is rarely simple, the Sindhis draw attention to this aspect by being ubiquitous as a business community, with a negligible professional class. The emergence of negative perceptions among the Gujaratis has roots in their hands-on market experience.

In the course of his conversation with me, Shankarlal Ahuja mentioned that he sends a 'good thought' by short messaging service (SMS) to his entire family everyday. Along with a 'good thought' that is spiritually inspiring, he also advises them everyday to never pay taxes. This casually made statement was in response to my question whether he thought there was any justification in considering Sindhis unethical businessmen. Prem Goplani, a chartered accountant from Bhavnagar testifies to the habit of tax evasion among Sindhis, "It is not that Gujaratis are all honest, but they are not this blatant. They will manipulate, but at least maintain books of accounts. The Gujarati bania gets terrified, while the Sindhis are just not bothered" (personal interview). It is true that immediately after Partition the pressures of earning quickly may have governed some of the casual business practices among Sindhis. However, the bania of Sindh was also adept at maintaining mystifying accounts that neither the poor haari nor the English officer could understand. It is perhaps a continuation of the same trait, exacerbated by the pressures of survival, which the Sindhis are still unwilling to give up. It would seem that the Sindhis have shed what seemed inconvenient to them, and have continued with traditions that seemed to make commercial sense. According to Anita Thapan, the Sindhi businessman has his own particular concept of morality. For him, irregularities in business practice are occupational hazards (2002, 40). In Bhavnagar, Harish Manglani, an owner of a biscuit factory, mentions that, "Sindhis here spend a lot of time and money in the 'diary' business; that is, they lend money at high rates of interest unaccompanied by any official papers. Earning quick cash has become their habit. I ask them to put money in schools, they say

1. Interestingly, this proverb is found in the states of Maharashtra, Madhya Pradesh and Uttar Pradesh as well.

'Asaankeh kero faido?' (How is it worthwhile for us?)" (personal interview).

In Surat, my interviews had begun first in Ramnagar, a camp turned township, with about six hundred and fifty Sindhi families. At the entrance of the lane that goes into Ramnagar, is a 'novelty store' (a generic title for sundry goods) owned by Thakur Motwani. After getting to know each other, he allowed me to be a curious onlooker in his shop. I began observing Thakurbhai at work. His business was retail in nature; hence it was entirely in cash with no bill transactions. I asked him, "Thakurbhai, how do you keep tabs on what you have sold if you don't make bills? Don't you pay taxes?" His brother Kanaiyo had also joined us in the meantime and he intervened, "You think we want to starve. How do we drive cars and wear diamonds by honest means? Business means theft. And mind you, this is Surat where nobody makes bills!" (personal interview). It can be observed that in some quarters at least, the Sindhis continue to provide reasons for being judged unethical businessmen.

It is not my concern to test the veracity of each perception, but to examine how the overwhelmingly negative perceptions (especially in the absence of any compensatory social interaction) can be internalised by the receiving community. The outward gaze of the persons without and the inward gaze of the insider collude to form a stigmatised identity. Such forms of stigma occur in historically marginalised communities such as the Dalits and tribals. They are usually not to be expected in a mainstream community 'known' for being wealthy and ostentatious. However, in its initial stages of resettlement, the Sindhis did appear both socially and economically marginal. The Dalit writer Kesharshivam on his appointment as mamlatdar (recovery officer) in Sardarnagar, a refugee camp in Ahmedabad, makes the following comparison:

> Like Dalits, the Sindhis also had to do hijrat. If the Dalits migrated
> en masse because of harassment, the Sindhis had to do hijrat to go
> away from religious fundamentalism. In the Sabarkantha district I
> had noticed that the tribals would starve rather than beg. I noticed
> similar qualities in the Sindhis. During daytime the man would earn

any which way he could, and somehow bring some money to the family. A Sindhi would take a basket of nuts and climb on trains to sell them. This community knows how to live with self-respect and self-reliance. This was a new experience for me. As such no other officer would have agreed to be appointed in this place. (2002, 351–52)

Stigma relativised

The sense of stigma is not uniform over all the sections of Sindhi society in Gujarat. The educated, westernised and socially privileged amils may have also encountered certain negative perceptions, but protected as they were by class and sophistication, the impact may not have been deep. Also, by and large, such a class did not come to Gujarat; it preferred to go to Delhi or Bombay. Those that did, did not have to live in the camps of Ahmedabad or Baroda, but joined the Gujarat government directly as much-privileged officers. Class continuities from pre-Partition and post-Partition lives is one of the least discussed aspects of Partition Studies. It determined the way people left, how they left, where they arrived and how were they received. A case in point is Lata Badlani, the wife of a former secretary with the Gujarat government (see chapter 4). After spending some months in Udaipur, her husband joined the Gujarat government. Unlike the large mass of Sindhis who lived in camps, and sold sundry things on railway platforms and pavements, the Badlanis moved in an elite circle where their acceptance was never an issue. It is possible therefore for her to say, "I don't think there is a sense of shame in being a Sindhi. There is less dividing me and my Punjabi or Gujarati friends, but more division between me and other Sindhis" (personal interview). The alienation of the amils from their community may be seen as a manifestation of some discomfort, but that phenomenon would not be peculiar only to the Sindhis. Hence, when the amils make choices outside the community through society and marriage, the choices are symptomatic of a larger process of elite cosmopolitanism and do not constitute an escape from their roots. There are cases of egalitarianism in the interaction of Sindhis with some communities in Gujarat. For instance, in the camp turned township of Ramnagar in Surat, the population consists of Sindhis and other Gujarati communities from the artisan classes such as potters and tailors. Here, the Gujaratis and Sindhis mix well and participate in each other's socio-religious functions. On the other hand, the upper caste Gujaratis from the elite colonies in Nanpara and City Light (Surat) look down upon the Sindhis living in their areas. The stigma varies with class as well as demography because neither the pressure on the Sindhis to assimilate nor the perception of threat is the same everywhere. The sociologist Achyut Yagnik sums up this difference succinctly:

> There are three cultural zones in what we now call Gujarat—
> Saurashtra, Kutch, and Gujarat. By Gujarat we mean non-Kutch and
> non-Saurashtra. The Sindhi experience in all three zones would be
> different. For instance, the Jadeja of Junagadh is not likely to resent a
> Sindhi because he himself is from Sindh. Similarly Kutch has had old
> links with Sindh, Kutchi is a dialect of Sindhi no matter what the
> Kutchis may think. It is in the third zone, dominated by the Jain–
> Vaishnav culture that Sindhis faced severe problems of identity. It is
> in this interaction that prejudices against Sindhis (their being 'half-
> Muslims' and non-vegetarians) figure the most. (personal interview)

The demographic coordinates are significant in the way Sindhis see themselves. For instance, the Sindhis of Godhra have both political and militant power. They are one of the most aggressive groups who locked horns with the Ghanchi Muslims of Godhra. A businessman from Godhra, Rajendra Makhijani, says, "Even if the Hindu Gujaratis here don't think much of us, nobody in Godhra can make a Sindhi feel shame. There is a confidence in the Godhra Sindhis, largely for the 'wrong' reasons!" (personal interview).

If the Sindhis of Godhra established their reputation as an aggressive community, those in Kutch, says Lakshmi Khilani, "came as early settlers, and not as refugees. We created opportunities for people here. The Kandla Port drew people from all over the country so that Gandhidham has become one of the most cosmopolitan places in Gujarat" (personal interview). Kutch shares the cultural fluidity of Sindh because of the presence of nomadic tribes who were both Hindus and Muslims at the same time. It was among the 'border Sindhis' of Kutch that a manuscript of the well-known Sufi piece "Shah jo Risalo" by Shah Abdul Latif was found. The Lohanas of Kutch celebrate the birth of Darya Lal, whom the Sindhis prefer to call Jhulelal. Having said that, such similarities do not make an idyllic relationship between the Kutchi Lohanas and the post-Partition Sindhis. The former tend not to acknowledge their shared culture with the Sindhis and identify themselves as 'Gujaratis' who have more in common with the upper caste and upper class Gujaratis of Ahmedabad or Vadodara. The Institute of Sindhology, established in Kutch to preserve and nurture Sindhi language and culture, finds more support from the nomadic Sindhi singers (Muslim by faith) living in the remote deserts of Banni than from the middle class Kutchis.

LANGUAGE AND IDENTITY

The first generation of migrants was rooted in its memories and had a sense of continuity with its past, but was too busy piecing its life together. Moreover, the pragmatism of this generation disallowed any sentimentality for the past. It evoked too much pain and was best not remembered. Intermittently, it may have communicated its memories of Sindh, but the midnight's children (born in the 1940s and 1950s) were growing up in a different world, where Sindh seemed remote and irrelevant. Their own ambivalence about being Sindhi did not allow them to pass on a legacy of pride in Sindhiness to the next generation. The absence of history and a past continued, and has now created a generation that operates in what Anita Thapan calls a "cultural vacuum" (2002, 131). For this third generation, Sindhiness is a cluster of undesirable traits and the easiest way to distance oneself is to not speak Sindhi—the only historical marker of this linguistic identity. We examine this phenomenon in the self-perceptions of the urban, third generation, college-going Sindhi boys and girls in Gujarat.

My first investigation was with a Sindhi student, Bhumika Udernani, in the college where I teach. One of my colleagues recommended Bhumika to me by saying, "She is so smart looking, you would never be able to tell she's a Sindhi." When I asked Bhumika what she felt when people told her that she did not look like a Sindhi, she smiled and said, "I feel very happy. It's a compliment." Pained and amused by the familiarity of this response, I began with her the first in a chain of interviews with young men and women.

Bhumika Udernani belongs to a business family that has lived in Ahmedabad since 1949. Her father has an electronics shop on Relief Road where Sindhi traders in electronic goods own most of the shops. Bhumika's mother is a homemaker. While her parents speak in Sindhi with each other, Bhumika and her siblings insist on speaking only in Hindi with them. "It used to irritate us when they spoke to us in Sindhi. So even they have switched over to Hindi." The only person with whom Bhumika tries her Sindhi is her maternal grandmother, her naani. "My naani likes to tell us about how she came to India during Partition. But I don't take the initiative and ask her. How do I, since I can't speak Sindhi?" Bhumika studied in an English-medium missionary school, which had a fair mix of many communities such as the Punjabis, Parsis, Malayalis. She admits that they never felt uncomfortable about being what they were, "In fact, they would smugly say, 'Oh I am a Punjabi' making me feel bad about my Sindhiness. I did not like that. There are such misconceptions about Sindhis—they are not educated, they are fat, and [the] boys join business. I have had to work hard to establish myself and not be ignored because I was a Sindhi. I have had bad experiences." Given the ubiquitous presence of Sindhis in business in Gujarat, Bhumika had no means of battling the stereotypes and citing Sindhis who had achieved distinction. In a world that values a bourgeois brand of success—the lack of education and the lack of what seemed refinement among Sindhis, left Bhumika apologetic. As a consequence, she has not only shed her language, but also finds it repulsive when a young Sindhi of her age appears ensconced in the language. "Nobody my age would like to be considered a Sindhi. When I see a girl of my age speaking in Sindhi, I feel, 'Oh my God, what have her parents done to her!' I can make out that they are from Kubernagar or Sardarnagar. It's embarrassing." Kubernagar and Sardarnagar are erstwhile camps now turned into townships. Bhumika lives away from such places, in a posh locality in the western part of Ahmedabad.

It would seem from Bhumika's example and from my own, that Sindhis studying in westernised schools carry the burden of such prejudices. This however, is not the case. Deepak Bhavnani who studies in a Gujarati-medium college also refuses to speak in Sindhi. "People in my college think Sindhis are some kind of inferior people." When I asked him what the basis of that perception was, he replied, "They say Sindhis are dirty, they eat meat and their homes stink." Unlike Bhumika, Deepak is surrounded by middle-class, non-westernised Gujaratis; therefore, his share of stereotypes is different. Nonetheless, the response to social condescension in both cases is the same—the shedding of language (personal interview).

Punit Padnani, a student of engineering in Ahmedabad does not admit any discomfort about being a Sindhi, but simply says, "I don't speak Sindhi. I am more comfortable with Gujarati." He has nothing against the language, he adds. However, gradually in the course of conversation, he expresses anger at how "...[the] media shows Sindhis in a very bad light. Why can't they show a decent-looking Sindhi professional?" (personal interview). A journalist with a prestigious English newspaper in Ahmedabad states that he dropped the suffix 'ni' from his last name because he sees himself as a non-Sindhi, "merely an Indian". His last name now gives the illusion that he is a south Indian, an identity that evokes in Gujarat the image of someone who is well-educated and has good English skills. At a conscious level, he does admit the difference between a mistaken identity and an alternative one.

While the lack of comfort with Sindhiness among the upwardly mobile, westernised Sindhis is quite visible, there is also a gradual erosion of confidence in the Sindhi heartlands, among those who are condescendingly called the campi Sindhis. The movement away from the camps is the aspiration of every Sindhi, but it is made possible by the denial of one's origins. Vidya Tewani and Krishna Ahuja are two of my students who lived in Kubernagar, studied in the Sindhi-medium schools there and came to St. Xavier's College to continue their studies.

The shift was almost like moving from a village to a city—destabilising and disorienting. Krishna was not fluent in either Gujarati or English and found it excruciating to go through with her education. She made no claims about not knowing Sindhi, for that is all she had. However, in her conversation to me she said, "I have to keep giving explanations of who I am. My classmates ask me why I look like a Muslim. Why do I wear such shiny clothes?" (personal interview). Krishna started wearing a cross around her neck during her days in college and found herself suddenly very 'interested' in Christianity. Vidya, on the other hand, retreated into a shell and made sure she read many English books to overcome her sense of inferiority. She told me, "No Sindhi girl in this college has come up and spoken to me. She wouldn't want to admit me as one of her own, because I am after all a Kuberi girl." The cleavages between the camp and non-camp Sindhis are analogous to the rich and poor classes. They began to come into effect with the migrant generation so that those who did not live in camps saw themselves as a superior class. In the second generation, the distance was already quite wide. Born in the 1950s, Maya Kodnani mentions how when she came to live in Kubernagar in 1988, "I was shocked. There was no education, no cleanliness. Everyone spoke in Sindhi. I found it difficult to adjust" (personal interview).

The examples quoted above are from the city of Ahmedabad. When I extended this investigation to other parts of Gujarat such as Kalol, Bhavnagar, Surat and Rajkot, the results were not vastly different. The only exception was the region of Adipur–Gandhidham in Kutch because the Sindhis there live in a close-knit community. Kutchi is a dialect of Sindhi (although the Kutchis never admit that) and Kutch, it must be remembered, is culturally close to Sindh. A socio-linguistic survey of the Sindhi community conducted by S.K. Rohra (1993) reveals a comfort with spoken Sindhi, but an unwillingness to go to Sindhi-medium schools. On the whole, the loss of language among post-Partition Sindhi generations has become an agonising issue for Sindhis in India, and Gujarat is not an exception.[2] The gradual closing

2. The well-known linguist, L.M. Khubchandani's research (1991; 1997) on this subject shows that as a language Sindhi may continue to exist among non-diasporic speakers of India such as the Tharis, Jaisalmeris and other border communities in Gujarat and Rajasthan.

down of Sindhi schools in India has threatened the identity of the Sindhis as a linguistic minority. A plethora of seminars, discussions and 'easy to learn' language kits betray the anxiety of the older generation about the likely extinction of the Sindhi language. On the whole, such discussions and seminars do not recognise the question of language as also one of identity, and their 'solutions' aim at the symptoms of what is a profoundly fractured sense of identity. Such anxieties are restricted to those engaged with Sindhi academia and literature. The large majority of Sindhis prefer to take a pragmatic view, "Just as we don't keep things in our shops that don't sell, Sindhi has no market now. There is no point in being sentimental about it," says Udhavdas Makhija (personal interview). The politician Maya Kodnani admits that, "I was myself never fluent in Sindhi. I grew up in a Gujarati locality and spoke only Gujarati. When we can't even send children to Sindhi-medium schools because there is no future [Where are the Sindhi colleges?], we can't force them to speak Sindhi. They need to know Hindi or English. I feel sorry about what is happening; it's almost as if to know Sindhi is to be backward" (personal interview). The issue of language is rife at many levels, beginning with an unresolved quarrel over script, but it is beyond the scope of our discussion here.[3]

By and large, the sense of shame is stronger in youngsters who come from business backgrounds for they find the mercantile ethos alienating, and the chasm between their aspirations and their business-minded parents', bewildering. During the stages when they have not yet made a distinct mark and broken stereotypes, their anxiety is most palpable. Once educated, they are no more in the prison of negative perceptions—perceptions that can now be countered. A chartered accountant, Prem Goplani, said confidently, "Now I am equipped to

3. After Partition, two schools of thought emerged over the question of script for writing in Sindhi in India. According to one, the Arabic script instituted by the British was no longer expressive of the 'Indian' reality of the Sindhis because every other language in India was written in Devanagri. While another group (comprising mainly of the old guard of writers such as Kirat Babani, Popati Hiranandani, etc.) believed that the identity of the Sindhi language lay in its Arabic script. The issue was never resolved, but remains arrested in the realm of history and its interpretation.

sit in any social circle in Bhavnagar. No Gujarati can make negative statements about me" (personal interview). It is more common to find young men camouflaging their embarrassment about Sindhiness as circumstantial or incidental in nature. Perhaps their notions of masculinity do not allow them to admit shame, or perhaps they know that they have far more choices than the women for taking what they want from the community and rejecting the rest. Among the young women, alienation from Sindhiness assumes a clearly articulated gendered perspective. The discussion below builds on the disaffection of young Sindhi women on the grounds of gender injustice.

GENDER AND IDENTITY

Historically speaking, Sindh has been a feudal and patriarchal society and in terms of everyday life, there was little to distinguish between Hindu and Muslim women. Writing about the Hindu women in nineteenth-century Sindh, Gobind Malhi notes:

> [The] preponderance of Muslim influence had brought purdah for Hindu women. Even in a city like Hyderabad, women of Amils and Bhaibandhs would not step out of their homes without their veils or akhris – thereby only one eye would see through the sole opening in the chadar. And women would leave their houses only for going to temples or to visit relations during religious and social celebrations. For girls, there was no education, or it ceased the moment they learnt how to read and write. (1988, 4).

We noticed early marriages and a lack of agency in the women's narratives of Partition.

We also referred to Prem Chowdhury's study (1996) on the Om Mandli which demonstrates the efforts to cast a distinctly Hindu woman in the nineteenth century. As mentioned earlier, the Om Mandli acquired a new avatar in independent India as the Brahmakumaris; it has undergone a change of form, if not of principle. The status of the women in a Sindhi household, especially among the business families in Gujarat, shows continuity from Sindh to independent India. There are changes in terms of external appearances; for instance, Sindhi women of the first generation stopped wearing suthan kurta because, "...my Gujarati neighbours said I looked like a Muslim. I had bought that house by telling the society committee that we were Brahmins from Sindh" (Nathani, personal interview). As far as the urban and post-migration generations are concerned, there are misleading signs of modernity in terms of westernised clothes and kitty parties. However, the underlying choices and compulsions between my mother's generation and her granddaughter's are only marginally different.

During my visit to Kalol, a small town in Gujarat, I came across two women (one married and the other unmarried) both of whom represented different aspects of gender discrimination fairly common in the community. Kiran Ramnani, the unmarried girl of the house had been made to abandon her studies. According to her, there were no decent colleges in Kalol and her brother did not want her to go to Ahmedabad to study. When I met her, she was to get married in a few months and spend the rest of her life in Kalol, in an extremely wealthy Sindhi household. Kiran was only seventeen; she had never set foot in college, or travelled alone. Her sister-in-law, Varsha Ramnani was nineteen and pregnant. She had dropped out of college in Ahmedabad, and had moved to Kalol after marriage. She told me that she looked forward to having a baby because, "I don't get to go out at all. My husband is at the shop all day. My mother-in-law would not let me step outside the house on my own. I feel a child will be a good pastime for me, I'd also get to go out on the pretext of dropping him at school" (personal interviews). If such is the case in the small town of Kalol, things are not any different in the diasporic lives of Sindhi women in Jakarta, Hong Kong and Manila. Writing about women there, Thapan notes, "attempts to transgress gender roles are few because Sindhi women have internalized the patriarchal system predominant in Sindh and they tend to conform to its norms" (2002, 55).

With the exception of certain educated amil families in cities like Bombay and Delhi, "A Sindhi girl is brought up with the idea that her principal aim in life is to get married" (Thapan 2002, 57). Vidya Tewani makes a shrewd observation in this context: "Whenever I ask [my] mother to have fun, to go out, to wear interesting clothes, she says, 'Now I am married, I can't do that.' If marriage is the end of life, how can it also be the goal of life? Why does she ask me to get married then?" (personal interview). Bhumika Udernani mentions that her mother is "worried about the fact that I don't have fair skin which is the only mark of beauty in Sindhi girls. She also asks me to grow my hair, stop playing basketball. She is not even particularly happy about my academic progress. She keeps reminding me that I only have to make rotis after marriage, what's the point of doing all this?"

Sunita Basantani, a student of literature in college mentions that she does not speak Sindhi and does not like Sindhi food. Sunita expressed a deep sense of rejection about her community which gives her no choices of any kind. "They treat women as objects. I am like property to my father. He would kill me if I fall in love with anyone. When I see television serials like "The Bold and The Beautiful" I feel I could also have lived that kind of life. But we live like Muslim women" (personal interview).

Urban and educated Sindhi girls feel frustrated not only about the choices they do not have, but also about the limited ones they have within the community. Sindhi boys prepare themselves for a life of business; they have little patience for academic education and grades. The boys in my own family were never regular students in college. They opt for certain 'practical' subjects such as commerce and accounts and eventually join the family business. A deeply entrenched view among Sindhi businessmen is that business sense is hereditary and has to be honed by experience and not education. This naturally does not motivate Sindhi boys to study well. The girls whom I interviewed feel that professionals are far more sensitive to the needs of women than businessmen. "I find the Sindhi men quite rigid and orthodox and if I were to marry one of them how would he be different from my father? I am in love with a Punjabi boy, but I just know my parents would create hell for me when they find out. They want me to marry not only a Sindhi, but a bhaiband," says Manisha Thadani, a twenty-year-old girl from Ahmedabad (personal interview).

Given these experiential accounts, I searched for responses from Sindhi men. The younger generation of Sindhi men, in their twenties and thirties, pay lip service to women's independence and 'allow' them some choices. However, the first and second generation vehemently disagreed with the view that Sindhi women are accorded unfair treatment, "Europe has been more exploitative of its women. We worship and respect our women and we don't make them do menial labour. When we first came to Gujarat, we were shocked to see women carrying weight and drawing carts. We would never do that. It is true that during Muslim rule, our women were also in purdah, but during the British period we got them out," says Jayant Relwani (personal interview). The one problem, with respect to many women, that Sindhi men were willing to grant was that of deti–leti. Hirabhai Sachdev, from Bhavnagar, mentioned that expectations of dowry had increased over the years: "Girls are beaten up for bringing inadequate dowry and marriages break up. We have tried very hard to stop the system, but people invent indirect ways of asking for it. Parents don't have the courage to refuse dowry, because they feel that the girls would be left without marriage. Sindhi organisations try and organise *samooh lagna* [group weddings], but only the very poor who can't afford to do deti–leti come for such weddings" (personal interview).

Young Sindhi women express a range of responses – from resignation to anger to rebellion – to this limitation of choices imposed by the patriarchal structure of their community. It is important for us to note their consciousness registers pain and they identify its source in Sindhiness. It matters little to them whether Sindhi patriarchy is merely an extension of a male-dominated society at large, or a historical continuation of Sindh. In the cluster of negative perceptions that engulf their lives, this becomes one more reason for disliking their community. They document their feelings, very often, by rejecting the language as also other aspects of their Sindhi identity.

RELIGION AND IDENTITY

In the biography of his father, Sadhu T.L. Vaswani, Hari Vaswani mentions, "Hindus in Sindh participated in the Muharram, the festival of the Muslims. They considered the *tabut* [image of a mausoleum] to be so very holy that they brought their newborn babes to it to be blessed. They also covered the *tabut* with their kerchiefs as a mark of respect and reverence" (1975/1999, 4). Similarly, the Sindhi Muslims attended the bhagat performances of Sant Kanwarram and listened to the Sufi songs of Sant Rochaldas. Several scholars have documented the widespread presence of Sufism[4] and its deep permeation in Sindhi society (see Markovits 2000; Ansari 1992; Parsaram 1924/2000). This tradition tends to be undermined by people with a 'purist Hindu' ideology because they tend to see it as an 'impurity' in Hindu identity. The well-known writer from Saurashtra, Jayant Relwani, has devoted considerable research to the articulation of the old links between Sindh and Kathiawar, to restore to a stigmatised present the dignity of a Hindu Rajput past. According to him, "We were given a soft dose of Islam through Sufi thought. It made us indolent and lazy. Meanwhile, the brand of Sikhism that came to us was also without its Khalsa element. It boiled down to reading sukhmanis and visiting gurudwaras. So we ended up not having a clear affiliation with anything and also lost our own culture. Sufi philosophy was *ishke mizazi* [divine love] it taught us to love." He goes on to say, "But it also weakened us" (personal interview). Jhamatmal Wadhwani comments, "It [Sufism] was a fringe phenomenon. It was to make Hindus Muslims in an indirect way" (personal interview). Sahib Bijani, co-director of the Institute of Sindhology, Adipur disagrees with this view and says, "People have this misconception that Sufism was Islamic. There were also a large number of Hindu Sufis. But now Sufism has disappeared from our lives because people don't want to be considered Muslims" (personal interview). The pirs borrowed ideas and images from both Hinduism and Islam and mocked equally the maulvis and the pandits, accusing

4. The use of the word 'Sufism' in this book derives from syncretic practices typical of Sindh rather than a description of a particular silsila or branch of formal Sufi sects.

them of misleading the people and taking them further away rather than closer to God. This radical, unmediated form of worshipping God continues to exist in certain pockets of Sindh.

When the third migrant generation of Sindhis of Gujarat listens to Abida Parveen (a Sufi singer from Sindh, Pakistan) or when my generation heard Runa Laila's (a Bangladeshi singer), "Damadam Mast Qalandar" it hardly occurred to them then and less so now, that these voices connect the Sindhis to their past. The discontinuation of this aspect of the Sindhis' life may be seen as the Sindhi's anxiety to become a part of the mainstream and hence relinquish all that s/he now associates with a distant, irrelevant and 'Muslim' past. In a state that is anyway divided along religious lines, the loss of syncretism becomes one more context that both contributes to and results from an anti-Muslim sentiment. We shall deal with this issue at some length later in the chapter. For now, let us look at another aspect of the ethno-religious complexion of the Gujarati Sindhi.

The rise of Jhulelal

Many narratives surround the origins of Jhulelal, the patron saint of Sindh. It is believed that around A.D. 951, when Mirkh Shah, the ruler of Thatta, Sindh, had threatened the Sindhi Hindus with forced conversion, they prayed to the river Indus. As a concretisation of their desire, a white-bearded god, sitting on a pallo (fish) emerged, and told them that he would take birth in the house of Ratan Shah in Nasarpur. This legend makes Jhulelal not only a saint of the Hindus, but carries a component of their resistance against what may be perceived as Muslim tyranny. However, there is also another legend that mitigates this sectarian element. According to this version, Jhulelal united the Hindus and Muslims of Sindh and asked them to worship him at the same place. The Jhulelal dargah in Sindh draws visitors from both communities even today. The Muslim names for Jhulelal are Tahir Shaikh, Zindah Pir and Khwaja Khizr. In the Muslim version of the tale, Jhulelal is not a white-bearded Hindu god (who looks like Brahma), but a faceless saint who was much revered. Apart from these

'Hindu' and 'Muslim' versions, there is another, more straightforward explanation for Jhulelal's existence. In it, Jhulelal is simply a water god (Darya Lal) who protected the Sindhi merchants sailing the Indus, from pirates and storms. Thus, as Parwani (b) mentions, "the iconography of Jhuley Lal represents a composite of the creeds", at least in pre-Partition Sindh.

In post-Partition India, the Jhulelal narrative has been simplified to one dominant version that privileges Muslim tyranny and underlines Hindu victimisation. In the mind of the Sindhis who came to India as atypical Hindus and were unaccepted by the mainstream, Jhulelal appeared as their own Hindu god. In the late 1960s, Ram Panjwani (a well-known Sindhi writer) propagated the celebration of the birth of Jhulelal as the Sindhi New Year. For a community that was scattered, and with the roots of its identity being elusive, there was a need to create a mythology in which all Sindhis could participate. Jhulelal is now projected as an avatar of Vishnu and more importantly, a vanquisher of Muslims. And yet, on the whole, the emergence of Jhulelal as a Sindhi icon is a relatively recent phenomenon, and his stories have not yet formed part of collective memory.

Growing up in the 1970s, I do not remember any celebration of cheti chand, the Sindhi New Year (also associated with the birth of Jhulelal). There were occasional visits to the tikaana which had Jhulelal among many icons such as Guru Nanak, Shiva, Rama, Krishna and Mira. It is more common now, in Gujarat and elsewhere, to see Sindhis celebrating cheti chand, although they may not always be aware of its mythology. In the cities of Ahmedabad, Vadodara, Surat and Kalol, the cheti chand celebration usually involves a procession that is carried out during the day and the singing of Hindi film songs at night. When I asked Bhumika Udernani if she knew who Jhulelal was, she replied or rather asked, "Some Sindhi promoter?" Bhumika's ignorance substantiates the absence of Jhulelal and his legends in everyday space. At the same time, there are indications that the postmodernist, hybrid Sindhi tikaana may well be reduced to exclusive Jhulelal temples in future. For instance, in Godhra, I was told by Tahilram Makhijani (a member of the migrant generation) that "Godhra did not have a Jhulelal temple until 1984. After the anti-Sikh riots in 1984, the

Sindhis here said we must distance ourselves from the Sikhs and we established a Jhulelal temple" (personal interview).

The rise in the cult of Jhulelal and the concomitant decline of the Sikh and Sufi elements in the Sindhis' practice of religion is not without coincidence. It is possible to conclude, in the words of Claude Markovits, that

> A redefinition of religious boundaries has been at work, towards a clearer affirmation of a Hindu identity. The Hinduism of the Sindhis first underwent a redefinition in India, where pressure to fit within 'mainstream' Hinduism became strong and led to a reshaping of beliefs and practices. The cult of Jhule Lal, de facto, identified as an avatar of Vishnu, has become the central marker of the new emerging religious identity of the Sindhi Hindus in India. Nankpanthism and Sufism, which were such crucial features of Sindhi Hindu beliefs, have been largely relegated to the background, when not openly repudiated. (2000, 285)

HARDENED IDENTITIES

The trajectory of the ethno-religious choices exercised by the Sindhis of Gujarat demonstrate their movement towards the 'Hindu fold', which is also a movement away from their past. As a symbolic statement of this new Hindu affiliation, the Sindhis of Gujarat prefer to support Hindu fundamentalist organisations which further feed into their anti-Muslim sentiment. They contribute significantly to the organisations' anti-Muslim, communal agenda. During Gujarat's infamous communal pogrom in February 2002, the Sindhi involvement was evident even in areas traditionally not known for Hindu–Muslim riots. In Kalol, for instance, Jeetu Ramnani (a fruit merchant) mentioned that, "There is one Muslim market here. The Sindhis and Gujaratis burnt it down. This happened here for the first time" (personal interview). Ramnani's family has been living in Kalol for the past thirty-seven years. His parents used to vote for the Congress, but, "Now that Congress has become a Muslim party, they vote for the BJP" (personal interview). There is a widespread acceptance of the BJP among the Sindhis. As Shankarlal Ahuja said, "You will find 90% of the

Sindhis with the BJP" (personal interview). Udhavdas Makhija mentioned to me proudly, "All my sons and my grandsons vote for the BJP. Now with L.K. Advani, it is our own party" (personal interview).

In Surat, Thakur Motwani stated, "They [the Muslims] are a scared lot after 1992. We looted their houses and shops during 1992. We thought enough was enough. But we did nothing to their women. This time, we didn't have to do anything" (personal interview). Thakur lives with his parents and grandparents in the colony called Ramnagar (also known as 'mini-Pakistan' because of a large Muslim presence). In the course of explaining the sociology of the camp, he said to me, "They also call it mini-Pakistan, because we look like Muslims to people here. *Asaan aahiyun bhi adha dyat*[5] (We are anyway half-Muslims)." Although Thakur is aware of the proximity Sindhis have culturally had with Muslims, he feels no hesitation in mentioning how, "Our boys looted and ransacked." His father testified to this and said, "The Muslim terrorism decreased after we settled down in Surat" (personal interviews). Ironically, these responses come with the knowledge that the grandmother in the house, Panjul Motwani, has no negative Partition memories of the Muslims. "It is not surprising that post-Partition Sindhis have become anti-Muslim," says Dinesh Bhatt, an archivist at the Gujarat State Archives (personal interview). "It is part of a world-wide phenomenon, to see [the] Muslim as a terrorist. Their parents had known a different reality, so they were never fanatic. I remember from childhood a Sindhi man in my village in Dakor. He would sell peanuts and grams. Every morning he carried a basketful on his head and kept distributing them to little children. I was a little child then and enjoyed receiving free peanuts from him. Some years later, I learnt that that old man had been a rich businessman in Sindh and yet I don't think I ever saw hatred in his eyes. He did not have children, but I am quite sure if he had had any, they would have been anti-Muslim".

In Bhavnagar, Prem Goplani and Hirabhai Sachdev mentioned that there were riots in Bhavnagar and that the Sindhis had been

---

5. The word 'dyat', used for Muslims, is a pejorative term. It means 'Muslim, dumb and illiterate'. It is also used generally for an uneducated, ill-bred person.

involved in burning down the Muslim shops during 2002. Goplani's mother, Ladi Goplani, told me in the course of the interview that she had no ill memories of the Muslims in Sindh. Hirabhai Sachdev mentioned to me that his grandfather had not been able to pay back a loan advanced by a Muslim friend. After Partition, he wrote letters to him and sent him back the money, "Until then, my grandfather could not sleep."

If Partition narratives have less poison than their interpretations by the second and third generation, it is not surprising that Maya Kodnani who has an RSS background and claims to have heard "horrible stories of what the Muslims did in Sindh", finds justification for these present actions in the past: "Who drove us away from Sindh? Muslims did. Sindhis [Hindus] were rich and settled. Muslims drove them away because they wanted their money. Once we came here, the Gujaratis thought we were Muslims. We had to become more Hindu than the Hindus to prove we were not Muslims" (personal interview).

The Narodia Patiya massacre that saw the most brutal burnings and rapes of Muslims perpetrated by members of three local communities, including Sindhis, was perhaps a consequence of becoming 'more Hindu than the Hindus'. It seems to elude Kodnani, that the mainstream is also using the Sindhis as cannon fodder. In a seminar on terrorism organised by the US–India Political Action Committee (USINPAC) in Washington D.C. on 16 July 2003, a delegate from Gujarat brought up the issue of state terrorism in Gujarat after its ethnic pogrom against the Muslims in February 2002. Another participant later reported on one speaker's views on the matter in an e-mail correspondence:

> However, Mr B. Raman... said that what happened in Gujarat was deplorable violence but not terrorism. He said that there were strong reasons for the violence. One, 58 people had been torched alive in Godhra. The second reason was that wherever violence was the highest had the largest concentration of Sindhis who had been forced to migrate from Sindh during the Partition and that they are emotionally very deeply affected by any violence in which Hindus are victims. (Bangarbale, 19 July 2003).

If Bangarbale's correspondence can be treated as a legitimate source, then the following implications can be teased out of Raman's statement. B. Raman's explanation of Gujarat's violent response can be seen as an attempt to gain legitimacy for mainstream Hindu Gujarat on several grounds. It portrays Hindu violence as a reaction to the Muslim provocation at Godhra. Secondly, it abrogates the responsibility to one single community—the Sindhis. It makes an implicit claim to understand the emotions of the Sindhis by drawing attention to their 'forced' migration. In the process, it is attempting to justify on behalf of the Sindhis, their present behaviour in the light of past experiences. In Raman's ostensibly sympathetic understanding of the Sindhis, we can read the danger for Sindhis—of being used as scapegoats.

During 2002, when the Sindhis of Ahmedabad, Vadodara, Bhavnagar and other parts of Gujarat showed signs of militant Hindutva, the Sindhis of Godhra – known for being the most militant in Gujarat – refrained from participating in any violence. Despite the fact that Godhra was the site where the train with fifty-eight Hindu passengers was burnt down, the Sindhis did not rise to the 'challenge' of being Hindus. They felt that their businesses would suffer and that "…it's all very well for the Gujaratis to have us do this. They tell everyone, 'We are not communal, the Sindhis and Muslims are fighting each other.' This time we decided with the Muslims that we would not bring the problem *into* Godhra—whatever had happened, had happened at the Godhra railway station" (Rajendra Makhijani, personal interview; also see Punwani, 2002a). The cases of the early Sindhi–Ghanchi riots in Godhra have pointed to the fact that the Sindhis and the Ghanchis of Godhra have fought over common spaces and shops. Their conflict has a class rather than a communal dimension to it. However, one of the reasons why this happened was because "…when the Sindhis came to Godhra during 1948, they were refused housing accommodation by the local Hindus who considered Sindhis non-vegetarian and socially inferior" (Engineer 1984, 250).

In the case of Kutch, there is economic interdependence without the burden of negative perceptions. Naoomal Samtani, an RSS activist from Sindh mentions with pleasure that "My sons are with the BJP.

But we have no complaints against the Kutchi Muslims. We do business with them. The Kutchi Muslim is very peaceful. V*aise bhi dhandhe mein matbhed nahin hota hai.* (In any case, there are no differences in business.)" (personal interview). The Sindhi Muslim writer Kaladhar Mutwa from Banni, Kutch, mentioned to me how much he owed to the Hindu Sindhis and also joked about how an 'RSS' type among them advised Kaladhar to start a shakha!

What emerges from the discussion so far is a post-Partition, hardened, anti-Muslim Sindhi whose affiliation with Hindutva may not always lead him to perpetrate violence (although 2002 does not bode well), especially if it hampers his business. The Sindhi community's shift to hardened identities is a result of multiple and complex contexts. It can be seen as having its roots in the developments in colonial Sindh, when organisations like the RSS and the Arya Samaj were supporting a minority whom they perceived as being in danger. It may have acquired reinforcement in the stray scuffles and riots during the Manzilgah episode in the winter of 1939. The Sindhi Muslims' acceptance of the Muslim League after 1941 – however ambiguous – may also have contributed to a perception that all Muslims were alike and that the Sindhi Muslims had betrayed the Hindus. The community also felt let down by the Congress at this point and took recourse to the RSS, which was more than willing to help. The Partition may have served as a moment of shedding doubts about whether or not Hindus and Muslims could live in peaceful coexistence. The influx of bitter and angry refugees into Sindh may have scarred their memory of Sindh. The displacement and dispossession in the wake of Partition may have found a scapegoat in one clear agency—the Muslim. The pressures of survival ensuing from Partition, particularly the competition for the houses and shops of the Muslims, may have further crystallised the Muslim into an enemy. The rejection from the local Hindu Gujarati community also contributed to a distancing, so that as Maya Kodnani implied, they *had* to hate the Muslim, to be accepted as Hindus.

Whether the Sindhis I witness in Gujarat would also be found equally stigmatised and (perhaps therefore?) communal in other states is difficult to say. It is equally difficult to say whether their hatred comes from witnessing the struggles of their parents or from their own experiences as Hindus whose credentials were not fully endorsed in Gujarat. In fact, my conversations with the migrant generations reveal a nuanced understanding and warm memories of Sindh, usually unscarred by hatred. The migrant generation knows that the Muslim haari was always poor, while the Hindu bania was always rich. S/he knows that there was no communal frenzy in Sindh, but an economic resentment. S/he also knows that the Sindhi Muslim was not the same as the immigrant Muslim who came to Sindh during Partition, angry and embittered.

So, are these nuances and stories not going over to the next generation, which has formed a seamless 'Muslim as enemy' narrative and has let Partition become one more illustration of that fact? Or has the post-Partition generation arrived at its own interpretation of Partition, filtered, as it were, through the anti-Muslim perceptions prevailing in Gujarat?

Having said that, there is an alternative view of history to which a Sindhi of Gujarat could take recourse. Here, s/he must remember that the Sindhi Hindus were a privileged community in Sindh. The amils controlled the bureaucracy, and the banias, trade. It was the Muslim tiller who was the most exploited and dispossessed, never the Hindu. The Sindhis of Gujarat would do well to remember that no matter what they may have been told by their RSS and Arya Samaji ancestors, no wealthy community that has the choice to migrate would continue to stay for centuries in a region where it faces 'persecution'. In the same view of history, the Sindhis of Gujarat must also remember that Jhulelal also has a Muslim name—Zindah Pir; that Kanwarram had a large Muslim following. The Sindhis of Gujarat may not know, do not know, that even today, Sindhi Muslims go to Hindu Sufi saints and pay their respects. They might also want to remember that their parents or grandparents had no memory of physical violence during the Partition. Finally, in their desire to become mainstream Hindus, they might want to remember that their exclusion has come not from Muslim quarters, but from Hindu quarters.

To sum up, this book has been an attempt to historicise and contextualise Sindhi Hindus without wanting to revive all practices Sindhi, It is not a plea for a 'back to the roots' movement. In fact, it seeks to support a self-critical attitude among the Sindhis who glorify themselves (as the inheritors of the Aryan civilisation), as well as among those who internalise stigma. It also seeks to create a sense of awareness among non-Sindhis who have engaged in the stigmatising process. It argues for a non-stigmatised Sindhiness into which individuals may enter, or not, as they wish. At times, identities can become prisons, especially if claimed unquestioningly. And yet, if the Sindhis were to assert 'Sindhiness' (a conglomeration of Hinduism, Sikhism and Islam) in a world asking for straitjackets, it would be a humane, sophisticated and historically consistent choice.

Appendix 1

Map of Sindh showing the routes of migration to India

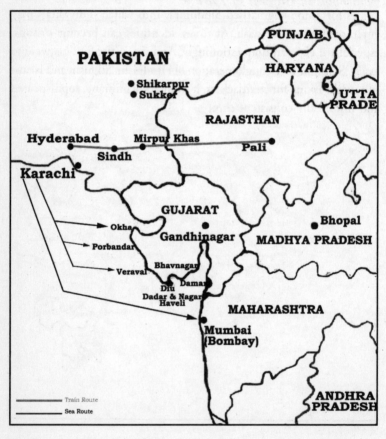

The map in Appendix 1 shows direct routes of migration from Sindh to Gujarat, Maharashtra and Rajasthan. The line from Hyderabad to Pali shows the only direct train route from Sindh. All other routes were by sea.

Appendix 2

Map of Gujarat showing the distribution of Sindhi-speaking households in Gujarat in 1981

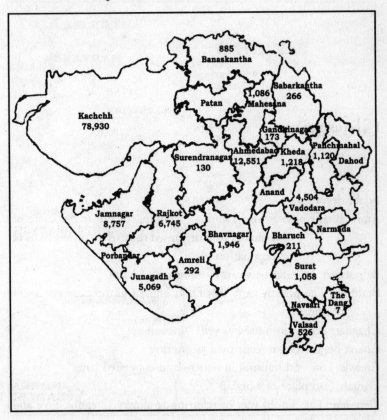

The district-wise map of Gujarat in Appendix 2 shows the number of Sindhi-speaking households in Gujarat based on the census of 1981. This kind of information has not been available in the subsequent censuses of 1991 and 2001.

Glossary

Adab: decorum

Amils/Bhaibands: Sindhi Hindus belonging to the trader caste of
    Lohanas who organised themselves on the basis of
    occupation

Bahasbaazi: Debates between Hinduism and Islam

Brahmin: The priestly caste that ranks highest in the caste system of
    India

Chaadar: Thick cloth used as veil

Chana-bugda: Gram seeds used as offering

Chawls: Low-end housing in narrow and congested lanes

Dargah: Sufi place of worship

Deti–leti: The Sindhi way of referring to dowry (literally, 'give and
    take')

Dyakto raaj: Rule by illiterate Muslims (pejorative usage)

Dyat: A pejorative reference, of being uneducated and ill-bred, to
    Muslims

Gurudwara: Sikh temple

Haaris: Landless labourers of Sindh

Haraami: Bastard

Hijrat: Exodus

Ishke mizazi: Divine love

Izzat: Honour

Jagir: Endowment of land

Kada: A thick bangle worn as a mark of Sikh identity

Kadhai: A large frying pan

Khandaani: Of respectable families

Kheti: Farming

Kothi: A large grocery store

Kshatriya: The warrior caste

Mamlatdar: Recovery officer

Maryada: Shame

Mohajjir: Immigrant

Nanakpanthi Hindus: Followers of Guru Nanak

Nirvasit: The homeless

Padayatras: Political campaigns undertaken by walking

Pallo: Fish

Peti: Cash box

Pir: Sufi saint

Pracharak: RSS member in charge of propaganda and recruitment of volunteers

Purusharti: The hard-working; those making an effort

Rangeen paani: Drinking water meant for Muslims (literally 'coloured water')

Riba: Charging interest (forbidden in Islam)

Safed paani: Drinking water meant for Hindus (literally 'pure water')

Sammoh lagna: Group weddings

Sangathan: Unity

Satsang: A gathering for the sake of listening to spiritual discourse

Shakha sanchalak: branch manager (in the RSS)

Shakti: Strength

Sharnathi: Refugees

Shikshak: Teacher/trainer in the RSS

Shuddhi: A purificatory rite practised by the Arya Samaj to bring the
 converted back to Hinduism

Shudra: The fourth and shunned caste in the caste system

Sufi bhagat: Mystics

Syeds: Muslim religious elite/teachers

Tabut: Image of a mausoleum

Tikaana: Sindhi temple

Vaishya: The trader caste, ranking third in the traditional caste system

Wadero: Elder of the community, usually an established landowner
 and village chief

Zari: Brocade business

References

PRIMARY SOURCES

Archival documents

Refugee files (1948–1949) and select archival documents. Baroda State Archives, Vadodara.
Police files. Junagadh Record Office, Gujarat State Archives, Junagadh.

Reports of government and other agencies

Annual Administrative Report. 1950. Rajkot, Saurashtra.
Baloch, N.A. 1982. Foreword to *The making of modern Sind: Documents on separation of Sind from the Bombay Presidency.* Islamabad: Institute of Islamic History, Culture and Civilisation.
Burton, Richard F. 1851/1998. *Scinde or the unhappy valley.* 2 vols. Delhi: Asian Education Services.

————. 1851/1993. *Sind revisited.* Vols. 1 and 2. Karachi: Department of Culture and Tourism, Government of Sindh.

Frere, Sir Bartle. 12 January 1855. Commissioner of Sind's Letter to Lord Elphinstone, Governor of Bombay.

Gazetteer of the Bombay Presidency, vol. 5, 1880. Bombay.

Gazetteer of the Province of Sindh, B. vol. 1, 1927. Karachi District.

Jotwani, Motilal. 1996. *Sufis of Sindh.* Delhi: Publications Division, Ministry of Information and Broadcasting, Government of India.

Khuhro, Hamida. 1982. Introduction to *The making of modern Sind: Documents on separation of Sind from Bombay Presidency.* Islamabad: Institute of Islamic Culture, History and Civilization.

Reddy, Jaganmohan P. 1971. *Report: Inquiry into the communal disturbances at Ahmedabad and other places in Gujarat on and after 18 September 1969.* Gandhinagar: Government of Gujarat.

Personal interviews: Gujarat, Pakistan and Mumbai (2002–2005)

Interviews conducted in Sindhi, English, Hindi and Gujarati

Advani, Bhugromal. 19 April 2003, Surat (Sindhi).

Advani, Parshram. 20 April 2003, Surat (Sindhi).

Ahuja, Krishna. 7 January 2003, Ahmedabad (Sindhi).

Ahuja, Shankarlal. 18 January 2003, Ahmedabad (Sindhi).

Asrani, Chara. 12 January 2004, Adipur, Kutch (Sindhi).

Babani, Kirat. 7 May 2004, Mumbai (Sindhi).

Badlani, Lata. 10 January 2003, Ahmedabad (English).

Basantani, Sunita. 2 March 2004, Ahmedabad (English).

Belani, Anju and Manhar. 25 March 2003, Rajkot (Sindhi and English).

Bhatt, Dinesh. 28 December 2005, Ahmedabad (Gujarati).

Bhavnani, Deepak. 8 March 2003, Ahmedabad (Hindi).

Bhurani, Naraindas. 15 February 2003, Ahmedabad (Sindhi).

Bhurani, Sunil. 15 February 2003, Ahmedabad (Gujarati).

Bijani, Sahib. 11 January 2005, Adipur, Kutch (Sindhi).

Chaman Lal. 7 September 2005, Karachi (Sindhi).

Dasani, Mulchand. 1 September 2005, Karachi (Sindhi).

Dharejo, Salam, 1 September 2005, Karachi (Sindhi).

Gehani, Ramchand. 12 January 2005, Adipur, Kutch (Sindhi).

Goplani, Ladi. 26 June 2003, Bhavnagar (Sindhi).

Goplani, Prem. 26 June 2003, Bhavnagar (Sindhi and Hindi).

Gurbani, Ishwari. 9 March 2003, Kalol (Sindhi).

Jaleel, Amar. 3 September 2005, Karachi (Sindhi and English).

Jambha, Banni. 26 June 2003, Bhavnagar (Sindhi).

Jethmalani, Harish. 27 April 2004, Vadodara (Sindhi).

Jesrani, Brij. 1 September 2005, Karachi (Sindhi).

Jonejo, Khalique. 1 September 2005, Karachi (Sindhi).

Karamchand, S. (Dr.). 27 April 2004, Vadodara (Sindhi).

Khilani, Lakshmi. 1 April 2004, Adipur, Kutch (Sindhi).

Kodnani, Maya. 10 January 2003, Ahmedabad (Sindhi).

Lilani, Ashok. 9 March 2003, Kalol (Sindhi)

Lilani, Radha. 9 March 2003, Kalol (Sindhi).

Makhija, Laxmandas. 10 June 2001, Mumbai (Sindhi).

Makhija, Udhavdas. 8 September 2002, Ahmedabad (Sindhi).

Makhijani, Rajendra. 24 December 2004, Godhra (Sindhi).

Makhijani, Tahilram. 24 December 2004, Godhra (Sindhi).

Manglani, Harish. 26 June 2003, Bhavnagar (Sindhi).

Memon, Siraj Ul Haq. 7 September 2005, Karachi (Sindhi and English).

Motwani, Kanaiyo. 19 April 2003, Surat (Sindhi).

Motwani, Panjul. 19 April 2003, Surat (Sindhi).

Motwani, Thakur. 19 April 2003, Surat (Sindhi).

Mulchandani, Tilli. 4 November 2004, Ahmedabad (Sindhi).

Mutwa, Kaladhar. 4 November 2005, Banni, Kutch (Sindhi).

Nathani, Draupadi. 31 June 2002, Ahmedabad (Sindhi).

Nawani, Gena. 2 April 2004, Adipur, Kutch (Sindhi).

Padnani, Punit. 6 April 2003, Ahmedabad (English).

Ramnani, Jeetu. 9 March 2003, Kalol (Sindhi).

Ramnani, Kiran. 9 March 2003, Kalol (Hindi).

Ramnani, Varsha. 9 March 2003, Kalol (Hindi).

Relwani, Jayant. 25 March 2003, Rajkot (Sindhi).

Rochwani, Chellaram. 12 September 2005 Ahmedabad (Sindhi).

Sachdev, Hirabhai. 26 June 2003, Bhavnagar (Sindhi).

Samtani, Naomal. 2 April 2004, Adipur, Kutch (Sindhi).

Samrat, Gangaram. 28 April 2003, Ahmedabad (Sindhi).

Sarki, Nuruddin. 2 September 2005, Karachi (Sindhi).

Tewani, Vidya. 1 March 2004, Ahmedabad (English).

Thadani, Manisha. 7 February 2003, Ahmedabad (English).

Thawani, Rochiram. 1 February 2003, Ahmedabad (Sindhi).

Udernani, Bhumika. 31 January 2002, Ahmedabad (English).

Vaswani, Nirmal. 2 April 2004, Adipur, Kutch (Sindhi and English).

Vazirani, Harish. 4 January 2003, Gandhinagar (English).

Vazirani, Prakash. 2 January 2003, Gandhinagar (English).

Wadhwani, Jhamatmal. 27 December 2004, Mumbai (Sindhi).

Yagnik, Achyut. 17 April 2004, Ahmedabad (Gujarati).

SECONDARY SOURCES

Published books and articles (English and Sindhi)

Advani, Berumal. 1946/2001. *Sindh jay Hindun jee tarikh* (History of Hindus in Sindh). 2 vols. Trans. Narain Sobhraj Kimatrai. Mumbai: Berumal Advani.

Agnivesh, Swami and Valson Thampu. 2002. *Harvest of hate: Gujarat under seige.* Delhi: Rupa.

Aiyer, Mani Shankar. 3 January 2001. The limits of the Hindu Rashtra. *Telegraph.*

Anand, Subhadra. 1996. *National integration of Sindhis.* Delhi: Vikas.

Anderson, Walter and Shridhar Damle. 1987. *The brotherhood in saffron: The Rashtriya Swayamsevak Sangh and Hindu revivalism.* Delhi: Vistaar.

Ansari, Sarah. 1992. *Sufi saints and state power: The pirs of Sind 1843–1947.* Cambridge: Cambridge University Press.

———. 2005. *Life after Partition: Migration, community and strife in Sindh 1947–1962.* Oxford: Oxford University Press.

Arnold, David and Stuart Blackburn. 2004. *Telling lives in India:*

Biography, autobiography and life history. Delhi: Permanent Black.

Atlani, Bhagwan. 1998. Virhange jo kahar (The torture of Partition). In *Virhango* (Partition), ed. Motilal Jotwani, 130–31. Delhi: Sindhi Academy.

Bangarbale, Srinivas. 19 July 2003. E-mail correspondence. Subject: USINPAC's seminar on terrorism – Some noteworthy items.

Basu, Tapan et al. 1993. *Khakhi shorts and saffron flags: A critique of the Hindu Right.* Hyderabad: Orient Longman.

Behrwani, Assandas. 1994. *Choithram Gidwani.* Bombay: n.p.

Bharti, Narayan. 1998. The Claim. In *Stories About Partition – II*, ed. Alok Bhalla, 219–22. Delhi: HarperCollins.

Braziel, Jana Evans and Anita Mannur, eds. 2003. *Theorizing diaspora: A reader.* Oxford: Blackwell.

Butalia, Urvashi. 1998. *The other side of silence: Voices from the Partition of India.* Delhi: Penguin.

———. 2001. An archive with a difference. In *The partitions of memory: The afterlife of the division of India,* ed. Suvir Kaul, 208–41. Delhi: Permanent Black.

Chawla, Thakur. 1998. 6 January 1948. In *Virhango* (Partition), ed. Motilal Jotwani, 46–47. Delhi: Sindhi Academy.

Cheesman, David. 1997. *Landlord power and rural indebtedness in colonial Sind 1865–1901.* Surrey: Curzon.

Chellani, Gobind. 1983. *Sindh ain Arya Samaj.* Delhi: Sunny.

Choksey, R.D. and K.S. Shastry. 1983. *The story of Sind.* Pune: Dastane Ramchandra.

Chowdhry, Prem. 24–31 August 1996. Marriage, sexuality and the female ascetic: Understanding a Hindu sect. *Economic and Political Weekly,* 2307–21.

Das, Durga, ed. 1972. *Sardar Patel's correspondence 1945–50.* Vol. 3. Ahmedabad: Navjivan.

———, ed. 1974. *Sardar Patel's correspondence 1945–50.* Vol. 10. Ahmedabad: Navjivan.

Das, Suranjan. 2001. *Kashmir and Sindh: Nation-building.* London: Anthem.

De, Shobha. 1994. *Sultry days.* Delhi: Penguin.

Deshpande, Shashi. 2004. *Moving on.* Delhi: Viking.

Engineer, Asghar Ali, ed. 1984. Case studies of five major riots. In *Communal riots in post-independence India.* Hyderabad: Sangam.

————, ed. 2003. *The Gujarat carnage.* Orient Longman: Hyderabad.

Epstein, Helen. 1988. *Children of the Holocaust: Conversations with daughters and sons of survivors.* New York: Penguin.

Gajra, Baldev T. 1986. *Sind's role in the freedom struggle.* Bombay: Bharatvasi.

Gandhi, M.K. 1927/1997. *An autobiography or The story of my experiments with truth.* Ahmedabad: Navjivan.

Gera, Nalini. 2002. *Ram Jethamalani: The authorized biography.* Delhi: Viking.

Gidumal, Dayaram. 1882. *Something about Sindh.* Hyderabad: Blavatsky.

Girglani, J.M. March 2003. A review of Seth Naoomal Hotchand Bhojwani. *Sindhi International,* 3.

Hansen, Thomas Blom. 2001. *Urban violence in India: Identity politics, 'Mumbai' and the postcolonial city.* Delhi: Permanent Black.

Hiranandani, Popati. 1981/1999. *Muhinjee hayati ja sona rupa varka* (The golden and silver pages of my life). Delhi: Sindh Akademi.

Jaisinghbhai, Bholanath. 1977. *Gujarat no rajkiya ane sanskritic itihas* (The political and cultural history of Gujarat). Vols. 5 and 9. Ahmedabad: Vidyabhawan.

Jones, Allen Keith. 2002. *Politics in Sindh 1907–1940.* Oxford: Oxford University Press.

Jotwani, Motilal, ed. 1998. *Gandhi on Sindh and Sindhis.* Delhi: Sindhi Academy.

Joyo, Ibrahim. 1947. *Save the Sind, save the continent: For feudal lords, capitalists and their communalism.* Karachi: Sindh Renaissance Association.

Kalelkar, Kaka. 1984. *Kalelkar Granthavali.* Vol. 5. Ahmedabad: Kaka Kalelkar Samiti.

Kalpana, Mohan. 1984. *Bukha, ishq ain adabu* (Hunger, love and literature). Hyderabad, Sindh: Gul Talpur, Sipi.

Kanungo, Pralay. 2002. *RSS's tryst with destiny: From Hedgewar to*

Sudarshan. Delhi: Manohar.

Kaul, Suvir, ed. *The partitions of memory: The afterlife of the division of India*. Delhi: Permanent Black.

Kesharshivam, B. 2002. *Purna satya* (The entire truth). Ahmedabad: Navbharat Sahitya Mandir.

Khan, Adeel. 2005. *Politics of identity: Ethnic nationalism and the state in Pakistan*. London: Sage.

Kennedy, Charles H. October 1991. The politics of ethnicity in Sindh. *Asian Survey* 31, no. 10, 938–55.

Khubchandani, L.M. 1991. Transplanted Sindhis. *Language, culture and nation building: Challenges of modernisation*, 84–94. Shimla: Indian Institute of Advanced Studies.

———. 1997. *Sindhi heritage: The dynamics of dispersal*. Delhi: Sindhi Academy.

Khuhro, Hamida, ed. 1981. Muslim political organisations in Sindh, 1843–1937. In *Sindh through centuries*, 170–79. Karachi: Oxford University Press.

———. 1998a. Masjid Manzilgah, 1939–40: Test case for Hindu–Muslim relations in Sind. *Modern Asian Studies* 32, no. 1, 49–89.

———. 1998b. *Mohammed Ayub Khuhro: A life of courage in politics*. Lahore: Ferozsons.

———. 1999. *The making of modern Sind: British policy and social change in the nineteenth century*. Karachi: Oxford University Press.

Kothari, Rita. 2004. Crossing the sea. In *Indian renaissance*, ed. Avadhesh Singh, 145–54. Delhi: Creative Books.

Kripalani, J.B. 2004. *My times*. Delhi: Rupa.

Kulkarni, Atmaram. 1995. *The advent of Advani*. Bombay: Aditya Prakashan.

Lambrick, H.T. 1972. *The terrorist*. UK: Ernest Benn.

Lari, Suhail Zaheer. 1994/2002. *An illustrated history of Sindh*. Pakistan: Pakistan Heritage Foundation.

Malhi, Gobind. 1988. *Sadhu Hiranand*. Delhi: National Book Trust.

Malkani, K.R. 1984. *The Sindh story*. Delhi: Sindhi Academy.

Malkani, Narayandas. 1973. *Nirali zindagi* (An unusual life). Mumbai: Navrashtra.

————. 1990. *Mirani Sindhi* (Sindh under the Mirs). Pune: Noble Enterprise.

Markovits, Claude. 2000. *The global world of Indian merchants 1750–1947: Traders of Sindh from Bukhara to Panama.* Cambridge: Cambridge University Press.

Mateke, Philemon. 1998. The separation of Sindh from Bombay presidency. In *Studies on Sind,* ed. Mughul Yakub, 131–60. Jamshoro: Pakistan Study Centre, University of Sind.

Menon, Ritu and Kamala Bhasin. 1998/2004. *Borders and boundaries: Women in India's partition.* Delhi: Kali for Women.

Mirchandani, Tekchand. 1920/ 2001. *Sindhwork and Sindhworkis.* Trans. Sarla Nari Kripalani. Pune: Sarla Nari Kripalani.

Moya, Paula. 2001. In *Reclaiming Identity: Realist Theory and the Predicament of Postmodernism,* eds. Paula M.L. Moya and Michael R. Hames-Garcia. California: University of California Press and Delhi: Orient Longman.

Napier, William. 1857/2001. *The history of General Napier's conquest of Scinde.* Karachi: Oxford University Press.

Naoomal, Seth. 1915. *Memoirs of Seth Naoomal Hotchand of Karachi.* Exeter: William Poland.

Oberoi, Harjot. 1994/1997. *The construction of religious boundaries: Culture, identity, diversity in the Sikh tradition.* Delhi: Oxford University Press.

Pandey, Gyanendra. 1990. *The construction of communalism in colonial north India.* Delhi: Oxford University Press.

Panjabi, Kavita. 2005. *Old maps and new legacies of the Partition: A Pakistan diary.* Calcutta: Seagull.

Parsaram, Jethmal. 1924/2000. *Sindh and its Sufis.* Adipur, Kutch: Institute of Sindhology.

Parsram, Zia. 1998. The curse of Pohu's mother. In *Freedom and fissures: An anthology of Sindhi Partition poetry,* ed. and trans. Anju Makhija, et al., 12, Delhi: Sahitya Akademi.

Patel, Kamala. 1985. *Mool sota ukhade* (The uprooted). Ahmedabad: R.R. Sheth.

Patel, Sardar. 1975. Letter to Purshottam Bhatt, 25 July 1948. In

Sardar Shree Na Patro – I (Letters of Sardar Patel). Ahmedabad: Sardar V. Patel Smarak Bhawan.

Pearce, Roger. 2001. *Once a happy valley: Memoirs of an ICS officer, 1938–1948*. Delhi: Oxford University Press.

Punwani, Jyoti. 15 April 2002a. Godhra revisited. *Hindu.*

———. December 2002b. A return to roots. *Sindhishaan* 1, no. 5, 6.

Rahman, Tariq. November 1995. Language and politics in a Pakistan province: The Sindhi language movement. *Asian Survey* 35, no. 11, 1005–16.

Rahman, Mahbubar and Willem Van Schendel. 2003. I am not a refugee: Rethinking Partition migration. *Modern Asian Studies* 37, no. 3, 551–84.

Rai, Alok. 1984. The trauma of independence: Some aspects of progressive Hindi literature 1945–47. *Journal of Arts and Ideas.*

Ramwani, Motiram. 1987. *Sindh ain asaanjo varso* (Sindh and our inheritance). Mumbai: n.p.

Rashdi, Ali Muhammad. 2003. *Sindh ways and days: A medley of memories, hunting, and sporting.* Karachi: Oxford University Press.

Ravikant and Tarun Saint, eds. 2001. *Translating Partition.* Delhi: Katha.

Relwani, Jayant. 1996. *Shamne Sindhu neer* (River Indus in my dreams). Ahmedabad: Laxmi Pustak Bhandar.

———. 2002. *Sindhupravaaha* (The flow of the Indus). Ahmedabad: Laxmi Pustak Bhandar.

Rioters torch 50 shops at Revdi Bazaar. 24 March, 2002. *Times of India.*

Rohra, S.K. 1993. *Socio-linguistic survey of Sindhi community.* Adipur-Gandhidham, Kutch: Institute of Sindhology.

———., trans. n.d. *Sangh* (Collective). Ajmer: Deepchand Trilokchand.

Sahni, Bhisham. 2001. *Tamas.* Delhi: Penguin.

Samrat, Gangaram. 1989. *Shud Ramayan* (Pure Ramayana). Ahmedabad: Gangaram Samrat.

Sathananthan, S. 2000. Sindhi nationalism and Islamic revolution in Pakistan. *International Studies* 37, no. 3, 227–42.

Satyani, Pirbhu Lal. 2005. *Hamey bhi jeeney do: Pakistan mai acchoot logon ki suratehal* (Let us also live: The plight of Dalits in Pakistan). Lahore: ASR Resource Centre.

Sethi, Harsh, ed. May 2002. Society under seige. *Seminar,* 513.

Sharma, Satish. 2000. Arya Samaj in Punjab. In *Social and political movements,* eds. Harish K. Puri and Paramit S. Judge, 93–101. Jaipur and Delhi: Rawat.

Sikand, Yoginder and Manjari Katju. 20 August 1994. Mass conversions to Hinduism among Indian Muslims. *Economic and Political Weekly* 29, no. 34, 2214–19.

Singh, Khushwant. 1988. *Train to Pakistan.* Ravi Dayal: Delhi.

Syed, G.M. 1949/1996. *Struggle for new Sindh.* Sehwan Sharif: Sain.

———. 1974. *Sindh ji kahani, Syed ji zubaani* (The story of Sindh by Syed). Ahmedabad: Kubernagar Press.

———. 1982. *Sindhua jee saanya* (Understanding Sindh). Mumbai: Introduced and published by Kirat Babani.

———. 1995. The case of Sindh: G.M. Syed's deposition for the court. Karachi: Naeen Sindh Academy.

Thakur, U.T. 1959/1997. *Sindhi culture.* Delhi: Sindhi Academy.

Thapan, Anita Raina. 2002. *Sindhi diaspora: Manila, Hong Kong and Jakarta.* Manila: Anteo De Manila University Press.

Trumpp, Ernest. 1872/1986. *Grammar of the Sindhi language.* Delhi: Asian Education Services.

Varadarajan, Siddharth, ed. 2002. *Gujarat: The making of a tragedy.* Delhi: Penguin.

Varshney, Ashutosh. 2002. *Ethnic conflict and civic life: Hindus and Muslims in India.* Delhi: Oxford University Press.

Vaswani, H.P. 1999. *A saint of modern India.* Pune: n.p.

Viswanath, Gita. Summer 1999. Writing the community: Sindhi literature as minority discourse. *Journal of Contemporary Thought* 9, 129–43.

Wadhwani, Jhamatmal, ed. 2004. *The voice of the nation* (Tribute to K.R. Malkani). Mumbai: Bharatiya Sindhu.

Wadhwani, Sangeeta. 2001. *Shakti in the city.* Delhi: Minerva Press.

Zaidi, Z.H. 1996. Patterns and trends of Sind politics (1936–1940). *Contemporary South Asia* 5, no. 1, 19–46.

Unpublished papers and dissertations

Menon, Jisha. 2004. Rehearsing the Partition: Performing nation, gender and violence. PhD diss., University of Michigan, Ann Arbor.

Parwani, Lata. n.d. (a). Communalism in the politics of Sindh: The Masjid Manzilgah case. Unpublished paper.

————. n.d. (b). Lal ja jhati sab cha'o Jhuley Lal! (Jhuley Lal and the invention of [Sindhi] tradition). Unpublished paper.

Ramey, Steven Wesley. 2004. Defying borders: Contemporary Sindhi Hindu constructions of practices and identifications. PhD diss., University of North Carolina.

Tejani, Shabnum. 2002. A pre-history of Indian secularism: Categories of nationalism and communalism in emerging definitions of India, Bombay Presidency (1893–1932). PhD diss., Columbia University.

Index

O

Okha, Baroda, 128
Om Mandli (Brahmakumaris),
        $33n^5$, 50, 164
opium trade from Malwa to
        China, 16

P

Padnani, Punit, 161
Pakistan, movement, 109
        support of Sindh, 53–54
        post-Partition state, 106
Pali, Sindhi Hindu refugees, 118
Panjwani, Ram, 170
        Kaidi, 31
Parmanand, Bhai, 59
Parsis, 20
Parsram, Jethamal, 10
Partition of Indian subcontinent,
        1947, ix–xiii, xvi–xviii, 1, 5,
        43, 45*ff*, 62, 64, 67, 68–74,
        76, 79–83, 94, 96, 98, 125,
        136, 155, 173, 175–76
        as heterogeneous experience,
        98–104
Patel, Kamala, 69, 100
Patel, Sardar Vallabhbhai, 54, 56,
        80–81, 117, 137
Pathans, 5, 91
patriarchal system, 165–66, 167
Pearce, Roger, 68, 72, 74, 78
peasantry, exploitation in Sindh,
        26
Peninsular War, 1815, 17
persecution, 6–8
Persian, official language of
        Sindh, 3
Persians, 17
Petlad, Baroda, 128
physical appearance of Sindhis,

xii, 149
Pirs, 13, 22, 29, 84
political consciousness of
        Muslims, 28, 29–31, 39
political economy of Sindh, 7, 15
political mobilisation of
        Muslims, 18
political power of Muslims, 12
politics, 70
        Hindu dominated, 50
pollution, ideology, 151
population and demographic
        distribution of Sindh, 13–14
        social demography, 20–21
poverty and dependence of
        Sindhi Hindu refugees in
        India, 114
power centres, 12–15
Pratap, Bhai, 140–2
Punjab, Hindu–Muslim riots, 73
        RSS activities, 62
        Sikhs and Aurangzeb,
        conflict, 5
Punjabis, ix, 87
Punwani, Jyoti, 149
Puran Anand, Pandit, 37
purdah, 33, 92, 97, 167
Puri, Rajpal Vishwambhar Nath,
        59, 61–62
purity and pollution, ideology of,
        8–9

Q

Qalandar, Shahbaz, 10
Quetta, Muslims and Pathans,
        clash, 74–75

R

rack-renting, 27
Rajasthan, 77